KNACK
MAKE IT EASY

CHICKEN
CLASSICS

KNACK

CHICKEN
CLASSICS

A Step-by-Step Guide to Favorites for Every Season

Linda Johnson Larsen

Photographs by Debi Harbin

KNACK
MAKE IT EASY

Guilford, Connecticut
An imprint of Globe Pequot Press

Copyright © 2010 by Morris Book Publishing, LLC

ALL RIGHTS RESERVED. No part of this book may be reproduced or transmitted in any form by any means, electronic or mechanical, including photocopying and recording, or by any information storage and retrieval system, except as may be expressly permitted in writing from the publisher. Requests for permission should be addressed to Globe Pequot Press, Attn: Rights and Permissions Department, P.O. Box 480, Guilford, CT 06437.

Knack is a registered trademark of Morris Publishing Group, LLC, and is used with express permission.

Editor-in-Chief: Maureen Graney
Editor: Katie Benoit
Cover Design: Paul Beatrice, Bret Kerr
Text Design: Paul Beatrice
Layout: Casey Shain
Cover photos by Debi Harbin
Interior photos by Debi Harbin

Library of Congress Cataloging-in-Publication Data
Larsen, Linda Johnson.
 Knack chicken classics : a step-by-step guide to favorites for every season / Linda Johnson Larsen ; photographs by Debi Harbin.
    p. cm.
 Includes index.
 ISBN 978-1-59921-617-1
 1. Cookery (Chicken) I. Title. II. Title: Chicken classics.
 TX750.5.C45L37 2010
 641.6'65—dc22
                    2009032195

The following manufacturers/names appearing in *Knack Chicken Classics* are trademarks:

Amazon.com®
Boboli®
Crock-pot®
Epinions.com®
Ibarra®
Taza®

The information in this book is true and complete to the best of our knowledge. All recommendations are made without guarantee on the part of the author or Globe Pequot Press. The author and Globe Pequot Press disclaim any liability in connection with the use of this information.

Printed in China

10 9 8 7 6 5 4 3 2 1

To my mother Marlene, who makes the best pan fried chicken in the world.

Acknowledgments

Thanks to my dear husband, Doug, for always being there for me, and to my agent, Barb Doyen, for all her help and support. And to my family and friends who love to eat what I make! And thanks to photographer Debi Harbin, for her wonderful work bringing the recipes to life.

Photographer Acknowledgments

Thank you to my three assistants for their help on this book: Michelle Feeser, Cliff Harbin, and Tina Jones.
—Debi Harbin

CONTENTS

INTRODUCTION

If chicken is on the table for dinner, everyone will be happy. This bird and its relatives, like the turkey and Cornish game hen, are easy to prepare and adapt to the foods and flavors of any cuisine. Children love chicken, and it is a nutritious addition to any family's diet.

Chickens are available in a dizzying array of cuts and types, ranging from boneless, skinless breasts and thighs to thin cutlets, whole chickens, wings, and giblets. The cook should prepare each cut a little bit differently for the most tender and juicy results. Whether you grill chicken, cook it in a slow cooker, stir-fry it in a wok, or cook it in a microwave, these tips and tricks will ensure the best results no matter what.

Every cuisine in the world has some recipes for chicken. Some are classic, like Chicken Paprikash or Lemon Chicken, and some are more adventurous, like Tandoori Chicken and Portuguese Chicken Stew. Simple roasted chicken can be flavored with curry powder or olives, and stir-fried chicken is delicious with anything from baby corn and water chestnuts to bell peppers and onions.

This tender and mild meat pairs perfectly with many flavors, including onions and garlic or peaches and thyme. You can make a mild chicken in a creamy sauce, a crisp chicken prepared with hot chile peppers, or a simple roast chicken with lots of herbs.

There are two types of heat used to cook chicken: wet and dry. Wet heat includes steaming, boiling, poaching, slow cooking, and braising. Dry heat includes baking, roasting, broiling, grilling, panfrying, and deep-frying.

It's important to distinguish between these two types of cooking, because the cooking temperatures are so different. Since water and steam are excellent conductors of heat,

poached and slow cooker chicken can be cooked at lower temperatures, around 180 to 190ºF. Chicken cooked in dry heat has to be cooked at a higher temperature, of at least 300ºF. Never bake or roast chicken at an oven temperature lower than 300ºF.

Cooking chicken can be tricky. Chicken breasts, because they are low in fat, can overcook easily and become tough and dry, even when cooked in wet heat environments. Cooking a whole chicken so the white meat is juicy by the time the dark meat is done is also challenging. Doneness tests are the most important indicator of when the chicken is perfectly cooked. You'll need an instant-read meat thermometer to safely prepare the recipes in this book.

Chicken that is cooked with bones and skin intact is more flavorful than boneless, skinless cuts. Marinating or brining the boneless types can add flavor and moisture. If you're concerned about fat and calories, you can still cook chicken with the skin and bone. Just remove the skin before eating; you'll eliminate almost all of its calorie and fat content. And the skin helps keep the chicken moist as it cooks.

Chicken can be cooked many ways. The microwave, the stovetop, the oven, the grill, the slow cooker, and the dual contact indoor grill are all good methods to use.

Cooking chicken in the microwave oven can be a bit tricky and isn't recommended if you have a person who is at risk for food poisoning in your family. Most microwaves have hot and cold spots, which can lead to overcooked or undercooked chicken. This can be dangerous. One of the ways to solve this problem is to cut the chicken into smaller pieces before microwaving it. Standing time is important in microwave cooking, too.

You can bake chicken in the oven and get several results. Roast chicken is cooked at a moderate temperature, usually

with the skin on, and is sometimes basted. Braised chicken is cooked in a pot with other ingredients, making it a wet heat form of cooking. Simply baked chicken is usually marinated or coated in something to add flavor and moisture. And you can "oven-fry" chicken at a high temperature to replicate deep-fried or panfried results.

Everyone has had panfried, sautéed, or stir-fried chicken. This is the fastest way to cook chicken, and it can be high calorie or low calorie, depending on how the chicken is handled. You can sauté chicken in some broth or other liquid, or fry it in an inch of peanut oil for crisp results.

Grilled chicken can be a challenge to make. It's tricky to cook the chicken thoroughly without drying it out. You'll learn how to make a graduated fire or use indirect grilling so you can brown the chicken, and then cook it to juicy perfection.

Once you learn how to prepare each cut and type of chicken perfectly, the sky's the limit. A simple panfried chicken breast can be transformed into a feast by the addition of pan gravy or some vegetables and fresh herbs. Learn how to stuff a chicken with herbs, and you'll know how to prepare delicacies like Chicken Kiev and Chicken Cordon Bleu.

Food safety is an important part of chicken preparation. You'll learn the best methods for handling chicken and how to clean your kitchen after preparation. You'll also learn how to determine the perfect doneness point so the chicken is safe to eat, yet still tender and juicy.

Always wash your hands before and after handling chicken. Be careful about splattering the juices around your kitchen, and always wash countertops and utensils with hot soapy water after use.

Chicken must be cooked thoroughly, every single time. There is no such thing as medium-well chicken. Well done is the rule. Chicken breasts must be cooked to 160ºF. The chicken should stand, covered, for 5–10 minutes so the temperature rises to 165ºF. And dark meat—thighs and drumsticks—must be cooked to 170ºF.

All the different parts of the chicken are cooked in different ways. I'm always surprised at how long it takes chicken wings to cook, while chicken breasts can be done in 12 minutes on the grill. A meat thermometer is a necessary piece of equipment whenever you're cooking chicken. It's a good idea to wash the thermometer probe between tests, too, so you don't recontaminate the meat. And make sure the probe isn't touching bone when you check the chicken's temperature.

Ground chicken and turkey are excellent substitutes for

ground beef and pork for those who are watching their fat intake. But because these products have less fat than their beef or pork counterparts, they must be prepared a bit differently. A chicken burger made with just ground chicken would be tough and dry, but one made with added ingredients like sautéed onions and breadcrumbs is moist and delicious.

Whether you cook chicken specifically to make sandwiches and salads or use a rotisserie chicken purchased at the supermarket, there are many delicious and super-easy precooked chicken recipes that are delicious and satisfying. Salads and sandwiches are easy to make when you have cubed cooked chicken on hand in the fridge or freezer.

And leftovers, those overlooked bonus points of cooking, are treated to a wonderful array of foods, flavorings, and cooking methods for the perfect end to the perfect bird. In fact, it's always a good idea to cook an extra thigh, breast, or leg so you'll have some chopped cooked chicken on hand at all times.

So let's get started learning about chicken and other poultry products, like turkey and Cornish game hens. Your repertoire will increase exponentially as you learn how to cook each part of the chicken. As you gain confidence in the kitchen, you will be creating your own masterpieces in no time.

KINDS OF CHICKEN

The types and variety of chicken you choose affect the final outcome

There are quite a few different kinds of chicken available in the market. These classifications separate the product depending on how it's raised.

Typically, factory-farmed chickens are treated rather brutally, kept indoors in small cages and not allowed much of a life. Many organizations have protested against chicken producers, so humanely farmed, or "sustainably farmed," chicken is on the increase.

As light has been shed on these practices, consumption of factory-farmed chicken has declined, while consumption of free range and sustainably farmed chicken has increased. Consumers care about the welfare of animals.

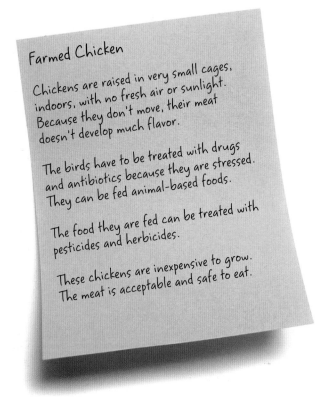

Farmed Chicken

Chickens are raised in very small cages, indoors, with no fresh air or sunlight. Because they don't move, their meat doesn't develop much flavor.

The birds have to be treated with drugs and antibiotics because they are stressed. They can be fed animal-based foods.

The food they are fed can be treated with pesticides and herbicides.

These chickens are inexpensive to grow. The meat is acceptable and safe to eat.

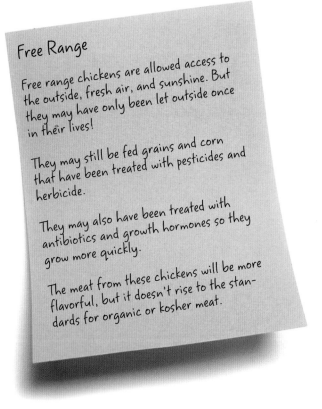

Free Range

Free range chickens are allowed access to the outside, fresh air, and sunshine. But they may have only been let outside once in their lives!

They may still be fed grains and corn that have been treated with pesticides and herbicide.

They may also have been treated with antibiotics and growth hormones so they grow more quickly.

The meat from these chickens will be more flavorful, but it doesn't rise to the standards for organic or kosher meat.

Many of these mistreated animals have to be treated with antibiotics and hormones. The effect of these products on human health really hasn't been studied. There does seem to be more concern about these practices in Britain and Europe than in the United States.

Free range and organic chicken is more expensive than factory-farmed chicken, but the difference in color, flavor, and texture is marked. If you have the choice, look for chickens raised under more humane conditions so you can enjoy your meal with better taste and a cleaner conscience.

Organic

- Organic chicken has to meet strict standards to be labeled as such.

- The birds must be fed only organic grains, raised on a farm that has been chemical-free for at least three years.

- The chickens are not given hormones, drugs, or antibiotics to help increase growth or size.

- And the birds roam outside, with access to fresh air and sunshine.

Kosher

- Kosher chickens are prepared under very humane standards. The bird is kept as stress-free as possible.

- These chickens are naturally more expensive, but their taste and texture may be worth it to you.

- Rabbinical inspectors check the birds to make sure they are healthy before slaughter.

- These chickens are fed only grain, are free range, and aren't given antibiotics. Their feed may have been treated with chemicals, however.

TYPES OF CHICKEN
Chickens are labeled according to their size and age

Chicken types vary according to how old the bird is, which dictates how each should be prepared. Young chickens can be prepared using any method, while older birds need special care to become tender and juicy.

Chickens are harvested very young. The oldest usually aren't even a year old. This makes their meat tender and juicy, but not as flavorful as other meats.

Because chickens have little fat and little connective tissue, they cook more quickly than other meats. A whole chicken, roasted in the oven, can be finished in about an hour, while the same size cut of beef needs several hours to become tender.

Chicken labels can be confusing. The terms are vague, so it's important to know what they mean.

KNACK CHICKEN CLASSICS

Capon

- Capons are castrated male chickens that are fed a fattening diet, and are about 8–9 months old. They weigh about 6–10 pounds.

- The meat of the capon is very flavorful and tender. They're great for making slow-roasted chicken.

- These chickens can be harder to find than regular broilers or roasters. You may need to specially order them.

- Capons tend to have more white meat than dark, which benefits those who like that type of meat.

Broiler-Fryers

- These chickens weigh 2–4 pounds. You can prepare them using any cooking method.

- The birds are usually about 12 weeks old when harvested. They can be grilled, fried, stir-fried, or broiled.

- These are the most versatile of chickens, and are the type most commonly found in the supermarket, whole or in parts.

- Dry heat methods are used to cook this type of chicken quickly. Marinades and sauces help enhance flavor.

"One hundred percent natural" means the poultry doesn't have artificial ingredients, but it can be fed grain mixed with preservatives, and there's no outside monitoring of this term. "Grain fed" should mean the birds were not fed animal products, but that isn't guaranteed.

So what should you do? Ask questions! If you buy your chicken in a supermarket, as most Americans do, ask the butcher what these names mean. Look for chickens raised by reputable farmers, and try to buy organic birds if you can.

Roasters

- Roasters are chickens that are a little older, about 3–4 months. They weigh 4–7 pounds.

- They have more flavor than broiler-fryers, along with a higher fat content that allows them to be cooked longer.

- These chickens can also be cooked on a rotisserie, either in the oven or on the grill. Dry heat, for a relatively short time, is best.

- With more flavor, these birds are also good for recipes like Chicken Cacciatore.

Stewing Hens

- These are mature chickens at least 10 months old. They are larger, and usually weigh around 5–7 pounds.

- The chicken is best used in stews, soups, or the slow cooker. The meat is tougher because the bird is older, but it is very flavorful.

- The hens have stopped laying eggs, which is traditionally when they have been used for meat.

- Stewing hens aren't often found on the market anymore; they were more common in the 20th century.

OTHER POULTRY

Chickens aren't the only birds in the poultry world

Other poultry you can find in the supermarket includes Cornish game hens, turkey, poussins, ducks, and game birds.

Cornish game hens are tiny, usually 1–2 pounds in weight. The larger hens can serve two people. Their flavor is stronger than regular chickens. These hens cost more than chickens do, pound for pound, as they are considered a specialty item. They are easy to overcook because they are so small; be sure to cook just until the temperature reaches 165ºF.

All Americans are familiar with turkey. These large birds weigh 10–24 pounds and are usually served at Thanksgiving. But they are a great choice for other times of the year, and turkey parts, especially the tenderloin, can make a quick and delicious meal.

Duck isn't a meat commonly consumed in this country. The

Turkey

- Turkeys are rich and flavorful. When properly cooked, they are also juicy. Overcooked turkey is unfortunately common.

- Follow directions carefully for roasting the turkey, especially if you want to stuff it.

- Turkeys range from 10–25 pounds. The smallest turkeys are females, while the largest are males, also known as toms.

- Cook thawed turkeys for about 20–25 minutes per pound. Increase that time to 35–40 minutes per pound when the bird is stuffed.

Cornish Hen

- A Cornish hen, or Cornish game hen, is a cross between a Cornish and White Rock or Plymouth Rock chicken.

- They are very small, less than 2 pounds apiece. Figure 1 bird per serving. They are tender and juicy, as they are usually only 5–6 weeks old.

- A poussin is the British name for what Americans consider a Cornish game hen.

- The poussin, however, is much smaller, about half the age and half the size of the Cornish hen.

meat is very fatty, and cooking it involves removing fat that renders in the heat. Ducks are very strongly flavored, and are usually served with a citrus sauce.

Game birds include partridge, pheasant, and quail. These birds have quite a strong flavor, which is aptly described as "gamey." This flavor is bold and earthy. Brining the birds can help reduce this intense flavor. When you serve these birds, be sure to read any instructions that come with the bird and follow cooking directions carefully each time.

YELLOW ● LIGHT

All of these birds are usually sold frozen. You must thaw them carefully, according to the package directions. Never thaw at room temperature. Thaw in the refrigerator or under cold running water. You can cook your turkey frozen; see the chapter on turkey.

Duck

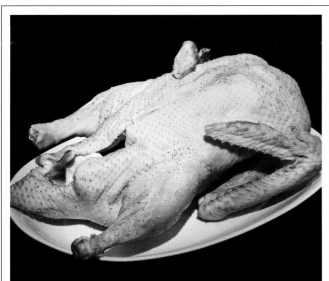

- Duck is usually roasted or braised. Roasting helps remove the fat and makes a crisp skin.

- Braising makes the duck tender and helps mute the strong gamey flavor of the duck.

- Duck meat is much darker than the meat from other birds. It pairs well with red wine, port, spices, and rich fruits.

- To help remove the fat, steam the duck to melt it before roasting or braising.

Game Birds

- Game birds are usually special order, unless you have a hunter in the family.

- Because the birds are strongly flavored, they are usually cooked with ingredients like oranges, onions, figs, and root vegetables.

- Be careful to remove any buckshot or birdshot if the bird you are preparing is wild.

- These birds are often lower in fat than farm-raised birds, so they need added fat, like bacon or butter, for flavor.

5

HERBS & SPICES
Fresh or dried herbs and spices can turn your chicken into a feast

Because chicken is so mildly flavored, it can be paired with every herb and spice on the planet. The addition of some chopped parsley can transform chicken and dumplings, while curry powder makes a fabulous Tandoori Chicken, and hot chile peppers turn grilled chicken into a Tex-Mex feast.

Herbs are the edible leaves of plants. They include rosemary, chervil, oregano, thyme, basil, savory, sage, tarragon, bay, dill, lavender, fennel, marjoram, mint, parsley, cilantro, and verbena. These herbs are available fresh or dried.

When substituting dried herbs for fresh, or vice-versa, remember that 1 tablespoon of fresh chopped or minced herbs is equal to 1 teaspoon dried herbs.

You can give dried herbs more flavor by crushing them between your fingertips before adding to the recipe.

KNACK CHICKEN CLASSICS

Nutmeg with Grater

- For the most intense flavor, use whole spices and grind or grate them yourself.

- Microplane graters are great for this type of use. You can find nutmeg graters that come in a jar that holds the whole nutmeg.

- A mortar and pestle can be used to grind spices; break them up first with your hands.

- Or you can use a spice grinder or a small coffee grinder, used only for grinding spices.

Ground Spices

- Ground spices you buy already ground will lose flavor after a few months.

- Smell the spices. If you don't jump back from the strength of the aroma, discard the spice and buy new.

- Curry powder is made of a blend of spices, including cinnamon, pepper, saffron, coriander, cumin, ginger, mace, and garlic.

- You can make your own spice blends. Make your own curry powder or chili powder.

Chopping dried herbs together with fresh herbs like parsley can also enhance the flavor.

Spices, which are the roots, berries, seeds, and bark of plants, include cinnamon, turmeric, cardamom, allspice, bay leaf, cloves, paprika, nutmeg, cumin, mustard, saffron, and pepper. Seeds include sesame seeds, fennel seeds, cumin, and dill. Curry powder and chili powder are spice blends, not individual spices.

Some spices improve when they are heated. Curry powder, for instance, is enhanced when it is cooked.

······· GREEN ● LIGHT ·······

Herbs can be grown in pots in your backyard or on a stoop. You don't need a whole garden to grow herbs for cooking. In fact, you can grow enough herbs in pots to dry or freeze for use in the winter. Herbs like water and sunlight.

Windowsill Herbs

- You can buy kits for growing herbs on a windowsill. Most herbs require direct sunlight.

- You can create your own windowsill herb garden. Use small pots, pick a good dirt mix, and add some seeds.

- Be sure to water your mini garden well, but don't drown the seeds.

- The dirt should be a light mix, combined with peat moss, sand, or Perlite. Place the pots on a tray to protect your windowsill.

Dried Herbs

- You can dry your own herbs by using a food dehydrator. It can be difficult to dry herbs in the oven, but it's possible.

- Keep dried herbs tightly sealed in a glass or plastic container, in a cool, dry place away from light.

- Just as with spices, smell the herbs before you use them. If they don't smell very intense, buy a new jar.

- Herbs don't have to be expensive. Look for tiny jars with only about a tablespoon per jar.

SAUCES

Sauces range from simple butter sauce to complex Alfredo or marinara

The best sauces for chicken use the chicken. When chicken is browned in fat, it will leave behind small browned pieces, called drippings, that have a lot of flavor. Deglaze the pan with vegetables or some type of liquid to dissolve the drippings into the sauce.

For the easiest pan sauce, just season and brown chicken, then add liquid to remove drippings. Return the chicken to the pan and simmer until done.

Chicken can also be paired with other sauces. Simmer the broth used to deglaze the pan until it's thick, then swirl in butter to make a simple and flavorful sauce. If the sauce is very reduced so it coats the chicken, it's called a glaze.

Simple Pan Sauce

- The secrets to a simple pan sauce are to brown the chicken thoroughly, use a flavorful liquid, and season it well.

- Chicken broth or stock is one of the best liquids for making a pan sauce, but you can use marinades or liquids from vegetables or fruits.

- For a nice finish for a simple pan sauce, swirl in a tablespoon of butter at the last second.

- Taste the sauce before serving and add more salt or pepper if necessary.

Reduction

- The point of reduction is to concentrate and increase flavor.

- So you have to start with high quality ingredients. Use homemade or boxed stocks, and don't be afraid of herbs and spices.

- When reducing a sauce, watch it carefully. It can go from burnished and perfect to burnt in seconds.

- You can reduce sauces right in the pan over high heat, or reduce liquid, then add to the pan to create a sauce.

The next step up is a white sauce, made by cooking flour in fat, then adding broth and milk or cream. This sauce can be flavored with citrus juices, herbs, fruits, or vegetables. If made with cream, it's called an Alfredo sauce. When cheese is added, it becomes a cheese sauce.

Pasta sauce, made with tomatoes and usually served over cooked linguine or spaghetti, turns plain chicken into Chicken Parmesan.

And of course, chicken in barbecue sauce is called barbecued chicken.

•••••••••••••• RED ● LIGHT ••••••••••••••

Never partially cook chicken and then save it, even in the refrigerator or freezer, to cook later. It may be tempting, especially in a recipe that calls for browning chicken, making a sauce, then returning chicken to the sauce to finish it. Always fully cook chicken immediately for food safety reasons.

Glaze

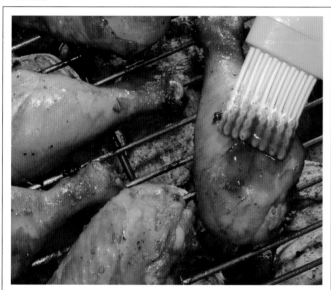

- A glaze can be made from a sauce that has been reduced to a syrupy consistency.

- It can also be made from a liquid mixture, thickened or not, that is brushed onto chicken that is then grilled or broiled.

- A glaze is usually shiny and highly flavored. It can be used on skinless chicken or skin-on chicken parts.

- Glazes usually have some sweet ingredients so they will brown, thicken, and turn shiny in the heat.

Gravy

- Turkey gravy, that bane of Thanksgiving hosts, can be made several ways.

- You can just add a slurry of flour and water to the drippings remaining in the pan; stir vigorously with a whisk.

- Or make a roux with fat and flour, then add broth made from the giblets and turkey neck.

- The secret to the best gravy is adding enough salt. Keep adding salt and tasting. When the flavor blooms, you've added enough.

COATINGS
Crisp, crunchy, or velvety coatings all help preserve juiciness

Whether you like skin-on or skinless chicken, coating adds texture and flavor. You can coat chicken with anything from a simple marinade to seasoned flour, breadcrumbs, cheese, or batter.

Make sure the chicken is dry before starting the coating process. A thin layer of flour can help the egg wash, batter, or other breading stick more thoroughly. Chilling the coated chicken before browning, grilling, or frying will also help the coating adhere.

So the coating will stick to chicken, you can dip the chicken in beaten egg, buttermilk, or other dairy products like milk, cream, or soft cheeses. Other wet ingredients can be combinations of egg and water, buttermilk and mustard, yogurt, and herbs. Use your imagination to come up with ingredients

Dredging

- To dredge means to immerse in a dry ingredient, then shake off the excess.

- Chicken is usually dredged in flour to help create a sauce, or before dipping into an egg mixture, then into crumbs.

- The dredging helps the coating adhere to the slippery chicken.

- You can put flour on a plate and dip chicken into it, or put it into a plastic or paper bag. Add the chicken and shake until coated.

Coating

- Breadcrumbs can be soft (made from fresh bread) or dried (made from dried bread). Add dried herbs for more flavor.

- Panko, or Japanese breadcrumbs, is a specialty product that makes an exceptionally crisp crust.

- Ground crackers can be purchased or made by placing crackers in a plastic bag and pounding.

- Make your own coating by combining anything from grated cheese to crushed pretzels to potato flakes, chips, or ground nuts.

for the wet layer that will add flavor as well as something for breadcrumbs or cracker crumbs to stick to.

You can make coatings from soft bread or dried bread, cracker or pretzel crumbs, crushed nuts, or grated cheese.

Batters should be thick enough to stick to the meat, but not so thick that the coating doesn't cook through. The coated chicken can be microwaved, panfried, deep-fried, baked, grilled, or broiled. A few minutes rest on a wire rack before cooking will help the coating set so it stays on the chicken.

ZOOM

To help with cleanup, when you're coating chicken keep a wet hand and a dry hand. Use one hand to dip the chicken into the dry ingredients, and the other to work with the wet ingredients. Or cover your hands with small plastic bags as you work.

Marinade

- Chicken can be marinated to add flavor and moisture, and to make the chicken very tender.

- White meat usually should only be marinated for a few hours in the fridge, or it can become mushy.

- A marinade combines an acidic ingredient like buttermilk or lemon juice with herbs, seasonings, and a bit of oil.

- The marinade can be discarded after use, or used to make a sauce or glaze added during cooking.

Batter

- Battered chicken is almost always deep-fried. Dredge the chicken in flour first, then dip it into batter.

- Then cook the chicken immediately in oil heated to 375°F.

- Battered chicken can also be used in Chinese recipes, like Sweet and Sour Chicken.

- There are batter mixes on the market, or you can just make your own. Batters are made of flour, liquid, seasonings, and sometimes leavening.

11

WHOLE CHICKEN

A whole chicken is usually prepared by grilling or roasting

The first time you look for a whole chicken in the supermarket, you may be surprised how small they are. A roasting chicken is usually only about 3–4 pounds.

Because the chickens are so young when harvested, they are very tender, but need some help in the flavor department. They will roast or grill quickly and are easy to season with herbs and spices.

When you buy chicken parts, you are basically buying a whole chicken minus the back. These parts are easy to season, cook, serve, and eat. You can purchase bone-in or boneless, skin-on or skinless, depending on your tastes and how you plan to cook the chicken.

When cooking whole chickens, food safety has to be at the forefront. Stuffing the birds can be risky, as the temperature

Whole Chicken

- Whole chickens are sold frozen or fresh. They are quite perishable and should be cooked or frozen within 2 days.

- Open the package over the sink, as there is usually quite a bit of liquid in the chicken.

- Remove the giblets, if any, rinse the chicken, and pat dry with paper towels.

- Then you can stuff the bird, season it, truss it if you'd like, and roast or grill.

Chicken Parts

- Chicken parts come in several different assortments. You can find breasts, cut-up chicken, thighs, or wings.

- There should not be much juice in the package, and the meat should be firm.

- The color of the chicken doesn't matter too much. There should not be too much fat on the bird.

- Some packages are assembled with more than 2 breasts or drumsticks for larger families.

inside the stuffing in the center of the bird must reach 165ºF. An accurate food thermometer is an important tool when working with chicken.

Compare prices when you're buying chicken. Sometimes the whole birds are a better deal than the parts. If you want parts, you must cut up the chicken. This isn't difficult; just follow the lines of the bird and use a sharp knife. Work carefully and save the back for stock.

•••••••••••••••••••• GREEN ● LIGHT ••••••••••••••••••

Freeze any leftover chicken pieces or parts and collect them in your freezer to make homemade stock. When you have about 2 pounds of the parts, cover with water, add some chopped vegetables, salt, and pepper, and simmer 3–4 hours.

Food Safety

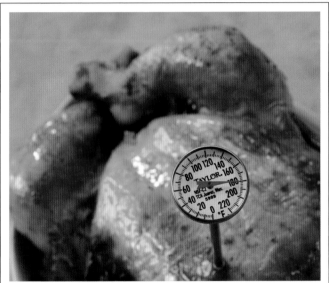

- A meat thermometer, whether regular or instant-read, is a necessity for safety.

- Always wash your hands, utensils, and work surface before and after working with raw chicken or poultry.

- Refrigerate chicken promptly, both while raw and after cooking. It should not be at room temperature longer than 2 hours.

- Never store raw poultry above fresh foods; the juices can drip onto the food.

Doneness Tests

- There are ways other than temperature to check doneness.

- However, these are just tests. For true safety, you have to check the internal temperature of the bird.

- One test is to prick the chicken. If the juices run clear, with no tinge of pink, the chicken may be thoroughly cooked; check the temperature.

- When roasting a whole chicken, if the drumstick is loose in the joint when rotated, the chicken is ready to be tested.

BREAST

The chicken breast can be bone-in or boneless; this simple meat takes on many cuisines

Chicken breasts are also known as the white, or light, meat. They can be found in several incarnations.

Bone-in, skin-on chicken breasts are the most common. They are actually made of one breast split in half. For the best flavor and the juiciest result, cook chicken on the bone with the skin on.

Boneless, skinless chicken breasts are a great convenience and time saver. You can bone breasts yourself with a sharp knife. Just pull off the skin and cut the meat away from the bone. Reserve the bone and skin in the freezer for home-made stock.

Chicken cutlets are chicken breasts that have been cut into

Bone-in Breasts

- Bone-in chicken breasts have more flavor than bone-less meat. There are several ways to add more flavor.

- You can gently loosen the skin from the flesh and add salt and pepper, fresh herbs, spices, or condiments like mustard.

- Then just smooth the skin back over the flesh and cook the chicken breasts as usual.

- Bone-in, skin-on breasts take longer to cook than boneless; about 40–50 minutes in a 350°F oven.

Boneless, Skinless Breasts

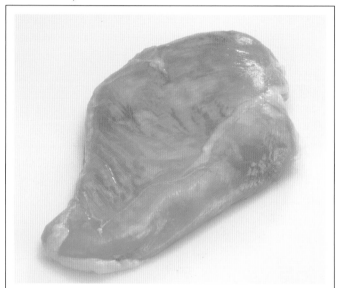

- Boneless, skinless chicken breasts are ready to use— as is, or cut into strips or cubes.

- Use a sharp knife to cut the breasts into smaller pieces. To make it easier, freeze the breasts for 10–15 minutes.

- Boneless, skinless chicken breasts are often marinated for more flavor.

- Add the chicken to the marinade, cover, and refrigerate for 8–24 hours. Any longer, and the meat can become mushy or tough when cooked.

thinner pieces. These cook very quickly, usually only for a minute or two on each side. They can be breaded or coated in a seasoned flour mixture to help preserve moisture.

Chicken fingers are usually made of the chicken tenderloin. This is a small piece of meat under the breast. If you trim your own bone-in breasts, you'll see the tenderloin; it's closest to the bone. The tenderloin usually has a strong tendon running through it that should be removed before cooking.

However you cook chicken breasts, be sure not to overcook them or they can become dry. Cook just to 160ºF.

ZOOM

Chicken breasts are very low in fat. Most of the fat is in the skin. If you cook the breast with the skin on, the chicken will remain more moist and tender, but as long as you don't eat the skin, the fat content of the meat doesn't increase.

Cutlets

- Cutlets can be cut thin or pounded thin. If pounded, the cutlets have a tendency to shrink when cooked.

- You can cut your own cutlets. Just cut a boneless, skinless chicken breast in halves or thirds horizontally.

- To pound cutlets, cut chicken breasts in half crosswise. Place between sheets of plastic wrap and gently pound.

- Sauté or quickly panfry these cuts so they don't overcook. Coat them in breadcrumbs or seasoned flour.

Chicken Fingers

- Chicken fingers are just breast meat cut into strips. They come from the breast itself or the tenderloin.

- If using the tenderloin, cut across each one to make shorter strips.

- You may want to use a knife to pull out the tough tendon that runs along the tenderloin.

- Marinate the strips in buttermilk or a lemon marinade, then coat in flour and breadcrumbs. Bake or fry until crisp.

15

WINGS

The chicken wing is usually served as an appetizer

Chicken wings are an inexpensive cut of the bird that can be cooked and flavored in many ways.

Chicken wings can be purchased whole, or cut into "drummies." This is the meaty part of the wing, with the thinner part and the tip cut off. The drummies, if you buy them separately, are more expensive per pound than the whole wing, especially considering that you can serve the thinner part of the wing and save the tips to make a stock later.

Wings have a surprising amount of meat on them. They can be deep-fried, panfried, grilled, broiled, or roasted.

Chicken wings are almost never skinned before use. The skin keeps the meat moist and tender and adds a lot of flavor, and really is about half of the chicken wing eating experience. If you are going to slow cook chicken wings, you should brown

Whole Wings

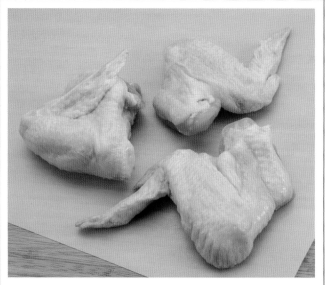

- Whole wings are almost never served as-is; they are cut apart into several pieces.

- The wings each weigh about ⅓ of a pound. A serving of wings for an appetizer is 4–6 wings per person.

- You can freeze whole wings, then thaw them in the refrigerator overnight.

- Chicken wings can be used to make a rich stock. Simmer the wings for about 1 hour, then remove the wings and the meat; return bones and skin to the stock and continue simmering.

Chicken Drummies

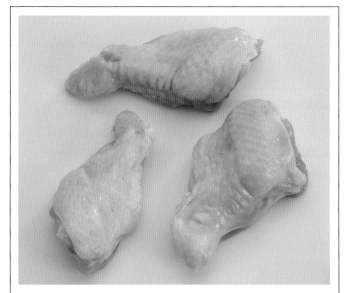

- Chicken drummies are the meaty part of the wing; they are prepared by the butcher and marketed as such.

- You can make chicken drummies look like little drumsticks by pulling the meat off one end of the bone.

- Pull the meat over the bone and use your knife to scrape the bone clean.

- Then cook the drummies by broiling, baking, or deep-frying until the temperature reaches 170ºF.

or broil them, either before or after slow cooking, so the skin isn't flabby.

Wings are usually very strongly seasoned, simply because they are served as appetizers. A dry rub, a marinade, or a crisp coating adds great flavor and texture and makes the wings seem more substantial.

Serve your chicken wings with a dipping sauce, made of anything from salsa to sour cream and mustard, to enhance the flavor.

· · · · · · · · · · · GREEN ● LIGHT · · · · · · · · · · ·

There are three parts of the wing: the thick part, a thinner part that is just as long, and the tip. If you serve a lot of chicken wings, cut them apart yourself and save the tips for stock. Use a sharp knife and work carefully.

Wing Tips

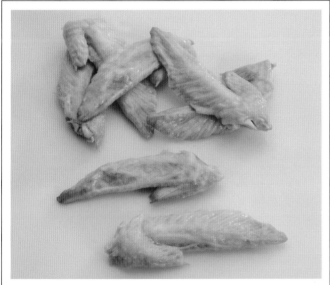

- Wing tips are usually not sold in the supermarket. You may ask the butcher for them, if the store sells drummies.

- When you use the wing tips to make stock, don't remove them to take off the meat.

- Cook the wings in the broth for the entire time. They will add a nice flavor to the stock.

- You can add the wings to the broth mixture frozen; they will thaw in a few minutes as the stock simmers.

Cut-up Chicken Wings

- This is what the three sections of the wing look like. It's important to cut the wings through the joint.

- Don't splinter the bone or you won't be able to serve the wings.

- Cutting the wings exposes more of the skin, making them cook evenly and providing more surface for breading and sauce.

- The wings are often sold in large bulk packages called family packs.

DRUMSTICKS

Drumsticks are kids' favorites; their tender meat is flavorful

Chicken drumsticks are fun to make and fun to eat. Children especially love them; they are tender and juicy and come with a built-in handle.

You can cook chicken drumsticks with or without the skin. If you're going to make a crisp coating for the drumstick, it is better to remove the skin. That way you can savor the crunchy coating without worrying about extra fat and calories.

The drumsticks are dark meat, which means they take longer to cook than white meat. But they also stay more moist and tender because they contain more fat.

You can do lots of fun things with drumsticks. Coat them with crushed taco chips, bake until crisp, and serve with a dipping sauce made of sour cream and salsa. Or skin the drumsticks, marinate in a curry mixture, roll in breadcrumbs,

Whole Drumstick

- Drumsticks marinate very well; the tender meat absorbs the flavors easily.

- Whole drumsticks with skin should be cooked until the skin is crisp, unless you are going to remove it before eating.

- If you do remove the skin before eating, you will remove much of the fat in the product while keeping the meat moist.

- To get a crisp skin, grilling, frying, baking, or broiling are the preferred methods.

Skinless Drumstick

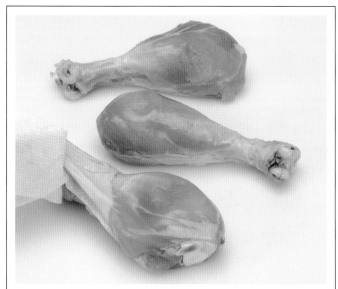

- To remove the skin before cooking, grip the drumstick firmly and pick up a paper towel with your other hand.

- Use the paper towel to pull the skin away from the flesh, starting at the bone.

- You can discard the skin or save it in the freezer to use for making broth or stock.

- Drumsticks should be cooked to 170–175ºF. The temperature will rise about 5ºF after cooking.

and broil. Serve with a sauce made from mango chutney and plain yogurt. The possibilities are endless.

You can usually buy drumsticks in a family or bulk package, which is useful if you want to serve them to a family or crowd. Or you can buy a whole chicken, cut it up, and freeze the drumsticks until you have accumulated enough to serve to your family or guests.

YELLOW LIGHT

When serving drumsticks to your kids, they should be served while hot, but you don't want them to burn their fingers. Wrap the thin part of the drumstick with foil and a paper towel so it's easy for them to grip the drumstick. Small pot holders would also work to protect their hands.

Turkey Drumstick

- Turkey drumsticks are also available in bulk packages. The drumsticks weigh about 1 pound each.

- About half of the drumstick is meat, which means each has about ½ pound of meat, which serves 2 people.

- Turkey drumsticks, like the whole turkey, are a good choice for brining. Use any brine recipe.

- Drumsticks are a good source for dark meat; cook in the slow cooker or braise until the meat falls off the bone.

Baked Drumsticks

- Baking, or "oven-frying," drumsticks is the healthiest way to cook them if you want crisp skin.

- Put the drumsticks on a rack after being coated with flour or breadcrumbs, which allows the heat to circulate evenly.

- This prevents having one soggy side, which can occur when the drumsticks are baked in a sauce or on the pan.

- Bake at a relatively high temperature, at least 400ºF, for a crisp finish.

THIGHS

Chicken thighs, or dark meat, are tender and juicy no matter how they are prepared

Chicken thighs are becoming very popular as a single cut. Their taste is rich and meaty, and it's very difficult to overcook them. They are a wonderful choice for slow cooker recipes.

For those who like dark meat, chicken thighs are perfect. They are also less expensive than chicken breasts and have more flavor. They are high in fat, however.

You can find chicken thighs bone-in or boneless. They are easy to bone if you'd like to buy the bone-in type and do it yourself. As always, save the trimmings for stock.

Cook chicken thighs to an internal temperature of 170ºF. They will still be moist, tender, and juicy at this temperature.

Often in the supermarket, you'll find the thigh/leg combi-

Bone-in Thighs

- Bone-in, skin-on thighs should be plump and meaty, heavy for their size, and evenly colored.

- There shouldn't be too much fat on the thighs. You can trim off excess fat and save it for making stock.

- Thighs have twice the amount of fat of boneless, skinless chicken breasts, but it's about the same as in beef or pork.

- Allow 2 chicken thighs per person, as they are smaller than the breast.

Boneless, Skinless Thighs

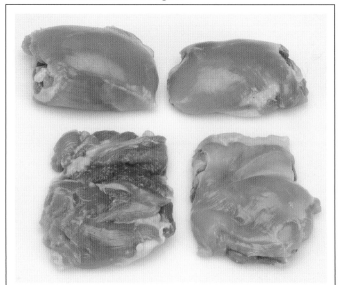

- You can purchase boneless, skinless thighs or make them yourself, depending on the cost per pound.

- Save the bone and skin in the freezer to make stock. Package in a freezer bag and freeze up to 6 months.

- To remove the skin yourself, grasp it with a paper towel and pull it off.

- Using a sharp knife, trim off any excess fat and cut the meat away from the bone.

nation. Compare prices per pound. If this combination is a better buy, purchase them and separate the thigh from the drumstick at the joint. Freeze the drumsticks for later use.

Even with a stronger flavor than chicken breasts, thighs are delicious using every ethnic flavor in the world. Tex-Mex thighs can be made spicy with jalapeño peppers and chili powder. Use them in a stir-fry with a teriyaki marinade. Or season them with citrus juices and fresh herbs for a French twist.

Turkey Thighs

- Turkey thighs, especially if they are boneless and skinless, are a great way to get a lot of dark meat.

- Just put them in the slow cooker with some water, onions, carrots, salt, pepper, and herbs.

- Cover and cook on low for 8–9 hours until the meat reaches 170ºF.

- Chop the meat and freeze it; freeze the broth too, and use in recipes from chicken salad to casseroles.

Slow-Cooked Thighs

- Slow cooking is a great way to cook thighs. They can cook on low up to 9 hours without becoming dry.

- You can brown the thighs first, especially if you leave the skin on, for more color and flavor.

- To decide if bone-in or boneless thighs are a better buy, realize that 25 percent of the thigh by weight is bone.

- If the cost of the boneless thighs is more than 25 percent higher, bone-in is a better buy.

BONES & GIBLETS
Bones and giblets have their uses: making stock and gravy

Chicken bones are very valuable. The flavor and body they provide to homemade chicken stock is incomparable. If you've never had homemade stock, you are in for a treat. Even the best boxed stocks will taste salty and weak next to homemade stock.

Roasting the bones, especially if there is meat or fat still attached to them, adds great depth of flavor to your stock.

By the way, if bones are used in the recipe, it's called stock. If only the meat and skin are used, it's called broth.

Giblets are the internal organs of the chicken. They usually include the heart, liver, neck, and gizzard. The liver can be used to make Chopped Chicken Liver, a hearty and old-fashioned appetizer. And the other parts can be used to make stock or broth for Giblet Gravy.

Chicken Broth

Chicken Broth

2 pounds chicken bones and trimmings

1 onion, chopped

3 cloves garlic, cut in half

2 carrots, sliced

2 tablespoons olive oil

8 cups water, divided

3 stalks celery, sliced

1/4 cup celery leaves

1 1/2 teaspoons salt

1/4 teaspoon pepper

1 teaspoon dried thyme

1 teaspoon dried basil

- Preheat oven to 400ºF. Place bones, onion, garlic, and carrots in roasting pan and drizzle with olive oil.

- Roast for 40–50 minutes until bones are dark golden. Place in 4-quart slow cooker.

- Rinse roasting pan with 1/2 cup water and add to slow cooker with remaining ingredients.

- Cover ; cook on low 8–9 hours. Strain broth, discarding solids. Skim fat; freeze broth in 1¾ cup portions to substitute for 14-ounce cans chicken broth.

The giblets usually come in a paper package in the center of the chicken. They are more commonly found in whole turkeys. For Thanksgiving, gravy made from a broth of the giblets has a rich and deep flavor.

There are some recipes that are made just from the giblets, but they are not common. The taste of these recipes is very rich and takes some getting used to.

Giblet Gravy

Giblet Gravy

Giblets from turkey or chicken

3 cups water

1 onion, chopped

2 cloves garlic, minced

1 teaspoon salt

1/8 teaspoon pepper

1/4 cup butter or drippings

1/4 cup flour

- Rinse the giblets and place in saucepan. Add water, onion, garlic, salt, and pepper and bring to a simmer.

- Reduce heat to very low and simmer for 2–3 hours, adding more water if necessary. Strain broth, reserving giblets.

- Discard the neck; chop the remaining giblets finely. Melt butter or drippings in saucepan.

- Add flour; cook and stir until light golden brown. Add enough of the broth to make a smooth gravy. Stir in giblets; simmer 10 minutes.

FOUR BEST TOOLS

You need certain tools to cook a large range of chicken recipes

You don't need a lot of fancy equipment to cook chicken to perfection, but the tools and appliances you do have should be top quality. Buy the best equipment you can afford.

A frying pan is the first tool to buy. With it, you can panfry, stir-fry, sauté, braise, and roast chicken, as long as the pan is ovenproof. And it should be. An ovenproof pan gives you the most flexibility.

The pan should be heavy, made of stainless steel, cast iron, or anodized aluminum. The pan should have moderately high sides that are gently sloping. A 10-inch frying pan is basic, with an integral handle or a handle attached with steel rivets.

A roasting pan is the best choice for cooking the Thanksgiving turkey, as well as more than two whole chickens at once.

Frying Pan

- Several different frying pans are nice to have on hand. An 8-inch pan can double as an omelet pan.

- A 10-inch pan will be the one you'll reach for most often, and a 12-inch pan is useful for panfrying large batches.

- The pans should be ovenproof; that is, with handles made to withstand high heat.

- But make sure those handles will stay cool on the stovetop; they should be hollowed out or made of slightly different material.

Roasting Pan

- A roasting pan is large and heavy, with sides that are about 3 inches tall.

- A roasting pan with attached handles should be made of stainless steel, clad aluminum, or anodized aluminum.

- A wire rack is a great way to help the chicken keep its shape without trussing. A rack also helps the chicken brown.

- Some roasting pans come complete with a rack, or you can buy one separately at any kitchen supply store.

It is large and heavy and, if well made, will last a lifetime.

Tongs are important for handling chicken, whether you're dipping it in batter, removing it from oil, or turning stuffed chicken breasts in a frying pan. The tongs should be spring-loaded, so you don't have to pry the handles apart.

And a slow cooker will turn chicken thighs or breasts into a sumptuous feast from any corner of the world. A five-quart oval is a good size to hold different cuts of chicken, and will serve a family of six easily.

Spring-Loaded Tongs

- Several pairs of tongs will help make cooking chicken easier.

- Spring-loaded tongs are held open automatically, so the only action you have to perform is closing them.

- It's too difficult to pry open tongs and then close them again, so make sure your tongs have this capability.

- Tongs come in various lengths and strengths. Longer tongs are good for working on the grill or over a deep fryer.

Slow Cooker

- Slow cookers have changed dramatically in the last 10 years. You can buy them in sizes from 1½-quart to 8-quart.

- Oval slow cookers seem to work best when cooking chicken parts; they will accommodate more bulk.

- A 4- or 5-quart slow cooker should meet most of your cooking needs. Look for several heat settings, delayed start, and keep-warm settings.

- Slow cookers are safe to use with chicken; just remember to use your meat thermometer.

METHODS

FRYING & STIR-FRYING
Chicken cooks beautifully with these dry heat methods

Fried chicken is a classic Southern recipe that melts in your mouth when correctly cooked. Deep-frying chicken can be tricky, and there are several rules to follow.

You need a thermometer to check the temperature of the oil. And the chicken has to be coated in a certain number of layers to develop a crisp crust.

Stir-frying is an art unto itself. If you are really into this healthy kind of cooking, get a good heavy Chinese wok and spatula for most authentic results. If you only stir-fry a few times a month, a heavy skillet and long handled spatula will work just fine. Just have all of the ingredients prepared and ready to go before you start cooking, and keep the food moving in the skillet or wok.

Panfrying is a close cousin to deep-frying, but the food isn't

Deep-Fried Chicken

- To deep-fry chicken, you'll need a very heavy pan with sides at least 3 inches deep.

- You can use a deep fryer. But never fry food in a pressure cooker; you're just asking for disaster.

- Add 4–6 cups of oil to the pan. Be sure that you leave at least 2 inches of head space between the oil and the top of the pan.

- The best oils to choose have a high smoke point, and include canola, corn, peanut, and safflower oils.

Chicken Stir-Fry

- Oils with a high smoke point make the best stir-fries. Make sure the wok or pan is dry before you add oil.

- All of the ingredients should be chopped, sliced, or diced to the same size so they cook at the same time.

- Have all the ingredients by the stove, in order of use.

- Stir constantly as you add the food to the hot oil. Cook just until the chicken is done and vegetables are crisp-tender.

completely immersed in the hot oil. You can panfry food in just a quarter inch or less of oil.

You can "fry" in the oven with a few methods. Cooking at very high heat will make the coating on the chicken sizzle, replicating the heat of the oil. Or you can place the chicken in a thin layer of fat in the oven.

Panfried Chicken

- Foods qualify as panfried if the oil only covers them halfway. The food is turned during cooking.

- Always use a long handled, sturdy spatula and handle the food with care so you don't splash oil as you turn.

- Any water or liquid will cause spattering when added to the hot oil, so stand back when you add it.

- You can keep deep-fried or panfried food warm in a 200ºF oven while you finish cooking all of the food.

Oven-Fried Chicken

- Oven fried chicken is usually coated with breadcrumbs or crushed cereal to mimic the crisp outer shell of deep-fried foods.

- You can use panko, or Japanese breadcrumbs, dried crumbs, soft fresh crumbs, or crushed cereal.

- Even potato flakes, crushed pretzel or cracker crumbs, or cheese can help create a crisp coating on oven-fried chicken.

- You can cook a large batch of chicken at one time when oven-frying, and the food will have fewer calories.

METHODS

POACHING

From the French word meaning, "to smile," poaching makes a velvety chicken

Chicken that is poached is very creamy, with a velvety flesh and super smooth texture. Poaching is a fat free cooking method that uses wet heat.

Wet heat is important because no liquid will evaporate from the chicken as it cooks. Some of the water will be squeezed out as the protein fibers shrink in the heat, but they will be

reabsorbed into the meat as the chicken cools.

Cool poached chicken in its poaching liquid for the most tender and soft results. Remove the chicken from the pan and place it in a heatproof container. Pour enough poaching liquid over the chicken to almost cover it. Cover the container and place it in the refrigerator until the chicken is cold.

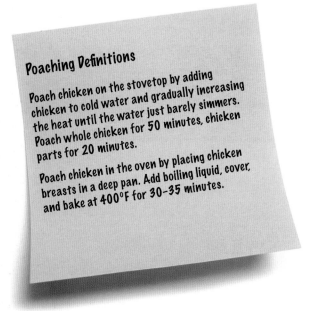

Poaching Definitions

Poach chicken on the stovetop by adding chicken to cold water and gradually increasing the heat until the water just barely simmers. Poach whole chicken for 50 minutes, chicken parts for 20 minutes.

Poach chicken in the oven by placing chicken breasts in a deep pan. Add boiling liquid, cover, and bake at 400°F for 30-35 minutes.

Poach Chicken on Stovetop

- You can poach chicken with its skin on and bone in, or remove both the skin and the bone.

- It is easier to work with boneless, skinless pieces of chicken.

- Check the chicken frequently as it poaches to make sure the water stays just below a simmer.

- This means that the bubbles will rise to the surface but break just below the surface. The temperature of the liquid should be no more than 180°F.

You can add ingredients to the poaching liquid to add flavor. Poaching produces a very mild chicken flavor, which is delicious for classic chicken salads and sandwiches. Poach the chicken in chicken broth, and add onions, lemon, garlic, and herbs to the liquid. Cooling the chicken in flavored poaching liquid will add flavor, too.

Poaching is an excellent way to cook boneless, skinless chicken breasts, because they can easily dry out using dry heat methods. You can also poach a whole chicken. Save the poaching liquid as broth.

METHODS

Poached Chicken

- Cool the chicken completely before slicing or chopping. This allows the juices to redistribute throughout the meat.

- You may find that a jellylike substance has formed in the liquid as it cools. Just scrape that off the chicken.

- Add the jelly to the poaching liquid and freeze it; it will add lots of flavor to chicken recipes.

- Slice the chicken firmly but gently using a very sharp knife, and use immediately in recipes or freeze for later use.

Poach Chicken in Oven

- For oven poaching, the liquid has to be brought to a boil. It takes too long for that first volume of liquid to heat in the oven.

- Place the chicken in the pan on the oven rack and then pour in the boiling liquid to prevent spilling.

- Be careful removing the pan from the oven; it will be very heavy.

- Cool the chicken the same way you do stovetop poached meat.

SLOW COOKER

The slow cooker produces tender, juicy chicken, but timing is everything

The slow cooker, commonly known by the brand name Crock-pot, is a wonderful appliance to help you cook moist, tender, and juicy chicken. It cooks at low heats: 180°F for low, and 200°F for high. While this seems low, it's wet heat, since the slow cooker is an enclosed cooking appliance.

This wet environment transfers heat more easily, so the

food cooked in the slow cooker is safe.

Chicken breasts can still overcook in the slow cooker. Newer slow cookers cook at a slightly hotter temperature than older models, so some older recipes may have to be adapted. With a new slow cooker, boneless, skinless chicken breasts cook in about 5–6 hours. Start testing them with a

Slow Cooker

- A true slow cooker typically consists of a metal unit that contains the heating coils, with a power cord.

- A removable stoneware or metal insert is common; this helps facilitate cleanup.

- The lid is made to fit closely to the insert, which creates a slight seal as the food cooks.

- If an appliance has heating coils just on the bottom, it is not a true slow cooker. A true slow cooker has heating coils all around the sides and bottom.

How to Fill It

- A slow cooker is filled differently from other appliances. Vegetables cook more slowly, so they are placed on the bottom.

- Meats can be browned before being added to the slow cooker for color and appearance improvement.

- Meats are placed on top of vegetables because they cook more quickly. Chop or slice to the same sizes.

- Add liquid according to the recipe instructions. Remember, there's no evaporation with this cooking method.

meat thermometer at that point. The slow cooker is a wonderful way to cook dark meat. This cut of meat can cook for up to 9–10 hours, making it ideal for long-cooking recipes. You can start a recipe using chicken or turkey thighs or drumsticks at 7:00 a.m., and get home at 5:00 p.m. to a perfectly cooked dinner.

Follow the directions for using your slow cooker carefully. Food has to be added in a certain order, and some foods have to be pre-cooked. Enjoy using this appliance.

· · · · · · · · · · · GREEN ● LIGHT · · · · · · · · · · ·

Because there is little or no evaporation in the slow cooker, if you are making a conventional recipe in this appliance, reduce the liquid amount by about one-quarter. The close-fitting lid and steam create a slight seal that also helps cook food more quickly.

Frozen vs. Thawed Chicken

- There is some controversy about using frozen or thawed chicken in the slow cooker.

- If you have a family member who falls into a high risk group, don't cook frozen chicken in the slow cooker.

- Frozen meat is kept in the danger zone of 40–140°F too long in this appliance.

- Frozen boneless, skinless chicken breasts will not dry out as quickly as thawed breasts.

Chicken in Slow Cooker

- Don't cook a whole chicken in the slow cooker. It may not get hot enough soon enough to make it safe to eat.

- Chicken breasts cook most quickly. Even cubed or chopped dark meat doesn't cook as quickly as white meat.

- When you layer chicken in the slow cooker, try to keep the layers even.

- An oval slow cooker is usually the best choice for cooking chicken, as the shape accommodates the meat.

OVEN & STOVETOP

Any chicken can be cooked in the oven or on the stovetop

Your oven and stovetop are used to bake, broil, and fry chicken. You really don't need any other appliances to cook chicken.

Make sure that your oven and stovetop are in good working order. Keep the appliances clean, and frequently check to make sure that the oven temperature settings are accurate.

Panfrying or deep-frying chicken takes some care. Hot oil can be dangerous and needs to be handled very carefully, but the results can be sublime. Fried chicken includes stir-fried recipes.

Roasting is probably the easiest chicken cooking method. You can season the chicken with just salt and pepper and put it in the oven, or add more spices and herbs. Stuff the chicken with just a cut lemon or a more complicated mixture. Any

Panfried Chicken

- Panfried chicken is easy to make as long as you follow a few rules.

- Keep the temperature as constant as possible for even results. You may need to increase or decrease the temp during cooking.

- Don't move the chicken until it releases easily from the pan. When it's ready to turn, it will release.

- Most panfried chicken, even deep-fried chicken, has to be covered during some of the cooking time so it will cook through.

Roasted Chicken

- Chicken is best roasted at a fairly high temperature. The skin becomes crisp and golden while the meat stays tender.

- You can baste chicken with anything from seasoned oils to chicken broth, but that's not necessary.

- A pan gravy can be made from the drippings of a roasted chicken.

- Just add some broth to the drippings and boil down to make a simple sauce, or add a cornstarch slurry for gravy.

way you roast a chicken, it will be delicious.

You can bake chicken and get moist and juicy or crisp results depending on how the chicken is prepared. Baking chicken at a lower temperature (never lower than 300°F) makes a soft and velvety result. High temperatures and coatings like breadcrumbs and crushed cereal yield a crisp outer layer.

Special pans can help you roast chicken to perfection. Some model themselves on the "beer can chicken" method, which yields a very flavorful bird.

· · · · · · · · · · · · RED ● LIGHT · · · · · · · · · · · · · ·

Never leave food unattended on the stovetop or under the broiler. An accident can happen in seconds. If you do need to leave the kitchen, turn the burners off and remove the pan from the heat. Cover the pan to keep the food warm. Don't interrupt cooking for more than 1 hour.

Broiled Chicken

- Most ovens have a broiler right in the oven cavity. The top heating coils turn on and stay on.

- There's usually no way to regulate a broiler's temperature. You maintain control by the distance from the heat and by turning and moving the food.

- Checking the temperature of broiled chicken is very important.

- You can set up two racks at different distances from the heating coils for even more control during cooking.

Chicken in Roaster

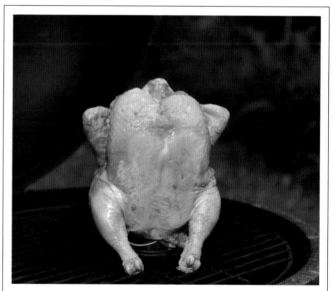

- These roasting pans mimic the method used in Teriyaki Can Chicken.

- The chicken is placed with its cavity wedged onto a small cup. The cup holds flavoring ingredients like beer, chicken broth, or a combination of herbs and spices.

- As the chicken roasts, the flavoring ingredients boil and steam and flavor the chicken from the inside out.

- Fat drips away into the round moat, so the chicken ends up tender and juicy with a crisp skin.

METHODS

GRILL
The hot, quick cooking method of the grill works best on certain cuts

Your grill—whether charcoal or gas, on the patio or an electric dual contact grill—can cook chicken to perfection.

Never use a charcoal or gas grill indoors; that's the first rule. Make sure you understand how the grill works and follow the manufacturer's instructions on care, cleaning, and safety to the letter.

It's a good idea to have several different temperature areas

on a grill. You can accomplish this on a gas grill by just turning off one of the burners. On a charcoal grill, leave an area free of coals, or build a graduated layer of coals from none to four or five deep. You can move the chicken around on these different areas as it cooks. Use the highest heat areas to brown the chicken and for quick cooking. The medium heat areas are used for thicker pieces and slower cooking.

Scrub Grill

- The grill rack cleans more easily when it's hot. Use a wire brush to scrub the rack after cooking.

- You should also clean the rack before you start cooking. Heat the grill with the lid closed, then scrub the rack.

- There are lots of tools available to make grill cleaning easier, including motorized brushes.

- Lightly oil the rack with a towel dampened with oil. Hold the towel firmly with tongs.

Quickly Grill Boneless Chicken

- Boneless chicken can be cooked skin-on or off. This meat cooks quite quickly, so it should be cooked on medium coals.

- You can pound boneless pieces of meat so they cook evenly and very fast.

- Cook these cuts over medium coals. You can start them over high coals, then move to medium coals to finish.

- Brining and marinating these cuts of chicken before grilling adds flavor and helps keep the meat moist and juicy.

Grill racks must be clean before you begin. Oil the rack to prevent sticking, or use special nonstick cooking sprays made just for the grill.

Always be careful with your grill. Never leave it unattended. Keep a fire extinguisher handy. Set the grill on a sturdy fireproof surface away from trees and shrubs. And safely dispose of coals in a metal fireproof bucket after they have completely cooled.

Kebabs

- Kebabs can be made on metal or on bamboo skewers. If you use bamboo, soak the skewers in water for 30 minutes before using.

- Metal skewers are the best choice for recipes that cook longer than 8–9 minutes, because bamboo can burn even if soaked.

- You can find all kinds of kebab holders and racks in specialty cooking stores.

- These products help you turn the kebabs so the food cooks evenly, and prevents food from falling off the skewers.

Grilled Whole Chicken

- Whole chicken can be cooked straight on the grill, as a beer can chicken, or on a rotisserie.

- If you use a rotisserie, follow the manufacturer's instructions to the letter.

- Whole chickens are usually grilled over indirect heat so they cook through before the outside burns.

- It's easiest not to stuff the chicken with an edible mixture. Stuff with lemons, garlic, and herbs instead to add flavor without compromising safety.

METHODS

35

CHICKEN WITH 40 CLOVES OF GARLIC

Garlic becomes mellow and sweet when roasted with a tender and juicy chicken

This elegant and classic recipe literally does use 40 cloves of garlic. But, since the garlic is cooked slowly and for a long period of time, the cloves become very soft, with a mellow and sweet flavor that is the perfect complement to chicken.

The garlic can be served with the chicken, stirred into mashed potatoes or rice pilaf, or just piled on a plate. In that case, offer some warm French bread and tell your guests to smash the soft garlic onto the bread.

Along with some excellent bread, serve this dish with roasted green beans or asparagus, and a fruit salad made with grapefruit, apples, and pears. A dry white wine is the perfect accompaniment. *Yield: Serves 4*

Ingredients

1 (4-pound) roasting chicken

2 tablespoons butter

$1/2$ teaspoon salt

$1/8$ teaspoon white pepper

$1/2$ teaspoon paprika

$1/2$ lemon

1 fresh sprig of thyme

1 fresh sprig of oregano

3 stems fresh flat-leaf parsley

$1/4$ cup chopped celery leaves

$1/4$ cup olive oil

$1/2$ cup chicken broth

$1/4$ cup dry white wine

40 cloves garlic, unpeeled

Chicken with 40 Cloves of Garlic

- Pat chicken dry and rub outside with butter. Sprinkle with salt, pepper, and paprika.

- Stuff chicken with a lemon half, thyme, oregano, parsley, and celery leaves, then place in large roasting pan.

- Add olive oil, broth, and wine to pan and add garlic. Cover with foil and place in 375ºF. oven.

- Roast for 90 minutes, then uncover and roast 15–20 minutes longer until chicken registers 180ºF. Remove chicken and garlic from pan and serve.

Slow Cooker Garlic Chicken

Make recipe as directed, except use chicken parts. Season, then brown them in butter. Place herb sprigs, celery leaves, and garlic in bottom of 4-quart slow cooker. Top with chicken. Add 2 tablespoons oil, and ¼ cup each broth and wine. Cover; cook on low 8–9 hours.

A whole chicken should cook to an internal temperature of 180ºF. Because of the different masses and density of the flesh, the whole bird has to cook to a higher temperature for food safety reasons.

Prepare Garlic

- To get 40 cloves of garlic, you'll need about 3 whole heads.

- Separate the cloves from the head with your fingers. Discard excess papery covering by making a small cut with a knife, then pulling off the skin.

- You can peel the garlic or leave it unpeeled. If it's peeled it will become softer than unpeeled garlic.

- For an easy way to peel garlic, blanch it in boiling water 2–3 minutes, then drain and slip off the skins.

Stuff Chicken

- Don't overstuff the chicken or it may split during cooking, which isn't attractive.

- To truss the chicken, use cotton kitchen twine; tie around the legs and under the chicken, then around the wings.

- You can also just place the herbs on top of the chicken, or tuck underneath in the roasting pan.

- Serve with some toasted garlic bread, French bread, or mashed potatoes for the soft and sweet garlic.

WHOLE CHICKEN

ROAST CHICKEN
Roasting chicken concentrates its flavor and makes crisp skin

Roast chicken is the classic Sunday meal that is easy to prepare and satisfying to eat. Roasting the bird is simple. You can flavor it any way you like, cook it alone in a pan, or tuck vegetables around it for a one-dish meal.

When the chicken roasts, the skin gets crisp, and the fat melts and seasons and flavors the bird. The drippings remaining in the bottom of the pan are perfect for making flavorful gravy.

Recipes for roasting chicken can call for oven temperatures ranging from 325 to 450ºF. All will work well, as long as you keep an eye on the internal temperature. The chicken is done when the temperature in the thigh registers 180ºF. *Yield: Serves 4*

KNACK CHICKEN CLASSICS

Ingredients

1 (4-pound) roasting chicken

4 whole fresh sage leaves

2 teaspoons fresh thyme leaves

4 cloves garlic, slivered, divided

1 teaspoon salt

1 teaspoon paprika

1/4 teaspoon pepper

1 small lemon, quartered

1 stalk celery with leaves, chopped

3 tablespoons butter

1 cup chicken stock

Roast Chicken

- Rinse chicken and pat dry. Loosen skin on breast and place sage leaves, thyme, and half of garlic on flesh.

- Smooth skin back over flesh. Sprinkle with salt, paprika, and pepper.

- Place remaining garlic, lemon, and celery in cavity. Place chicken on rack in roasting pan and rub with butter.

- Pour stock into pan. Roast at 350ºF for 90–120 minutes until temperature registers 170ºF. Let stand, covered, 15 minutes before carving.

38

Gravy

Skim the fat from the juices or use a fat separator. Cook 2 tablespoons flour in 2 tablespoons butter until bubbly. Place roasting pan on burner and add 1 cup chicken broth; scrape off drippings. Add to pan with butter mixture; simmer 10–12 minutes until gravy thickens.

ZOOM

To truss a chicken, place breast side up on top of kitchen twine. Pull the twine over the wings and cross the twine. Wrap one end of twine around each drumstick and pull until the legs cross. Tie the twine and cut the ends short. You can stuff the chicken before trussing.

Place Herbs under Skin

Carve Chicken

- Place the herbs in a pleasing pattern on the flesh of the chicken. However, the pattern doesn't matter unless you're serving the chicken whole at the table.

- Smooth the pattern down and then carefully pull the skin back over. Try to keep the herbs in place.

- You can use other herbs if you'd like; fresh basil and oregano will give a different taste.

- Dried herbs can be substituted for the fresh; just use one-third of the amount.

- Place chicken breast side up on a carving board. Pull on the leg and cut in between the leg and thigh, popping the joint. Repeat on other side.

- Remove the wings. Then make a cut along the sides of the breastbone.

- Cut parallel to the work surface at the bottom of the breast. Remove the whole breast and slice.

- Arrange all the meat on a platter and serve immediately.

WHOLE CHICKEN

CHICKEN VERDE

Whole chicken is simmered until falling off the bone, then shredded and mixed with a green sauce

Chicken Verde, or chicken in a green sauce, is a classic Mexican or Tex-Mex recipe. The tender chicken is mixed with a sauce made from tomatillos, bell peppers, and spicy hot chile peppers.

This mixture can be used in many ways. Use it as a filling for enchiladas, burritos, or tacos, or just serve it over hot cooked rice or pasta. It can be layered in a casserole dish with tortillas and sour cream, then baked until bubbly.

The chicken is simmered to make sure it remains tender, moist, and juicy. You can simmer the chicken ahead of time. Shred it and mix with some chicken broth to keep it moist. *Yield: Serves 6*

Ingredients

- 1 (4-pound) whole chicken
- 1 onion, quartered
- 3 whole cloves garlic
- 2 teaspoons salt
- Water to cover
- 2 tablespoons olive oil
- 1 onion, chopped
- 3 cloves garlic, minced
- 1 jalapeño pepper, minced
- 2 cups tomatillos, chopped
- 1 green bell pepper
- 1/2 cup green salsa
- 1/2 cup chopped cilantro
- 1/2 teaspoon ground cumin

Chicken Verde

- Place chicken in pot. Add quartered onion, whole garlic, and salt; cover with water.

- Simmer for 1½ hours until chicken is tender. Remove and shred meat; discard skin and bones. Reserve broth.

- In large saucepan, heat oil; cook chopped onion and minced garlic 4 minutes. Add jalapeño, tomatillos, bell pepper, green salsa, chicken, and 1 cup broth.

- Bring to a simmer; add cilantro and cumin. Simmer 20–30 minutes until mixture is blended. Serve over rice or in enchiladas.

White Meat Verde

Make recipe as directed, except poach bone-in, skin-on chicken breasts in liquid for 20–30 minutes until done. Shred chicken, mix with ⅓ cup broth, and set aside. Make the verde sauce as directed. Serve with warmed tortillas and guacamole.

Slow Cooker Chicken Verde

Make recipe as directed, except use 2½ pounds boneless, skinless chicken thighs. Place vegetables in bottom of 4-quart slow cooker. Top with chicken, salsa, cilantro, and cumin. Cover and cook on low 7–9 hours. Remove chicken, shred, and stir back into sauce; cook uncovered on high 30 minutes.

Remove Chicken from Bones

- When the chicken is done, it will literally fall off the bone. Remove it from the broth with a large strainer or sieve.

- Let the chicken cool for 10–15 minutes until you can handle it. Pull the meat off the bones and skin.

- You can reserve the bones and skin to make stock. And make sure to reserve all of that stock.

- Cool the stock, remove the fat, and freeze in 1-cup portions to use in soups, sauces, and gravies.

Simmer Chicken in Sauce

- The chicken is simmered in the sauce just long enough so it absorbs some of the flavor from the peppers.

- If you'd like a spicier sauce, use more jalapeño peppers, or add a habanero or dried ancho chile.

- To prepare the tomatillos, remove the papery skin and rinse them well. Then chop and cook in the sauce.

- Green salsa can be found right next to the regular red salsa in the international foods aisle.

WHOLE CHICKEN

ROASTED HERBED CHICKEN
Brining chicken before roasting adds incredible flavor

Chicken roasted with herbs is nothing new, but chicken first brined, then roasted with herbs is quite different.

Brining chicken forces moisture and flavor into the meat. Brine is a combination of water, salt, sugar, and sometimes spices. The chicken has to be refrigerated while in the brine.

Rinse the chicken and discard the brine. Don't worry; you won't rinse away any flavor. Pat the chicken dry before adding any herbs or flavoring. As the chicken roasts, the skin will become crisp and the flavor of the herbs will make its way into the meat. Let stand for 10 minutes after roasting while you make the gravy, and then carve it at the table. *Yield: Serves 4*

Ingredients

6 cups warm water

$^1/_3$ cup salt

$^1/_3$ cup sugar

1 teaspoon dried thyme

1 teaspoon dried oregano

1 teaspoon dried basil

1 (4-pound) roasting chicken

1 tablespoon fresh thyme leaves

$^1/_4$ cup chopped fresh basil

2 teaspoons fresh oregano leaves

$^1/_2$ lemon

$^1/_4$ teaspoon pepper

2 tablespoons butter

$^1/_2$ cup chicken broth

$^1/_2$ cup water

Roasted Herbed Chicken

- First brine the chicken: Combine 6 cups water, salt, sugar, and dried herbs in large pot.

- Add chicken; weight with plate and refrigerate 12–18 hours.

- Drain chicken, rinse, pat dry. Combine fresh herbs and rub half under skin. Place half in cavity along with lemon.

- Sprinkle with pepper and rub with butter. Place in pan, add broth and ½ cup water. Roast at 350ºF for 2 hours until 180ºF.

Grilled Herbed Chicken

Brine chicken as directed, and place herbs and butter under skin. Preheat a grill using indirect heat, with a drip pan in the center of the coals. Add chicken; cover and grill for 40–50 minutes, turning with tongs frequently, until chicken registers 180°F. Wrap in foil and let stand 10 minutes.

Pan Gravy

Remove the chicken, cover with foil, and set aside. Pour the pan juices into a sauté pan, making sure to include the brown bits. Add more chicken broth if necessary. Combine 2 tablespoons flour with $1/4$ cup water and add along with $1/2$ teaspoon each salt, pepper, and thyme; simmer until thickened.

Brine Chicken

- The chicken has to be fully submerged in the brine to properly absorb the water and flavorings.

- Place a heavy plate on top of the chicken when it's in the brine to keep it under the surface of the water.

- Don't worry about the amount of salt used in the brine. The chicken flesh doesn't absorb much of the salt.

- It's the concentration of salt and sugar in the brine that forces liquid into the cells of the chicken.

Roast Chicken

- Broth helps prevent the drippings from burning and provides the base for pan gravy.

- You can use all water or wine instead of the broth if you'd like. Add more dried herbs for flavor.

- When the chicken has finished roasting, it must stand for a few minutes so the juices can redistribute.

- Cover the chicken with foil to keep warm and let stand 10–15 minutes while you make the gravy, then serve.

WHOLE CHICKEN

CHICKEN PAPRIKASH

Paprika adds a gorgeous color and spicy flavor to tender chicken

Chicken Paprikash is a classic Hungarian dish that combines paprika with chicken, simmered slowly in a rich and flavorful sauce made with onions, tomatoes, and sour cream.

There are three kinds of paprika; sweet, hot, and smoked. Sweet is traditionally used in this recipe, but you can use hot or smoked if you'd like a kick of flavor. Or combine two or three of the types for a complex depth of flavor.

This rich dish should be served with spaetzle, or tiny dumplings. You can find those in the freezer section of the supermarket. Or serve with medium or wide egg noodles to soak up the delicious sauce, along with a baby spinach salad and some glazed carrots. *Yield: Serves 6*

Ingredients

1 (4-pound) whole chicken, cut into serving pieces

¹/₃ cup flour

1 teaspoon salt

¹/₄ teaspoon cayenne pepper

2 tablespoons paprika, divided

1 tablespoon butter

2 tablespoons olive oil

1 onion, chopped

4 cloves garlic, minced

1¹/₂ cups chicken broth

3 tomatoes, peeled, seeded, and diced

1 cup sour cream

Chicken Paprikash

- Pat chicken dry. Combine flour, salt, pepper, and 2 teaspoons paprika; dredge chicken.

- Melt butter and olive oil in large pan. Brown chicken, skin side down, removing from pan as it cooks.

- Add onion and garlic; cook 4 minutes. Add chicken with remaining paprika, broth, and tomatoes.

- Cover and simmer for 60–70 minutes until chicken registers 170ºF; remove chicken. Add spoonful of juices to sour cream; return to sauce; cook until thickened.

Slow Cooker Chicken Paprikash

Make recipe as directed, dredging chicken, browning it, then cooking the onion and garlic. Combine with chicken, chicken broth, paprika, and tomatoes in 4-quart slow cooker. Cover and cook on low 8–10 hours. Combine some of the liquid and sour cream; add to slow cooker; cook 20 minutes on high.

Paprika is made from dried sweet or mildly spicy bell peppers that are ground until a fine powder is produced. It is used in eastern European cuisine in paprikash as well as goulash and other stews. If the peppers are smoked first, smoked paprika is the result. The spice is rich in vitamin C.

Brown Chicken

- If you'd like a milder dish, you can use less paprika; reduce the total amount to 2 teaspoons.

- To dredge the chicken, push it into the flour mixture, then lift up and gently shake to remove excess flour.

- Brown the chicken slowly; don't let it burn. You want the flour on the skin to caramelize for flavor and color.

- Remove the chicken as it browns. Don't crowd the chicken in the pan; cook in batches if necessary.

Finish Sauce

- The flour used to dredge the chicken should help thicken the sauce. Browning it helps increase its liquid-absorbing capacity.

- If the sauce isn't thick enough for your taste, stir a tablespoon of cornstarch into the sour cream mixture.

- Simmer for just a few minutes until the sauce blends and thickens.

- Place the chicken on the serving platter and pour the sauce, onions and all, evenly over. Pass with noodles.

WHOLE CHICKEN

CHICKEN A L'ORANGE
Orange, garlic, and ginger combine to make a delicious sauce

Chicken a l'Orange, or chicken in orange sauce, is a classic French recipe that sounds very fancy, but it's easy to make and delicious to serve. This recipe was originally made with duck. The sweet, tart flavor of the orange helps cut through the richness of the duck's flavor. Chicken is much milder, but the combination of chicken and orange is wonderful.

Both orange juice and orange zest are used to give this recipe a depth of flavor. The zest has more aromatic oils than the juice, so don't omit it from the recipe.

Serve this dish on a rice pilaf made with thyme and chicken broth to help soak up the delicious sauce, and some roasted asparagus. *Yield: Serves 4–6*

KNACK CHICKEN CLASSICS

Ingredients

1 (3-pound) whole chicken, cut into serving pieces

¼ cup orange juice

¼ cup flour

1 teaspoon orange zest

½ teaspoon salt

⅛ teaspoon white pepper

2 tablespoons butter

1 tablespoon olive oil

1 onion, chopped

1 tablespoon grated gingerroot

2 cloves garlic, minced

⅓ cup orange juice

2 tablespoons honey

2 tablespoons lemon juice

1 cup chicken broth

1 tablespoon minced fresh rosemary

Chicken a l'Orange

- Rinse chicken and pat dry. Dip chicken in ¼ cup orange juice; let stand 10 minutes.

- Mix flour, zest, salt, and pepper; dredge chicken. Melt butter and olive oil in large pan; brown chicken; remove.

- Add onion, ginger, and garlic; cook 4 minutes. Return chicken to pan. Mix ⅓ cup orange juice, honey, lemon juice, broth, and rosemary.

- Pour over chicken. Cover and simmer for 30–40 minutes until chicken registers 170°F.

Slow Cooker Chicken a l'Orange

Make recipe as directed; brown the dredged chicken and place on top of onion, garlic, and ginger in 4-quart slow cooker. Add remaining ingredients; cover and cook on low 8–9 hours. If you'd like, thicken the sauce by adding a slurry of cornstarch and water.

Chicken a l'Orange with Veggies

Make recipe as directed, except add 3 carrots, sliced, 2 stalks celery, sliced, and another onion to the pan. Increase orange juice to ²/₃ cup. Cover pan and simmer the mixture as directed until the chicken reaches 165ºF.

Dredge Chicken

- You can marinate the chicken in the orange juice up to 8 hours in the refrigerator for a more intense flavor.

- Make sure to mix the orange zest in the flour mixture very well so it is evenly distributed.

- You can make this dish using bone-in, skin-on chicken breasts.

- The recipe can easily be doubled or tripled; just use 2–3 whole cut up chickens.

Simmer Chicken

- Instead of the honey, use brown sugar or regular sugar. The dish needs some sweetness for balance.

- To add even more orange flavor and thicken the sauce, stir in ⅓ cup of orange marmalade with the broth and rosemary.

- If you're making this for adults, add a few tablespoons Grand Marnier liqueur for a snappy orange flavor.

- Garnish this dish with fresh rosemary sprigs and thinly sliced oranges.

WHOLE CHICKEN

47

CRISP FRIED CHICKEN
The secret to crisp fried chicken is to refrigerate after coating

Crisp fried chicken is the American ideal. The perfect fried chicken has a crisp and crunchy but tender skin, moist meat, lots of juices, and lots of flavor.

The chicken doesn't have to be immersed in a deep fryer in order to be labeled "fried." All you need is about 1/2 inch of oil in the pan. The chicken is browned first, skin side down, and cooked until brown, then turned.

The chicken has to be covered in order to cook evenly. This won't affect the crispness of the coating, while allowing the chicken to thoroughly cook all the way through.

Cornmeal and flour is the classic coating combination, but you can use cracker crumbs, breadcrumbs, or even a batter. *Yield: Serves 6*

Ingredients

6 bone-in, skin-on chicken breasts

1 teaspoon salt

1/4 teaspoon pepper

1 teaspoon paprika

3/4 cup flour

1/4 cup cornmeal

1 teaspoon dried thyme leaves

1/2 teaspoon dry mustard

1/2 teaspoon baking powder

1/2 cup buttermilk

1 egg, beaten

1/2 cup canola oil

Crisp Fried Chicken

- Pat chicken dry and sprinkle with salt, pepper, and paprika.

- On plate, combine flour, cornmeal, thyme, mustard, and baking powder; mix well. Combine buttermilk and egg in bowl.

- Dip chicken into flour mixture, then egg mixture, then again into flour mixture to coat. Place on wire rack; chill 2 hours.

- Heat oil in deep saucepan to 375ºF. Add chicken, skin side down; cook 7 minutes. Turn and cover; cook 11–15 minutes longer until done.

Crisp Batter-Fried Chicken

Season chicken as directed. Combine 1½ cups flour, 1 teaspoon paprika, ¼ cup cornmeal, ¼ teaspoon pepper and 1 (12-ounce) can beer; mix. Heat 1 inch of oil to 375ºF. Dip chicken into batter; fry, turning once, for 30–35 minutes until done.

Crisp Panko-Fried Chicken

Make recipe as directed, except substitute 1 cup panko breadcrumbs for the flour and cornmeal. Dip chicken into buttermilk mixture, then into seasoned breadcrumbs just once; refrigerate. Fry as directed in 1 cup of peanut oil until done.

Dip Chicken

- Keep one wet hand and one dry hand to minimize mess and make it easier to handle the chicken.

- It's important that the chicken is coated in the flour mixture twice. The first coat helps the egg mixture adhere.

- The second coat helps seal in the juices while the chicken cooks, and makes the crispy coating.

- You can use any combination of herbs and spices to season the flour used for the coating.

Cook Chicken

- A deep-frying thermometer is important to regulate the temperature of the oil.

- The temperature will drop about 25 degrees when you add the chicken; keep an eye on the heat.

- Drain the chicken on paper towels after cooking; let it stand 5 minutes so the juices redistribute.

- The chicken can be kept warm in a 200ºF oven up to 45 minutes while you fry the rest.

CHICKEN BREASTS

LEMON CHICKEN
This classic dish is light and healthy

Lemon and chicken were made for each other. The sweet, tart flavor of the lemon complements the mild tenderness of the chicken breasts.

Boneless, skinless chicken breasts work best in this recipe because they cook quickly and they are so simple the lemon flavor really sings.

Marinating the chicken will help make it super tender, and the lemon flavor will penetrate the flesh. Don't marinate the chicken longer than 8 hours.

It's important not to overcook the chicken in this recipe. Cook until a meat thermometer reads exactly 160ºF. Remove the pan from heat and cover; let stand 5 minutes. The temperature will rise to 165ºF. Serve with hot cooked long-grain rice scented with fresh thyme and lemon zest. *Yield: Serves 6*

Ingredients

¹/₃ cup fresh lemon juice

1 teaspoon grated lemon zest

¹/₂ teaspoon salt

¹/₈ teaspoon white pepper

¹/₂ teaspoon paprika

1 teaspoon dried thyme leaves

6 boneless, skinless chicken breasts

2 tablespoons olive oil

2 cloves garlic, minced

1 lemon, thinly sliced

¹/₄ cup chicken broth

Lemon Chicken

- In baking dish, combine lemon juice, zest, salt, pepper, paprika, and thyme.

- Add chicken breasts; turn to coat. Cover and refrigerate for 2 hours.

- Heat olive oil in large skillet. Add garlic; cook for 2 minutes. Drain chicken, reserving marinade; brown chicken on first side.

- Turn chicken and top each with a lemon slice. Add marinade and broth to pan and bring to a simmer. Cover and simmer 15–18 minutes until chicken is done, 160ºF.

Slow Cooker Lemon Chicken
Make recipe as directed, except don't brown the chicken. Layer the seasoned chicken, garlic, and lemon slices in a 3¹/₂-quart slow cooker; pour lemon juice, zest, and broth over all. Cover and cook on low for 5–6 hours until chicken is done.

Grilled Lemon Chicken
Marinate the chicken in the refrigerator for 6 hours. Prepare and preheat grill. Drain chicken; combine marinade with broth. Season chicken with salt and pepper and brush with oil. Grill over medium coals for 7–10 minutes, brushing once with marinade, until done.

Marinate Chicken

Brown Chicken

- This marinade is quite strong, so the chicken isn't marinated for a long time.

- If you'd like to marinate the chicken overnight, reduce the lemon juice to ¼ cup and add ¼ cup chicken broth.

- Turn the chicken several times in the marinade so it is coated evenly.

- You can use a bottled marinade if you'd like. Look for it in the condiment aisle of the supermarket.

- The chicken shouldn't brown very long; just long enough so it releases easily from the pan, about 3–4 minutes.

- If you'd like more sauce, increase the chicken broth to 1–2 cups.

- To thicken the sauce, remove chicken and add 1–2 tablespoons cornstarch mixed with ¼ cup water.

- Simmer, stirring with wire whisk, until sauce is thickened. Return chicken to sauce; simmer 1 minute to reheat, then serve.

CHICKEN BREASTS

TANDOORI CHICKEN

Chicken marinates in a flavored yogurt sauce for a velvety texture

Tandoori is a method of cooking food in a clay pot. The meaning has been adapted to refer to chicken that has been marinated in a mixture of garam masala and yogurt.

Yogurt is slightly acidic, so it is a natural marinade. It makes the chicken velvety and tender, unlike any other treatment. The chicken can marinate for a long time in this mixture.

Broiling the chicken keeps the meat moist and tender, while creating a crisp and fairly dark crust on the outside. This very high, dry heat cooks the chicken quickly.

Serve the chicken with mango chutney, lemon and lime wedges, and lots of hot cooked basmati rice. A sweet and spicy spinach salad would be a great complement. *Yield: Serves 6*

Ingredients

6 boneless, skinless chicken breasts

1 cup plain yogurt

1 teaspoon salt

1 tablespoon curry powder

1 tablespoon grated gingerroot

$1/2$ teaspoon garlic powder

1 teaspoon paprika

$1/2$ teaspoon ground coriander

$1/8$ teaspoon white pepper

2 tablespoons lime juice

Tandoori Chicken

- In glass baking dish, place chicken. Combine yogurt, salt, curry powder, gingerroot, garlic powder, paprika, coriander, pepper, and lime juice in small bowl.

- Brush yogurt mixture over chicken; turn and brush on the other side. Coat chicken heavily.

- Cover chicken and refrigerate for 4–24 hours. Place chicken on broiler pan.

- Broil chicken 8–10 minutes on each side, turning once, until meat thermometer registers 160ºF. Let chicken stand 5 minutes, then serve.

Marinate Chicken

- You can add other ingredients to the curry powder mixture. Grated orange rind, lemon rind, or dried chiles would be good.

- Always marinate chicken in the refrigerator, even if the marinating time is only 30 minutes.

- Cover the dish tightly with plastic wrap or foil so the flavors don't transfer to other foods in the fridge.

- This will also prevent flavors from foods in your refrigerator from transferring to the marinating chicken.

Chicken under Broiler

- To broil chicken, arrange on a broiling pan or rack. Always preheat the broiler.

- Arrange the oven rack about 6 inches from the oven coils before you turn on the oven.

- Most ovens must be open in order for the broiler to work. Check your oven manual to make sure.

- Watch the chicken carefully when under the broiler. It can go from beautifully browned to burned in a matter of seconds.

CHICKEN BREASTS

BAKED CRISP CHICKEN

A flavorful crisp coating makes this tender and juicy chicken delectable

Baked crisp chicken is just as delicious as fried chicken, and has much less fat and fewer calories. You can also use your imagination with coatings.

The typical coatings for baked crisp chicken include crushed crackers, dried or fresh breadcrumbs, cornmeal, or crushed cereal. Other more unusual ingredients include ground oatmeal, rice flour, and panko breadcrumbs, which are very crisp.

For chicken that is completely crisp on both sides, place the chicken on a rack in the baking pan. Elevating the chicken lets the hot air circulate all the way around, making the coating crisp. *Yield: Serves 6*

Ingredients

¹/₄ cup buttermilk

¹/₄ cup Dijon mustard

1 shallot, minced

¹/₂ teaspoon paprika

1 teaspoon salt, divided

¹/₈ teaspoon white pepper

1 teaspoon dried thyme leaves

6 boneless, skinless chicken breasts

1 cup soft fresh breadcrumbs

¹/₂ cup quick oats, ground

2 tablespoons butter, melted

Baked Crisp Chicken

- In small bowl, combine buttermilk, mustard, shallot, paprika, ½ teaspoon salt, pepper, and thyme.

- Dip chicken in this mixture to coat both sides, then place in baking dish, cover, and refrigerate 2–4 hours.

- Combine breadcrumbs, oats, remaining salt, and butter on plate; mix. Coat chicken in this mixture.

- Place chicken on rack in roasting pan. Bake at 400ºF for 20–25 minutes until chicken registers 160ºF on meat thermometer.

Baked Cornmeal Chicken

Make recipe as directed, except use $1/2$ cup cornmeal and $1/2$ cup flour in place of the breadcrumbs and ground oats. Omit the minced shallot in the marinade and add 2 cloves garlic, minced. Coat chicken, then bake as directed until done.

Panko Chicken

Panko breadcrumbs come from Japan. They are very crisp and light. Use these breadcrumbs in place of the fresh breadcrumbs. Omit the ground oats and the melted butter. Place chicken on rack and back as directed until done.

Marinate Chicken

- Buttermilk is a slightly acidic ingredient, so it tenderizes the chicken just like yogurt.

- Never marinate chicken longer than 24 hours, or it can become mushy.

- You can add other herbs or spices to your marinade. Thyme, basil, oregano, curry powder, chili powder, or lemon zest would be delicious.

- Or use a mixture of yogurt and lemon juice, with some dried marjoram, salt, pepper, and minced garlic.

Coat Chicken

- When you remove the chicken from the marinade, don't wipe it off.

- Just shake off the excess and dip into the bread-crumb mixture. The marinade will flavor the chicken and help the coating adhere.

- Preheat the oven for at least 10 minutes before you add the chicken.

- The relatively short baking time at a high temperature is what makes the coating crisp, while the chicken stays moist.

CHICKEN KIEV

This simple, classic recipe is perfect for entertaining

Classic Chicken Kiev is a very rich dish. Traditionally, the chicken rolls are deep fried until done. This version lightens things up by just sautéing the chicken in some olive oil, then baking in the oven.

The trick to making Chicken Kiev is to gently but thoroughly pound the chicken so it is large enough to completely encase the butter mixture. The butter melts in the heat of the oven, so when you slice into the chicken, seasoned butter pours out.

Follow the directions carefully and handle the chicken with care, and you will have success.

This dish should be served with hot cooked rice or a rice pilaf to soak up the wonderful butter sauce. Pair it with a fruit salad and glazed carrots. *Yield: Serves 6*

Ingredients

2 cloves garlic, minced

1 teaspoon salt, divided

$1/2$ cup butter, softened

1 teaspoon lemon zest

2 tablespoons lemon juice

2 tablespoons minced parsley

6 boneless, skinless chicken breasts

$1/8$ teaspoon white pepper

2 eggs, beaten

2 cups soft fresh breadcrumbs

$1/3$ cup olive oil

Chicken Kiev

- Mix garlic with ½ teaspoon salt until a paste forms. Add butter, lemon zest, juice, and parsley. Divide into 6 2-inch x ½-inch sticks; freeze until firm.

- Place chicken on plastic wrap; sprinkle with remaining salt and pepper. Pound until ¼ inch thick.

- Top with butter sticks; roll up. Dip in eggs, then breadcrumbs; refrigerate 1 hour.

- Heat oil in pan; brown chicken on all sides, 5 minutes, turning carefully. Bake at 375°F 20–25 minutes until done.

Baked Chicken Kiev

Make recipe as directed, except chill the coated and filled chicken for 2–3 hours. Cover and bake in a preheated 350ºF oven for 30 minutes. Uncover and bake 25–35 minutes longer until coating is crisp and brown and chicken is done.

Deep Fried Chicken Kiev

Make recipe as directed, except chill the coated and filled chicken for 5–6 hours. Place 3 cups peanut oil in a large, heavy saucepan; heat to 375ºF. Two at a time, gently lower the chicken rolls into the hot oil; fry for 12–15 minutes or until chicken is golden brown and done.

Pound Chicken

- Place the chicken on the plastic wrap smooth side down.

- Pound the chicken using a meat mallet or a rolling pin. Work gently, starting from the inside and working out.

- You can secure the chicken bundles with toothpicks if you'd like, but the chicken should just stick to itself.

- If you do use toothpicks, be sure to carefully remove them before serving, or warn your guests about them.

Fill Chicken

- The secret to success includes pounding the chicken completely and gently, and handling the filled bundles with care.

- Always use tongs or a spatula to move the chicken; never a knife or fork.

- A knife or fork may pierce the chicken and the coating, and the butter will run out into the pan.

- If the butter does run out, the chicken will still be delicious. Make a gravy with the butter and drippings left in the pan.

CHICKEN BREASTS

CHICKEN CORDON BLEU

Chicken stuffed with Swiss cheese and ham is a classic

Chicken Cordon Bleu is a classic French dish that is made by stuffing boneless, skinless chicken breasts with thinly sliced ham and Grùyere or Swiss cheese.

The chicken is then coated in breadcrumbs, fried, and baked until golden. When you slice into the chicken, the melted cheese runs out in a golden stream.

Though this dish seems complicated and fancy, it's actually quite simple. It uses just four main ingredients: chicken, ham, cheese, and breadcrumbs.

This recipe has more flavor and is easier to eat than other Cordon Bleu recipes, because the ham is chopped and mixed with the cheese. Each bite contains the perfect balance of ham and cheese. *Yield: Serves 6*

Ingredients

6 boneless, skinless chicken breasts, pounded ¼ inch thick

½ teaspoon salt

⅛ teaspoon pepper

2 tablespoons Dijon mustard

1 cup chopped spiral-sliced ham

1 cup diced Swiss cheese

½ cup shredded Grùyere cheese

¼ teaspoon garlic powder

2 eggs, beaten

¾ cup dried breadcrumbs

1 teaspoon paprika

2 tablespoons butter

2 tablespoons olive oil

2 tablespoons flour

1 cup chicken broth

½ cup heavy cream

Chicken Cordon Bleu

- Sprinkle chicken with salt and pepper; spread with mustard. In bowl, combine ham, Swiss, Grùyere, and garlic powder. Divide among chicken.

- Roll up chicken; secure with toothpicks. Dip bundles into egg, then dip in mixture of breadcrumbs and paprika.

- Brown chicken in butter and olive oil mixture; place in 350ºF oven; bake 20 minutes.

- Meanwhile, add 2 tablespoons flour to skillet; cook 2 minutes. Add broth and cream; simmer 3–5 minutes. Pour over chicken and serve.

Slow Cooker Cordon Bleu

Top 6 boneless, skinless chicken breasts with 2 cups shredded Swiss and roll each in 1 slice boiled ham. Place 2 chopped onions in 4-quart slow cooker; top with chicken bundles. Pour over 1 cup chicken broth, 1 (16-ounce) jar Alfredo sauce, and ½ cup Parmesan cheese. Cook on low 7–8 hours.

Cordon Bleu Casserole

Combine 2 pounds cooked, cubed chicken with 2 cups cubed ham and 2 cups diced Grùyere cheese. Add 1 (16-ounce) jar Alfredo sauce, 1 teaspoon dried thyme, and 1 cup chicken broth. Place 3 cups cooked rice in 2-quart casserole; pour chicken mixture over. Bake at 350ºF for 45–55 minutes.

Stuff Chicken

- It's important to use the best ham you can find in this recipe; it's the key flavor.

- Using chopped ham and diced cheese makes this dish easier to eat, and prettier too.

- It's also easier to roll the pounded chicken around this mixture; there are no edges to poke through the meat.

- Be sure the toothpicks stick out of the bundles slightly so you can see them to remove later.

Brown Chicken

- You can prepare the chicken bundles ahead of time. Dredge in the egg and flour just before cooking.

- Brown the chicken over medium heat and turn frequently using tongs so bundles color evenly.

- After the chicken has baked, remove from oven and remove the toothpicks, using tongs.

- The drippings remaining in the skillet have a lot of flavor; they are incorporated into the sauce so they aren't wasted.

CHICKEN BREASTS

BUFFALO WINGS
Crisp and spicy wings are served with a creamy blue cheese sauce

There's been a lot of research done into the creation of Buffalo Wings. Historians now recognize the Anchor Bar in Buffalo, New York, as their origin. They were created by Teressa Belissimo, who needed a quick snack for some unexpected guests. Chicken wings were considered discards at that point, and her idea of tossing them in the deep fryer, coating them in a spicy sauce, and serving them with a blue cheese dressing was revolutionary. It's not easy to make the original recipe of the wings in a home kitchen, so many variations now exist.

Baking the wings is the easiest way to cook them, and healthier than frying, too. The celery serves as a cooling complement. *Yield: Serves 6–8*

Ingredients

¾ cup flour

1 teaspoon paprika

⅛ teaspoon cayenne pepper

½ teaspoon salt

2 pounds chicken wings, tips removed, cut apart at joint

3 tablespoons butter, melted

3 cloves garlic, minced

¼ cup finely minced onion

2 tablespoons tomato sauce

3 tablespoons hot sauce

1 tablespoon apple cider vinegar

4 stalks celery, cut into sticks

¾ cup mayonnaise

½ cup creamy blue cheese salad dressing

¼ cup crumbled blue cheese

Buffalo Wings

- In large bowl, mix flour, paprika, pepper, and salt; add chicken wings and toss to coat. Cover; place on rack in roasting pan, and refrigerate 2 hours.

- Bake at 350°F 40 minutes. Turn heat to 400°F; bake 10 minutes longer.

- Melt butter; cook garlic and onion 6 minutes. Remove from heat; add tomato sauce, hot sauce, and vinegar.

- Toss wings in onion sauce. Serve with celery and a sauce made by mixing mayonnaise, salad dressing, and blue cheese.

• • • • RECIPE VARIATIONS • • • •

Fried Buffalo Wings
Prepare recipe as directed, except after coating and refrigerating the wings, heat 2 cups peanut oil in a heavy, deep saucepan to 375ºF. Add half of the wings; fry 10–12 minutes until crisp. Fry second batch, then toss all together with the tomato sauce mixture.

Grilled Buffalo Wings
Prepare recipe as directed, except after coating and refrigerating the wings, prepare and preheat grill. Brush grill rack with oil. Grill wings over low coals for 15–20 minutes, turning several times, until chicken is done. Toss with tomato sauce mixture and serve immediately.

Prepare Wings

- The wings are tossed in the flour mixture and refrigerated to help form a crisp coating.

- Don't refrigerate the wings longer than 2 hours, or the flour coating will be absorbed into the skin.

- Make the tomato and onion sauce while the wings are baking in the oven.

- You can make the tomato sauce ahead of time; refrigerate it, then bring to a simmer while the wings are baking.

Toss Wings with Sauce

- Like the traditional recipe, the wings are coated with a hot tomato sauce before serving.

- You can buy Buffalo Wing sauce at the supermarket and use that instead of the homemade variety.

- Make the sauce as hot or as mild as you like by varying the amount of hot sauce you use.

- The blue cheese dip complements the sauce and helps cool the heat, as do the celery sticks.

BBQ WINGS

These spicy and tender wings bake to perfection

Barbecued wings have great flavor, are fun to eat, and can be a complete meal if eaten in quantity. They also make an excellent appetizer, especially before a cookout.

You can bake the wings in any barbecue sauce—your favorite homemade or purchased is just fine. You can also marinate the wings for 8–24 hours before baking them. Just be sure the sauce is cool before you add the wings, and marinate them in the refrigerator. Whether baked, broiled, or grilled, these wings should be heavily coated with a sweet and spicy tomato-based sauce. If you grill or broil the wings, baste them several times during cooking. And if you bake them, turn the wings several times so they build up a coating of the sauce. *Yield: Serves 6–8*

KNACK CHICKEN CLASSICS

Ingredients

2 tablespoons butter

1 tablespoon olive oil

1 onion, finely chopped

5 cloves garlic, minced

1/4 cup brown sugar

1/4 cup Dijon mustard

1/2 cup ketchup

1/4 cup tomato juice

3 tablespoons cider vinegar

1 tablespoon hot sauce

1/2 teaspoon dried oregano

1/2 teaspoon dried thyme

1/2 teaspoon salt

1/8 teaspoon cayenne pepper

2 pounds chicken wings, each cut into 3 pieces, tips discarded

BBQ Wings

- In medium saucepan, melt butter and olive oil; add onion and garlic. Cook 5 minutes.

- Add brown sugar, mustard, ketchup, tomato juice, vinegar, hot sauce, oregano, thyme, salt, and pepper; simmer 10 minutes.

- Prepare wings and place in roasting pan. Pour half of sauce over all.

- Bake at 400ºF 20 minutes, turn wings, and add remaining sauce. Bake 25–35 minutes longer, until wings are tender.

• • • • RECIPE VARIATION • • • •

Grilled BBQ Wings
Make recipe as directed, except cool sauce mixture, add wings, stir to coat, cover, and refrigerate 8–24 hours. When ready to cook, prepare and preheat grill. Remove wings from marinade; reserve marinade. Grill wings over low coals 15–25 minutes, brushing frequently with sauce. Simmer sauce; serve with wings.

ZOOM

You can dress up a purchased barbecue sauce by adding your own twist to the recipe. Taste the sauce and see if you think it's missing something. You can add honey, brown sugar, hot sauce, cooked onions or garlic, cayenne pepper, or any herbs or spices in your pantry.

Simmer Sauce

- The sauce can be simmered for a longer time before combining with the wings for a concentrated flavor.

- You can vary the herbs and spices used in the sauce. Omit the mustard, add horseradish, or use honey instead of brown sugar.

- Use marjoram and basil instead of the oregano and thyme. Add fresh herbs instead of dried.

- As soon as you combine the hot sauce with the wings, they should go into the oven.

Turn Wings

- Taste the sauce before you pour it over the wings and correct seasonings if necessary.

- You can add more salt, pepper, vinegar, hot sauce, herbs, or mustard to suit your taste.

- The sauce will thicken in the oven as it simmers. You must turn the wings to glaze them.

- You can pour the sauce into a serving bowl and serve it along with the finished wings for dunking.

CURRIED WINGS

Crispy broiled wings are first marinated in a sweet and sour curry sauce

Curry powder and chicken wings are a natural match. The mild and tender wings are perfectly complemented by the sweet and spicy blend of spices.

Broiling wings is a delicious way to get crisp skin and tender meat with little fuss or mess. You need to be careful when broiling wings because they will pop and spatter under the intense heat. Always use potholders to protect your hands and arms when turning wings under the broiler.

These wings can be served hot or cold. The glaze will form a slightly chewy, sweet and tart crust on the wings. To serve cold, cover and chill them for 4–5 hours before serving. *Yield: Serves 6–8*

Ingredients

2 tablespoons olive oil

2 cloves garlic, minced

2 shallots, minced

1 tablespoon curry powder

$1/4$ cup lemon juice

$1/2$ teaspoon salt

$1/8$ teaspoon pepper

$1/3$ cup honey

$1 1/2$ pounds chicken wings, prepared

Curried Wings

- In small saucepan, heat olive oil. Add garlic, shallots, and curry powder; cook 4 minutes; remove from heat.

- Add lemon juice, salt, pepper, and honey. Place wings in baking dish; pour sauce over. Refrigerate 6–24 hours.

- Reserve marinade; place wings on broiler pan; broil 6 inches from heat source 15 minutes, turning frequently.

- Brush wings with reserved marinate; continue broiling, turning, and basting, 10–15 minutes longer until done. Serve with Chutney Sauce.

• • • • RECIPE VARIATIONS • • • •

Chutney Sauce

In bowl, combine ½ cup mango chutney or blueberry chutney, ½ cup thick Greek yogurt or 1 cup plain yogurt, drained, 2 tablespoons minced green onion, and ½ teaspoon dried basil leaves. Cover and refrigerate for 2–3 hours before serving as a dipping sauce for the wings.

Grilled Curried Wings

Make recipe as directed, except marinate wings in the refrigerator 12–24 hours. When ready to cook, prepare and preheat grill. Remove wings from marinade; reserve marinade. Grill wings over low coals 15–20 minutes, brushing frequently with reserved marinade, until done. Discard marinade.

Cook Marinade

- The curry powder is cooked with the garlic and shallots because heat releases the essential oils in the spices.

- This intensifies the flavor and builds the aroma so the curry powder dominates the dish.

- If you would prefer more marinade, double the ingredients. You can then simmer the marinade for 2 minutes and serve with the chicken.

- Turn the chicken wings several times in the marinade while it's in the refrigerator.

Broil Wings

- There isn't a lot of marinade to brush on the wings, but use what's left in the dish to create a glaze.

- Adjust the oven rack to the correct level before you turn on the broiler. And let the broiler preheat for 5–10 minutes.

- Spray the broiler rack or pan with nonstick cooking spray before adding the wings so they don't stick.

- Watch the wings carefully as they broil. You want them to be deep golden brown but not burnt.

WINGS CASINO

A twist on Clams Casino, this excellent recipe is full of flavor

Clams Casino is a rich appetizer dish made by topping clams with a mixture of bacon, breadcrumbs, cheese, and cooked vegetables. Using chicken wings instead of clams reduces the cost, and makes the recipe easier. And the combination is delicious!

The classic casino mixture is piled on top of clams in the shell, then the whole thing is baked quickly in a hot oven.

The wings are made by first baking them, then topping with a bacon, vegetable, and cheese mixture.

These wings are delicious served with a glass of dry white wine before a meal of grilled steak or salmon, along with a spinach salad. For dessert, a lemon meringue pie would be perfect. *Yield: Serves 6*

Wings Casino

Ingredients

4 slices bacon

1 tablespoon butter

2 pounds chicken wings, each cut into 3 pieces, tips discarded

1/4 cup dry white wine

1 onion, finely chopped

4 cloves garlic, minced

1 green bell pepper, chopped

1/4 cup chicken broth

1 tablespoon lemon juice

1/3 cup grated Parmesan cheese

- Cook bacon until crisp in large skillet; drain, crumble, and set aside. Remove all but 2 tablespoons drippings.

- Add butter; brown wings on both sides; remove wings to baking dish; drizzle with wine.

- Bake wings at 375ºF 30–40 minutes. Meanwhile, add onion, garlic, and bell pepper to skillet; cook 5 minutes.

- Add broth and lemon juice; simmer 5 minutes. When wings are done, top each with a spoonful of vegetables, bacon, and cheese. Bake 10 minutes longer.

•••• RECIPE VARIATIONS ••••

Wings Rockefeller
Prepare and bake the wings as directed. For the topping, substitute 2 minced shallots for the onion. Omit green bell pepper; add 1½ cups chopped baby spinach and 2 tablespoons dry white wine; cook until tender. Add Parmesan, pile on cooked wings, and bake 5–10 minutes longer.

Wings Cocktail
Like shrimp cocktail; first prepare the wings as directed in the recipe, but don't make the casino topping. Serve the wings with a seafood cocktail sauce, either bottled or made by mixing ½ cup each ketchup and chili sauce with 2 tablespoons each mustard, lemon juice, and honey.

Brown Wings

- The wings are browned in some of the bacon drippings and butter for fabulous flavor.

- This browning step also helps create pan drippings from the chicken that flavor the vegetables as they cook.

- Make the vegetable topping while the wings are in the oven. It can stand at room temperature up to 20 minutes.

- If you want to prepare this partially ahead of time, just make the filling; don't brown the wings to bake later.

Top Wings with Vegetables

- Some of the topping will fall off the wings as they bake and as you serve them; that's okay.

- Just serve some toasted bread to sop up the leftover vegetables and juices, or spoon them back on the wings.

- Other vegetables that would be good in this mixture include chopped mushrooms, zucchini, or tomatoes.

- Add fresh or dried thyme, basil, and oregano to the vegetable mixture for even more flavor.

APRICOT WINGS

Sweet apricot preserves and nectar add color and flavor to these fun wings

Meat with fruit, especially chicken with fruit, is a fabulous combination. The sweet and tart flavor of the fruit complements the mild, tender, and buttery meat.

Apricots are one of the best fruits to use in glaze and sauce recipes for meat. Their sweet and tart balance is perfect, they are easy to find and delicious in canned form and as preserves, and the color is beautiful too.

You can make this recipe with peach nectar and peach preserves instead. Be sure to use a fruit that has some acidity, or the recipe will be too sweet.

Serve these sweet, tart, and sticky wings with beer or chilled white wine and lots of napkins. *Yield: Serves 6*

Ingredients

2 pounds chicken wings, cut into thirds, tips discarded

1 cup apricot preserves

1 onion, minced

3 cloves garlic, minced

³/₄ cup apricot nectar

1 tablespoon lemon juice

¹/₈ teaspoon cayenne pepper

2 tablespoons soy sauce

¹/₂ teaspoon ground ginger

Apricot Wings

- Prepare wings and place in large heavy-duty plastic bag. Add remaining ingredients.

- Seal bag and squish to knead. Place bag in bowl in refrigerator; marinate for 8–24 hours.

- Remove wings from marinade and place on baking sheet. Place marinade in medium saucepan.

- Bake wings at 375°F for 20 minutes; simmer sauce on low heat, stirring frequently. Brush wings with half of sauce; bake 10–15 minutes. Serve wings with sauce.

• • • • RECIPE VARIATIONS • • • •

Curried Peach Wings

Make recipe as directed, except use peach preserves and peach nectar in place of apricot preserves and apricot nectar. Omit ground ginger; add $1/2$ teaspoon dried thyme leaves and $1/8$ teaspoon black pepper.

Sticky Asian Wings

Make recipe as directed, except cook onion and garlic in 2 tablespoons olive oil. Add $1/3$ cup low sodium soy sauce, lemon juice, cayenne pepper, and ginger. Add $1/2$ teaspoon five-spice powder and $1/4$ cup honey. Bake wings as directed, basting with sauce.

Wings in Marinade

- Make sure that the onion is finely minced. This will intensify the flavor and ensure that no one bites into a big chunk of onion.

- You can marinate the wings longer than 24 hours, but don't go beyond 48 hours.

- Because they are dark meat, you don't run the risk of the wings becoming tough or mushy.

- You can take a shortcut by combining apricot preserves with sweet and sour or barbecue sauce.

Brush Wings with Sauce

- Keep simmering the sauce while the wings are baking. When you brush the wings with the marinade, they are not fully cooked.

- So you have to simmer the marinade for at least 2 minutes after you dip the brush in the marinade.

- For a really sticky glaze, instead of baking the wings for the last 10–15 minutes, broil them for 5–6 minutes.

- Serve the wings with sour cream mixed with a little apricot preserves for a cooling contrast.

WINGS SATAY
A ginger and peanut sauce envelops these tender wings

Satay is a barbecued main dish made of marinated chicken, pork, or lamb, usually threaded onto skewers. It's served with a sauce made of peanuts, soy sauce, gingerroot, and red curry paste.

For Wings Satay, the wings are marinated, then baked and served with a sauce made from peanut butter, curry powder and paste, and ginger. The mixture is very rich and complements the chicken. Rolling the chicken wings in peanuts adds a great layer of flavor and crunch.

You can substitute a bottled peanut sauce for the homemade sauce. Marinate the wings in that, or in the lemon juice mixture, then brush with the peanut sauce and continue baking. *Yield: Serves 6*

Ingredients

2 tablespoons olive oil

3 cloves garlic, minced

1 tablespoon grated gingerroot

¼ cup lemon juice

1 teaspoon chili powder

¾ cup chicken stock

2 pounds chicken wings, cut into thirds, tips discarded

¼ cup peanut butter

2 teaspoons curry powder

1 teaspoon red curry paste

1 cup finely chopped roasted peanuts

Wings Satay

- In small saucepan, heat olive oil and cook garlic and gingerroot for 4 minutes.

- Remove to bowl and add lemon juice, chili powder, and chicken stock.

- Add wings; stir and marinate in refrigerator for 2–8 hours. Drain wings, reserving marinade, and place on baking pan.

- Bake wings at 350ºF 20 minutes. Mix reserved marinade with peanut butter, curry powder, and paste; brush on wings. Bake 10–15 minutes longer. Roll in nuts and serve.

• • • • RECIPE VARIATION • • • •

Chicken Thighs Satay

Make recipe as directed, except use bone-in, skin-on chicken thighs. Marinate them for 8–24 hours, and then bake for 45 minutes. Brush with sauce, bake 10–15 minutes longer, and then broil until dark brown. Roll in peanuts and serve.

GREEN ● LIGHT

You can serve chicken wings as the main dish as long as you serve enough of them. If 3–4 wings is an appetizer serving, at least ½ pound is a main dish serving. Plan on ¾ pound per person just to be sure you have enough—leftovers are wonderful.

Marinate Wings

- The wings can marinate up to 48 hours for a more intense flavor, or if you want to make them ahead of time.

- For very spicy wings, increase the amount of chili powder, or add some curry paste or red pepper flakes to the marinade.

- For milder wings, omit the curry paste and reduce the chili powder amount.

- Place the wings on a rack for crisper skin, or just place them on the pan so they sizzle in the marinade.

Bake Wings

- Bake the wings until the internal temperature registers 170ºF.

- You can use the peanut coating step with other recipes, or roll the finished wings in pretzel crumbs.

- Discard any remaining marinade after you've finished coating the wings in the oven.

- Or, if you'd like to serve a dipping sauce with the chicken, add another ½ cup chicken stock to the marinade and boil 2 minutes.

PICNIC DRUMSTICKS
Crisp cereal makes a crunchy coating on tender drumsticks

What's a picnic without chicken drumsticks? Hot or cold, drumsticks are the perfect portable food, as long as you follow a few rules.

If you want to serve the drumsticks hot, pack them in an insulated container and serve within one hour of removing them from the oven or fryer. If you want to serve the drumsticks cold, make sure they are really cold. Refrigerate them overnight and pack in an insulated cooler.

The skin is removed on these drumsticks so you can enjoy the crisp and flavorful coating without worrying about the skin turning flabby.

Pack the drumsticks, in their insulated container, into a picnic basket with lots of napkins. For more fun, offer the Herbed Dipping Sauce. *Yield: Serves 4–6*

Ingredients

2 cloves garlic, minced

1/4 cup minced onion

1 tablespoon olive oil

3 tablespoons honey

3 tablespoons mustard

2 tablespoons cider vinegar

1 1/2 cups crushed crisp rice flakes cereal

1/2 teaspoon seasoned salt

8 drumsticks, skin removed

1/4 cup butter, melted

Picnic Drumsticks

- Preheat oven to 350ºF. In small saucepan, cook garlic and onion in olive oil 5 minutes; remove to bowl.

- Add honey, mustard, and vinegar; mix well. On plate, combine cereal and salt.

- Dip drumsticks in honey mixture, then roll in cereal mixture to coat. Place melted butter on baking sheet.

- Add drumsticks to sheet; bake for 45–55 minutes until chicken is thoroughly cooked. Serve warm or chill until cold.

Herbed Dipping Sauce

In small bowl, combine $1/2$ cup plain yogurt, $1/3$ cup sour cream, and $1/3$ cup mayonnaise. Add 1 tablespoon each chopped fresh dill, thyme, and basil. Stir in $1/2$ cup shredded Parmesan cheese and 2 chopped green onions. Refrigerate until serving time.

Spicy Picnic Drumsticks

Make recipe as directed, except increase garlic to 4 cloves and omit honey. Add 1 tablespoon chili powder, $1/2$ teaspoon pepper, and $1/4$ teaspoon cayenne pepper to the cereal mixture. Use crushed cornflakes instead of the rice cereal. Coat chicken and bake as directed until done.

Skin Drumsticks

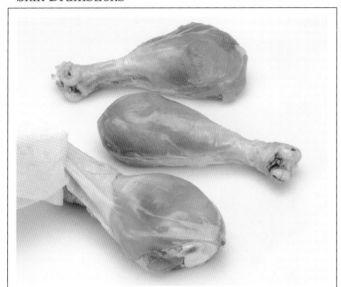

- Use paper towels to easily remove the skin from the drumsticks.

- Hold onto the drumsticks at the small end and, using a paper towel to hold onto the slippery skin, pull it off.

- You may need to use a knife to start loosening the skin, but it should come off relatively easily.

- You can prepare the honey mustard and the cereal coating mixture ahead of time; store them in airtight containers.

Coat Drumsticks

- Coat the drumsticks evenly in the mustard mixture, then, holding them by the end of the bone, shake off excess.

- Make sure that you measure the cereal after you crush it. If you measure the cereal, then crush it, you won't have enough.

- Place the cereal in a resealable plastic bag, close the bag, and roll over the bag with a rolling pin.

- You can gently turn the drumsticks over halfway through cooking time for more even browning.

OVEN-FRIED DRUMSTICKS
This old-fashioned recipe makes crisp chicken with less fat

Technically, this method isn't true frying. But with hot melted butter and a hot oven, oven-frying does a pretty good job of replicating deep-fried results.

It's important that both the butter and the oven be hot when you add the coated drumsticks to the pan and put the pan in the oven. If the butter isn't hot enough, the chicken coating will absorb it and become soggy. If the oven isn't hot enough, the chicken will steam in the butter rather than frying and won't be crisp.

With the skin removed, you can bite right into the crisp coating of this tender and juicy chicken and enjoy every morsel. Serve it with mashed potatoes and glazed baby carrots. *Yield: Serves 4–6*

KNACK CHICKEN CLASSICS

Ingredients

8 chicken drumsticks, skin removed

¹/₂ cup buttermilk

3 cloves garlic, minced

¹/₂ teaspoon seasoned salt

¹/₂ teaspoon ground cumin

1 teaspoon dried thyme

2 cups cornflakes cereal, crushed

¹/₂ cup flour

1 teaspoon paprika

¹/₃ cup butter, melted

Oven Fried Drumsticks

- Place drumsticks in large heavy-duty plastic bag. In bowl, mix buttermilk with garlic, salt, cumin, and thyme.

- Pour into bag with chicken; seal and knead to mix well. Cover and refrigerate for 8–24 hours.

- Preheat oven to 400ºF. Combine cereal crumbs, flour, and paprika on plate; roll chicken in this mixture to coat.

- Melt butter in jelly roll pan; add chicken, skin side down. Bake 35 minutes; turn and bake 20–25 minutes longer until done.

Oven-Fried Tex-Mex Drumsticks
Make recipe as directed, except add 1 tablespoon chili powder and $1/2$ teaspoon cayenne pepper to the buttermilk mixture. Marinate the chicken. Add 1 teaspoon crushed red pepper flakes to the cereal mixture. Bake chicken as directed.

YELLOW ● LIGHT

It's important that your oven temperature is accurate when baking and cooking. To check, you should have a reliable oven thermometer hanging on the middle rack in your oven. If that temperature doesn't meet the set temperature, have the oven serviced so it's accurate.

Coat Drumsticks

Turn Chicken

- Place the bag containing the chicken and the marinade into a large pan or casserole to prevent drips and leaks.

- The longer you marinate the drumsticks, the more tender they will be. You can add other herbs or spices to the marinade if you'd like.

- Just don't marinate them longer than 24 hours, or the flesh may become tough.

- Shake off the excess marinade and coat chicken. Discard any remaining marinade and coating.

- Make sure the butter is sizzling hot when you add the chicken. Add the chicken using tongs.

- Place the chicken carefully in the hot butter; it may splatter a bit as it touches the hot fat.

- Keep the oven door closed while the chicken is cooking; don't open the door to check or you'll lower the temperature.

- After 55 minutes of baking, check the temperature of the chicken. When it's done, drain briefly on paper towels and serve.

BBQ DRUMSTICKS
A spicy homemade barbecue sauce glazes these drumsticks

Grilling chicken adds a marvelous smoky flavor that complements the sweet and spicy barbecue sauce. It's easy to make your own sauce and control the ingredients, or if you have a favorite barbecue sauce, just use that.

Dress up a purchased barbecue sauce by adding your favorite ingredients. Mustard, hot peppers, honey, and herbs and spices are great additions to bottled barbecue sauce.

To use the sauce as a marinade and to serve it with the cooked chicken, you can either use separate quantities for the two uses, or simmer the marinade for a few minutes after you've finished basting the chicken as it grills.

Serve this delicious chicken with potato salad, chips, and cold beer. *Yield: Serves 4–6*

Ingredients

1 onion, chopped

4 cloves garlic, minced

1 jalapeño pepper, minced

3 tablespoons olive oil

$^1/_2$ cup cider vinegar

$^1/_2$ cup ketchup

$^1/_3$ cup brown sugar

3 tablespoons Dijon mustard

1 tablespoon soy sauce

$^1/_2$ teaspoon celery salt

$^1/_4$ teaspoon pepper

2 pounds chicken drumsticks

BBQ Drumsticks

- Cook onion, garlic, and jalapeño in olive oil 6–7 minutes. Remove to bowl; add vinegar, ketchup, brown sugar, mustard, soy sauce, celery salt, and pepper.

- Add drumsticks; turn to coat. Cover and refrigerate 8–24 hours. Drain drumsticks, reserving marinade.

- Prepare grill; place marinade in saucepan. Simmer.

- Grill chicken, covered, over medium coals for 15 minutes. Turn and start brushing with simmering marinade; grill 15–20 minutes longer until done. Serve with remaining marinade.

Mild BBQ Drumsticks

Make recipe as directed, except increase ketchup to ³/₄ cup. Omit the jalapeño pepper and reduce garlic cloves to 2. Add ¹/₄ cup honey to the barbecue sauce. Marinate the chicken in the refrigerator, then grill as directed, simmering the marinade and basting the chicken as it cooks.

Curried BBQ Drumsticks

Make recipe as directed, except add 1–2 tablespoons curry powder to the marinade. Omit the jalapeño pepper and substitute ¹/₃ cup honey for the brown sugar. Add 1 teaspoon cumin to the marinade. Marinate chicken and grill as directed. Serve chicken with mango chutney and toasted nuts and coconut.

Grill Drumsticks

- To prepare the grill, add coals or turn on the gas according to manufacturer's directions.

- After the coals are heated or the grill is up to temperature, scrape the grill rack to clean, then oil using oiled paper towels.

- Shake excess marinade off the chicken and place on the grill. Don't move the chicken until it lifts easily from the rack.

- When the chicken has cooked on both sides, keep it moving. You can move to cooler areas of the grill as it cooks.

Simmer Marinade

- Place the marinade in a pan and put that pan right on the grill to simmer while the chicken cooks.

- Use a silicone brush to spread the marinade on the chicken for easiest cleanup.

- Or you can bundle together some sturdy herbs, like rosemary and oregano, and use them as a basting brush.

- Stir the marinade frequently as it simmers so it doesn't burn. Let it cool slightly before serving with the chicken.

PESTO STUFFED DRUMSTICKS

A cheesy pesto mixture is stuffed under drumstick's skin

Pesto is a mixture of basil, Parmesan cheese, garlic, olive oil, and pine nuts blended into a paste. This Italian condiment is delicious with mild, tender chicken.

Drumsticks may not seem like a natural choice for stuffing, but they are. You just loosen the skin and place the stuffing in between the skin and the flesh. Smooth the skin back over the stuffing and you're ready to grill or bake the chicken.

Use your imagination when thinking of stuffings for drumsticks. A combination of cheeses and herbs with caramelized onions would be delicious, as would tapenade (olive paste) with fresh rosemary and lemon juice.

Serve these drumsticks with rice pilaf, a mixed vegetable salad, and lemon pie for dessert. *Yield: Serves 6–8*

Ingredients

1 (7-ounce) container basil pesto

1 (3-ounce) package cream cheese, softened

¼ cup grated Parmesan cheese

½ cup chopped walnuts

8 chicken drumsticks

3 tablespoons butter, melted

Pesto Stuffed Drumsticks

- Preheat oven to 375ºF. In small bowl, combine pesto, cream cheese, Parmesan cheese, and walnuts; blend well until combined.

- With your fingers, carefully loosen skin from drumsticks; do not remove completely.

- Divide pesto mixture among drumsticks. Stuff it under skin and over flesh; carefully smooth skin back over flesh.

- Place drumsticks in a roasting pan; brush with butter. Bake for 50–55 minutes until chicken is thoroughly cooked.

• • • • RECIPE VARIATIONS • • • •

Grilled Stuffed Drumsticks

Prepare recipe as directed, except after stuffing the drumsticks, refrigerate them while preheating the grill. Brush the grill rack with vegetable oil. Brush the drumsticks with butter, and grill, covered, turning frequently, for 30–40 minutes until drumsticks are done. Move the drumsticks to a cooler part of the grill if they get too brown.

Shrimp Stuffed Drumsticks

Make recipe as directed, except add 1 (6-ounce) can tiny shrimp, drained. Omit pesto; add 1 cup shredded Havarti cheese and ¹/₂ cup minced red bell pepper to the stuffing. Stuff drumsticks as directed, brush with butter, and bake as directed.

Loosen Skin and Stuff

- When you loosen the skin on the drumsticks, be careful not to tear it or the filling may leak out.

- Push the filling deep into the area between the skin and the flesh with a spoon or your fingers.

- Then pull the skin out and over the filling, smoothing it down as close as you can to the bone at the end.

- You can stuff the drumsticks ahead of time; cover and refrigerate until you want to bake or grill them.

Bake Drumsticks

- Preheat the oven for best results and so the chicken bakes evenly.

- The drumsticks can be coated in seasoned breadcrumbs or crushed cereal for a crunchy coating.

- You can turn the chicken as it cooks for more even browning, or place it on a rack for crisp skin. Let chicken stand 10 minutes after baking.

- You can serve these drumsticks with a dipping sauce made by mixing equal parts sour cream and pesto.

79

DEVILED DRUMSTICKS
Mustard and cayenne pepper flavor this easy recipe

"Deviling" food just means adding spicy ingredients that also color the food a deep red or gold. Cayenne pepper, paprika, and mustard are the ingredients used to get this combination.

These drumsticks are especially good for dipping. You can use a spicy mixture for the dip, like salsa mixed with yogurt or mayonnaise, or something cooling, like sour cream with mint and chopped cucumber.

If you're serving this recipe to kids, you can cut down on the mustard and cayenne pepper for a milder recipe. Don't omit the paprika; it adds a smoky sweetness.

Serve these drumsticks with mashed potatoes and steamed green beans. A mixed fruit salad with poppy seed dressing is a good complement. *Yield: Serves 6–8*

Ingredients

8 drumsticks, skin removed

1/4 cup yogurt

1/4 cup Dijon mustard

2 tablespoons grainy mustard

1/8 teaspoon cayenne pepper

2 tablespoons butter, melted

1 1/2 cups soft fresh breadcrumbs

1 teaspoon paprika

1/2 teaspoon seasoned salt

1/8 teaspoon pepper

Deviled Drumsticks

- Preheat oven to 400°F. Coat a jelly roll pan with nonstick cooking spray; set aside.

- In medium bowl, combine yogurt, mustards, cayenne pepper, and butter; mix well.

- On plate, combine breadcrumbs, paprika, salt, and pepper. Dip drumsticks in mustard mixture, then roll in breadcrumb mixture to coat.

- Place on wire rack in roasting pan. Bake for 35–45 minutes until drumsticks are thoroughly cooked.

Sweet and Sour Drumsticks

Make recipe as directed, except combine ¼ cup lemon juice, 3 tablespoons sugar, 2 tablespoons honey, ⅓ cup ketchup, and 1 tablespoon each soy sauce and cornstarch in small pan; simmer 5 minutes. Coat drumsticks in this mixture, roll in breadcrumb mixture, and bake on a wire rack until done.

Grilled Deviled Drumsticks

Leave skin on drumsticks. Make yogurt mixture as directed, except add ¼ cup ketchup and 1 teaspoon paprika. Omit breadcrumb mixture. Start grilling the drumsticks over medium coals. After 10 minutes, brush with yogurt mixture. Grill 35–45 minutes until drumsticks are done; discard yogurt mixture.

Dip Drumsticks

- You can marinate the drumsticks in the spicy yogurt mixture if you'd like.

- Just coat with the marinade, place in a glass baking dish, cover, and marinate in the refrigerator for 8–24 hours.

- You can make the yogurt mixture as spicy or as mild as you like. Add 1–2 jalapeños for more spice.

- Or omit the spicy ingredients and use mild yellow mustard and ketchup or mayonnaise; it's up to you!

Coat Drumsticks with Breadcrumbs

- The drumsticks should be evenly and thickly coated with the marinade.

- Dip the drumsticks and then hold over the marinade to let some of the excess drip off; then immediately roll in breadcrumb mixture.

- If you want to use dried breadcrumbs instead of the fresh, use about 1 cup. You can use seasoned breadcrumbs.

- Even with the skin removed, the marinade and breadcrumbs ensure that this chicken will be moist and juicy.

SANTA FE CHICKEN

Drumsticks broiled with a spicy glaze are served with a sour cream salsa mixture

Broiling drumsticks is a great way to cook them. The intense heat will make the skin crisp, and the skin protects the meat from the heat so it stays tender and juicy.

In most ovens, the broiler must be preheated, and the oven door must be left slightly ajar. The coils will stay bright red the entire time the broiler is on.

Once again, you can make this recipe as mild or as spicy as you'd like. A poblano pepper is a mild substitute for the jalapeños, or you can use habanero or even Scotch Bonnet peppers to increase the heat.

Serve with creamy potato salad, fresh fruit, and lots of tortilla chips. *Yield: Serves 4–6*

Ingredients

2 tablespoons olive oil

4 cloves garlic, minced

2 jalapeño peppers, minced

1 tablespoon chili powder

1 teaspoon ground cumin

$1/2$ teaspoon salt

$1/8$ teaspoon cayenne pepper

8 drumsticks

$1/2$ cup sour cream

1 cup chunky salsa

1 avocado, peeled and chopped

Santa Fe Chicken

- In small saucepan, heat olive oil; cook garlic and jalapeños for 2 minutes. Remove to bowl; add chili powder, cumin, salt, and pepper.

- Preheat broiler. Coat drumsticks in oil mixture and place on a sprayed broiler pan.

- Broil 8 inches from heat source for 20–25 minutes, turning occasionally; brush with more oil mixture twice during broiling time.

- Combine sour cream, salsa, and avocado; serve drumsticks with this mixture for dipping.

····· RECIPE VARIATIONS ·····

Chutney Chicken

Make recipe as directed, except omit jalapeños and chili powder. Add 1 tablespoon curry powder to onion mixture. Broil drumsticks as directed. Serve with dipping sauce made of $2/3$ cup sour cream, $1/2$ cup mango chutney, and $1/4$ cup toasted coconut.

Sticky Drumsticks

Make recipe as directed, except add $1/4$ cup each apple cider vinegar and low-sodium soy sauce to onion mixture along with $1/4$ cup honey. Omit jalapeño peppers, chili powder, and cumin. Coat drumsticks in this mixture and broil as directed, brushing with more sauce, until done.

Drumsticks under Broiler

- Arrange the rack at the proper distance from the coils before you turn on the broiler.

- For most purposes, the oven rack should be 6–8 inches from the hot coils.

- Whenever you cook food under the broiler, you must watch it very closely. It can go from beautifully browned to burnt in seconds.

- Turn the pan around from side to side and from front to back so the food cooks evenly.

Mix Dip

- Have fun using your imagination to create new dips for drumsticks. They can be sweet, savory, hot, or spicy.

- Combine your favorite flavors or browse through the spice aisle for more ideas.

- Good dip combinations include sour cream and grated cheese, fresh fruit with sweetened yogurt, or lots of chopped herbs with mayonnaise and sour cream.

- For a party, offer a selection of dips and drumsticks and let your guests mix and match.

CHICKEN NIÇOISE

Tender chicken is cooked with potatoes, wine, garlic, and olives

Niçoise literally means, "as prepared in Nice," a city in the south of France. The basic ingredients for any food prepared Niçoise style include olives, tomatoes, garlic, and anchovies.

Even if you don't like anchovies, please include them in this dish. The paste will melt into the sauce and they add a meaty dimension to the dish it's not possible to achieve with any other ingredient.

You can add other ingredients to this dish, including green beans, chopped cherry tomatoes, and different types of olives.

This really is a dish for company. Serve it with garlic-flavored couscous, roasted green beans, and some dinner rolls. Fresh fruit served over ice cream is a lovely finish to this flavorful dinner. *Yield: Serves 4*

Ingredients

8 bone-in, skin-on chicken thighs

1 teaspoon salt

$1/8$ teaspoon pepper

1 teaspoon dried thyme

1 teaspoon dried oregano

2 tablespoons flour

3 tablespoons olive oil

1 onion, chopped

2 shallots, minced

2 cloves garlic, minced

1 teaspoon anchovy paste

8 small red potatoes

$1/2$ cup dry white wine

1 cup chicken broth

1 (14.5-ounce) can diced tomatoes, undrained

1 sprig fresh rosemary

$1/3$ cup sliced Niçoise olives

Chicken Niçoise

- Loosen skin from chicken; sprinkle flesh with salt, pepper, thyme, and oregano; smooth skin back over.

- Dredge chicken in flour. Heat olive oil in large pan; add chicken, skin side down. Brown 5 minutes, then remove.

- Add onion, shallots, and garlic; cook 5 minutes. Add anchovy paste; stir.

- Add potatoes, wine, broth, tomatoes, and chicken; cover and simmer 40–45 minutes until done. Pull leaves from rosemary and add with olives; simmer 5 minutes. Serve over rice.

····· RECIPE VARIATION ·····

Slow Cooker Chicken Niçoise
Make recipe as directed; dredge chicken and brown in olive oil. Add onions, garlic, shallot, and anchovy paste to skillet and cook; place in 4-quart slow cooker with potatoes. Top with chicken; add remaining ingredients. Cover and cook on low 8–9 hours. Thicken broth if necessary with cornstarch.

ZOOM

Niçoise olives are a very distinctive variety of olive. The fruits are very small and shiny, with a deep burgundy color. Their flavor is quite sour and they taste very rich. If you can't find them, kalamata olives or Picholine olives are a good substitute.

Prepare Chicken

- By adding the seasonings directly to the chicken flesh, you will flavor the meat very well.

- Brown the chicken thoroughly in the first step. Don't remove the chicken until it releases easily from the pan.

- The chicken is removed from the pan so you can cook the remaining ingredients evenly and quickly.

- Set the chicken on a clean plate. Don't delay making the recipe; cook the remaining ingredients and proceed.

Return Chicken to Pan

- Add the potatoes, wine, broth, and tomatoes and stir the mixture well so the ingredients are evenly distributed.

- Then add the chicken, snuggling it down into the liquid and vegetables.

- Place the chicken evenly around the pan for a nice presentation and so the meat cooks at the same time.

- You can thicken the sauce by adding a mixture of 1 tablespoon cornstarch and 3 tablespoons water; simmer until thickened.

CHICKEN AMANDINE
Chicken coated with ground almonds is tender, juicy, and delicious

Amandine just means, "cooked with almonds." Chicken coated in a mixture of ground almonds, breadcrumbs, and herbs has a wonderful flavor. The coating becomes crisp and crunchy, while the chicken stays moist and tender.

The best almonds to use for this recipe are slivered almonds. They look like little sticks and have all the skin removed, so they grind evenly and don't have a bitter flavor. Toasting nuts

brings out their flavor by developing their oils, which accent the flavor of the chicken.

A simple yet flavorful sauce is made after the chicken is cooked. Serve this dish with rice pilaf to soak up the sauce, steamed asparagus, and a spinach salad made with strawberries. *Yield: Serves 4–6*

Ingredients

¹/₂ cup slivered almonds

¹/₄ cup dry breadcrumbs

1 teaspoon dried basil leaves

8 boneless, skinless chicken thighs

1 teaspoon salt

¹/₈ teaspoon pepper

1 egg, beaten

2 tablespoons olive oil

¹/₂ cup dry white wine

¹/₂ cup chicken broth

1 tablespoon lemon juice

1 tablespoon butter

Chicken Amandine

- Toast and grind almonds. Combine with breadcrumbs and basil on plate. Sprinkle chicken with salt and pepper.

- Coat chicken in egg, then dip in breadcrumb mixture. Heat olive oil in ovenproof pan; brown chicken on one side 4 minutes. Turn.

- Place in 375ºF oven; bake 30–35 minutes until done. Remove chicken; keep warm.

- Place pan on stovetop; add wine, broth, and lemon juice; boil, scraping up drippings. Swirl in butter and pour over chicken; serve immediately.

Pecan Chicken

Make recipe as directed, except substitute ³⁄₄ cup small pecan halves, toasted, cooled, and finely ground. Substitute 1 teaspoon dried thyme leaves for the basil leaves. Coat the chicken in egg, then in pecan/bread-crumb mixture, and prepare as directed.

ZOOM

Toast nuts by placing in a small dry pan over medium heat. Toss the nuts over the heat for 4–5 minutes until they are fragrant. You can also toast nuts in the microwave on high for 3–5 minutes, or bake them in a 400ºF oven for 8–10 minutes.

Toast Nuts for Coating

- Always let nuts cool after they have been toasted. If you chop or grind them immediately they'll get mushy.

- You can make the bread-crumb mixture ahead of time. Store it in the refrigerator, since the nuts contain perishable oils.

- Be sure to bake the chicken as soon as the first side is browned. Never partially cook chicken and hold it for later cooking.

- You can make this recipe with chicken breasts; double the coating mixture and bake for 25–35 minutes.

Bake Chicken

- Making a sauce while the chicken rests lets the juices redistribute in the chicken so it's juicy.

- To keep the chicken warm, place on a serving platter and cover with foil. Or you can put the chicken in a 200ºF oven up to 15 minutes.

- If you don't want to use white wine in this recipe, just substitute an equal amount of chicken broth or stock.

- Serve this recipe immediately while the coating is crisp and the sauce hot.

CHICKEN THIGHS

CHICKEN PICCATA
Tender chicken is cooked with lemon, capers, and stock

Chicken Piccata is a simple recipe that is full of flavor. When it's made with chicken thighs, it is also juicy, tender, and difficult to overcook.

Food cooked piccata-style uses lemons, olive oil, garlic, and capers to add flavor and brightness to the dish. Capers are the small buds of an evergreen plant that grows in the Mediterranean. They have a sharp, spicy flavor accented with salt.

They are usually found packed in brine, but you can also find them packed in salt. Rinse capers before use.

The sauce is made separately from the chicken so the chicken, which is coated in crumbs and cheese, stays crisp.

Classic accompaniments to Chicken Piccata include cooked rice and steamed zucchini. *Yield: Serves 4*

Ingredients

8 boneless, skinless chicken thighs

1 teaspoon salt

$^1/_8$ teaspoon pepper

$^1/_3$ cup flour

1 egg, beaten

$^1/_2$ cup dry breadcrumbs

$^1/_4$ cup grated Parmesan cheese

$^1/_2$ teaspoon dried oregano

3 tablespoons olive oil

2 cloves garlic, minced

$^1/_3$ cup lemon juice

$^1/_2$ cup chicken stock

$^1/_4$ cup capers, rinsed

1 tablespoon butter

$^1/_4$ cup chopped parsley

Chicken Piccata

- Flatten chicken and sprinkle with salt and pepper. Dredge in flour, then in egg.

- Combine breadcrumbs, cheese, and oregano; dredge chicken. Heat olive oil in large pan.

- Add chicken; brown on one side 4 minutes, then brown on second side 2 minutes. Remove to baking dish.

- Bake chicken at 375ºF 10–15 minutes. Place pan over heat; add garlic; cook 2 minutes. Add juice, stock, and capers; boil. Add butter, pour over chicken, sprinkle with parsley, and serve.

Simple Chicken Piccata

Make recipe as directed, except omit breadcrumbs, cheese, and oregano. Dredge chicken first in egg, then in flour. Brown chicken and bake as directed. Make sauce with drippings remaining in pan and serve sauce over chicken.

Pounded Chicken Piccata

Pound the chicken thighs until they are ¼ inch thick. Dredge in egg, then in flour; omit breadcrumbs, cheese, and oregano. Cook 4 minutes on each side until done; remove and keep warm. Make sauce in drippings from pan as directed. Do not bake the chicken.

Brown Chicken

- The chicken is coated first in flour, then egg, then the breadcrumb mixture so the coating stays on the chicken.

- You can season the bread-crumb mixture any way you'd like. Omit the cheese or add more herbs.

- It's important not to move the chicken when it's first added to the pan. Turn it when it releases easily.

- The chicken is cooked for just a few minutes on the second side before it is finished in the oven.

Make Sauce

- Make sure that you drain and rinse the capers before use. If you use capers packed in salt, rinse them twice.

- If you like lots of sauce, double the recipe. Pour some over the chicken and serve some on the side.

- The sauce for this dish isn't meant to be very thick. Boil it for 4–5 minutes until slightly reduced.

- The butter swirled in at the very end adds flavor and some body to the simple sauce.

CHICKEN FRICASSEE

Fricasseed chicken is cooked in your slow cooker with sausage

To fricassee means to cook or stew meat in a light-colored gravy. The recipe can be mildly seasoned, or made Cajun style, with lots of spices and peppers.

Andouille sausage is a highly spiced smoked sausage with a strong flavor that adds a rich depth of flavor to the recipe. You can substitute Polish sausage or salami for the Andouille.

The "Holy Trinity" of celery, bell pepper, and onion is a Cajun and Creole staple. The combination adds great flavor to this spicy dish.

Because this recipe makes such a wonderful sauce, you have to serve it with something like rice pilaf or mashed potatoes. A crisp green salad and some fresh fruit are cooling complements that round out the meal. *Yield: Serves 4–6*

Ingredients

³/₄ pound Andouille sausage, sliced

2 tablespoons olive oil

8 boneless, skinless chicken thighs

¹/₃ cup flour

1 teaspoon salt

¹/₄ teaspoon cayenne pepper

2 onions, chopped

3 cloves garlic, minced

1 (8-ounce) package mushrooms, sliced

3 stalks celery, chopped

1 green bell pepper, chopped

2 teaspoons Creole seasoning

1 bay leaf

¹/₂ teaspoon pepper

2 cups chicken stock

¹/₂ cup light cream

Chicken Fricassee

- Cook sausage until some of the fat is rendered; drain sausage on paper towels.

- Drain fat from pan. Add olive oil. Dredge thighs in mixture of flour, salt, and cayenne. Brown in oil; remove.

- Add onions, garlic, and mushrooms to pan; cook and stir for 6 minutes. Place in 4-quart slow cooker; top with chicken, sausage, celery, and bell pepper.

- Mix Creole seasoning, bay leaf, pepper, and stock; pour over food. Cover; cook on low 7–8 hours. Add cream; heat through and serve.

Oven Chicken Fricassee

Prepare recipe as directed. Brown sausage and chicken; cook onion, garlic, and mushrooms, then combine all ingredients except light cream into a 3-quart casserole dish. Cover and bake at 375°F for 60–70 minutes until chicken is done. Stir in cream, then serve.

Classic Chicken Fricassee

Make recipe as directed, except omit sausage, cayenne pepper, and Creole seasoning. Cook the coated chicken thighs in olive oil and remove; cook onions, garlic, and mushrooms. Combine in slow cooker, cover, and cook as directed.

Brown Chicken

Combine in Slow Cooker

- The only thickener in this recipe is the flour used to coat the chicken.

- Because the flour is browned, it will absorb more liquid during cooking in addition to keeping the chicken moist.

- The onions, garlic, and mushrooms are cooked in the chicken drippings to pick up a lot of the flavor.

- This cooking also helps the vegetables become very tender as they cook in the slow cooker.

- The longer cooking root vegetables are placed on the bottom of the slow cooker.

- The meats and tender vegetables are placed on the top because they cook more quickly.

- If the sauce isn't thick enough after cooking, you can add a cornstarch slurry.

- Or just turn the slow cooker to high and remove the cover for 20–30 minutes until some of the liquid has evaporated and the sauce is thicker.

91

INDIAN BUTTER CHICKEN
There isn't much butter in this recipe; yogurt is the tenderizer

While this recipe sounds rich, most of the sauce for this delicious recipe comes from yogurt. To keep the sauce thick, the yogurt is drained before being used in the recipe. This is a good technique to use when making any recipe with yogurt. Place the yogurt in a cheesecloth-lined strainer, put it into a bowl, then refrigerate it until most of the whey, or thin liquid, drains out. The resulting yogurt is thick and rich tasting.

Onions, garlic, tomatoes, curry powder, and ginger add the flavoring for this wonderful dish. You must serve it with hot cooked rice, preferably Basmati rice, to soak up the sauce.

Add a spinach salad and some nan or chapatti bread for an Indian feast. *Yield: Serves 4–6*

Ingredients

8 boneless, skinless chicken thighs, cubed

3 tablespoons lemon juice, divided

1/2 teaspoon salt

1 cup plain yogurt

1 onion, chopped

3 cloves garlic, minced

1 tablespoon vegetable oil

2 tablespoons butter

1 tablespoon grated gingerroot

1 tablespoon curry powder

1/2 teaspoon cumin

1/2 teaspoon ground coriander

1 bay leaf

1 (14.5-ounce) can diced tomatoes, undrained

1/4 cup heavy cream

1/3 cup ground cashews

Indian Butter Chicken

- Sprinkle chicken with half the lemon juice and salt; refrigerate 2 hours. At same time, put yogurt in cheesecloth-lined bowl; let drain in refrigerator.

- Cook onion and garlic in oil and butter for 6 minutes. Add remaining lemon juice, gingerroot, curry powder, cumin, coriander, and bay leaf; cook 2 minutes.

- Add tomatoes and drained yogurt. Add chicken; cover; simmer 20 minutes.

- Uncover; remove bay leaf. Add cream and cashews; simmer 10–15 minutes until thickened.

Slow Cooker Butter Chicken

Marinate chicken and drain yogurt as directed. Stir 1 tablespoon cornstarch into the yogurt. Cook onion, garlic, and spices as directed. Combine all ingredients in 4-quart slow cooker. Cover and cook on low for 7–9 hours until chicken is tender and sauce is blended. Remove bay leaf.

Curry Powder

In a small bowl, combine 1 tablespoon each ground coriander seeds, ground cumin seeds, and turmeric; 1 teaspoon each dry mustard, ground ginger, salt, and pepper, and $1/2$ teaspoon each ground cloves, cardamom, and cayenne pepper. Blend well and store in airtight container.

Prepare Ingredients

- While the yogurt drains, the whey is removed. This makes the yogurt thicker and gives it a richer flavor.

- If you can find thick Greek yogurt, you don't need to drain it. Most other yogurts should be drained first in this recipe.

- Vary the amount of spices used in this recipe according to your taste. You can use as little as 1 teaspoon each curry powder and ginger.

- You can substitute 3–4 red ripe tomatoes for the canned tomatoes. Peel, seed, and chop them before using.

Add Chicken to Sauce

- You can cut the chicken thighs into strips if you'd like for a different texture.

- Or use whole boneless, skinless chicken thighs. In that case, increase the cooking time to 30–35 minutes.

- The cashews are added to thicken the sauce and add a sweet and nutty flavor.

- Basmati rice, with its fluffy texture and popcorn aroma, can be found in the international foods aisle of the supermarket.

CHICKEN MOLE
Thighs simmer in a rich spice and chocolate sauce

Mole is a Mexican dish that uses chocolate to enhance the flavor and color of the sauce. The word evolved from the Aztec word "molli," which means stew or sauce. The recipes are handed down through the generations in Mexico.

Since chocolate was originally discovered and used in that country, it's appropriate that it is even used in main dishes there.

Chiles, onions, garlic, and spices like cinnamon and cumin add to the depth of flavor. If you can find Mexican chocolate to make this dish, use it. Some brands include Ibarra and Taza. The chocolate is made with cinnamon and nuts, so it has a grainier texture than the chocolate you are used to.

Enjoy this exotic dish with some iced tea. *Yield: Serves 6*

Ingredients

1 dried ancho chile

1 dried pasilla chile

$^1/_2$ cup boiling water

2 tablespoons butter

2 pounds boneless, skinless chicken thighs

2 tablespoons flour

1 teaspoon salt

$^1/_8$ teaspoon pepper

1 onion, chopped

3 cloves garlic, minced

$^1/_3$ cup raisins, finely chopped

1 (8-ounce) can tomato sauce

$^1/_4$ cup peanut butter

2 teaspoons chili powder

$^1/_2$ teaspoon cumin

$^1/_8$ teaspoon ground cloves

$^1/_2$ ounce unsweetened chocolate, chopped

$1^1/_2$ cups chicken broth

$^1/_4$ cup chopped fresh cilantro

Chicken Mole

- Soak dried chiles in water 5 minutes; drain, then chop chiles. Discard stems.

- Melt butter. Sprinkle chicken with flour, salt, and pepper; brown chicken 4 minutes. Remove from pan.

- Add onion, garlic, chiles, and raisins to pan; cook and stir 4 minutes. Puree using immersion blender.

- Stir in remaining ingredients except cilantro; bring to a simmer. Add chicken; simmer 40 minutes. Shred chicken and return to sauce. Serve over hot cooked rice with cilantro.

Slow Cooker Chicken Mole

Make recipe as directed, all the way up to pureeing the onion mixture. Combine all ingredients in a 4-quart slow cooker. Cover and cook on low for 8–9 hours. Remove chicken and shred, then return to sauce; cook uncovered on high 10 minutes; serve.

Cilantro Rice

Heat 1 tablespoon olive oil in pan; cook 3 cloves minced garlic and 1 teaspoon cumin 3 minutes. Add 1$\frac{1}{2}$ cups long-grain white rice; cook 3 minutes. Add 3 cups chicken stock; cover and simmer 20–25 minutes until tender. Add $\frac{1}{2}$ cup chopped fresh cilantro and 2 tablespoons butter.

Soak Chiles

- You can find dried chiles in the international foods aisle of most large supermarkets, or look in ethnic grocery stores.

- The chiles should be dry but not brittle. They should still be pliable, and be free of mold or wet spots.

- There's really no substitute for the soaked dried chiles in an authentic mole recipe, so do look for them.

- The chiles are spicy and hot, so use rubber gloves and don't touch your face or eyes when working.

Add Chicken

- You can use bone-in, skin-on chicken thighs for more flavor. Increase the cooking time to 55–65 minutes.

- To shred the chicken, remove it from the sauce. Use 2 forks to gently pull the chicken apart into rough pieces.

- Be careful to remove all bones and skin if you use bone-in chicken.

- This mixture is more like a stew, so can be served in bowls over rice or steamed vegetables.

CHICKEN THIGHS

CHICKEN STOCK

There's nothing better than homemade chicken stock

Chicken stock is made from the meat, bones, and skin of the bird. Stock is richer than broth, since the bones and skin add lots of flavor.

Broth can be a soup in itself. Simple heated broth, perhaps sprinkled with a few fresh herbs, is one of the most elegant first course recipes.

Browning the bones with some of the vegetables adds lots of flavor to the stock, and deepens the color. You don't have to brown the bones; just place all ingredients in a large pot, add the water, and simmer.

If you want to make stock in the slow cooker, place ingredients in a 3- or 4-quart appliance. Cook on low 7–8 hours, skimming the surface occasionally, until the stock tastes rich. *Yield: 8 cups*

Ingredients

2 pounds cut-up chicken

3 whole cloves

1 onion, quartered

4 stalks celery

1-inch piece gingerroot, peeled

$^1/_2$ cup chopped celery leaves

2 carrots, quartered

2 teaspoons salt

9 cups cold water

Chicken Stock

- Place chicken in large soup pot. Stick the whole cloves into 1 quarter of the onion and add to chicken with the rest of the onion.

- Add celery, gingerroot, celery leaves, carrots, and salt. Pour cold water over all.

- Simmer 1 hour. Remove chicken; remove and reserve meat for another use. Return bones and skin to pot.

- Simmer 4–5 hours longer, covered, until stock tastes rich. Strain and refrigerate; freeze up to 4 months.

Slow Cooker Chicken Stock

Make recipe as directed, except combine all ingredients in a 4- or 5-quart slow cooker. Cover and cook on low for 8–9 hours. Strain the broth, remove fat, and freeze as directed. You can brown the chicken and onions in the oven before making the stock if you'd like.

Chicken Broth

Make recipe as directed, except use 1 pound cooked, cubed chicken meat, both light and dark, in place of the whole cut-up chicken. Simmer the broth for 2 hours total. No need to remove the chicken from the pot; just discard after broth is done.

Simmer Stock

- You can brown the chicken pieces in the oven or on the stovetop before you begin for a richer taste.

- Heat some olive oil in a large pan and brown the chicken well on the skin side. Place in the pot and add remaining ingredients.

- Or bake the chicken and carrots in a 400ºF oven for 50–60 minutes until browned.

- The stock should just simmer, but not boil. Occasionally skim off foam and discard.

Strain Stock

- The foam, or scum, on the top of the broth consists of protein combined with fat and impurities in the food.

- If you don't skim it off, the soup will be cloudy. The stock also needs to be strained.

- Remove all of the large pieces of food with a slotted spoon or sieve.

- Then pour the broth through a strainer into a large pot. Refrigerate overnight, then remove the fat layer on top.

CHICKEN NOODLE SOUP

Noodles and chicken simmer together in a flavorful stock

Everyone's grandma had the best recipe for chicken noodle soup. There's a good reason it's so popular: it's inexpensive, easy to make, and literally is a cure-all for illness.

Research has shown that chicken soup will actually made you feel better when you have a cold. The heat, the vitamins and minerals from the stock and vegetables, and the steam are magic remedies.

Homemade stock makes the best Chicken Noodle Soup, but boxed stocks are a good compromise. Onions, garlic, and carrots are de rigueur, but you can add your favorites.

Egg noodles are the classic pasta, but you can use any size or type of pasta. Just cook according to the package directions until al dente. *Yield: Serves 6*

KNACK CHICKEN CLASSICS

Ingredients

1 tablespoon butter

1 tablespoon olive oil

2 boneless, skinless chicken breasts

4 boneless, skinless chicken thighs, cubed

1 teaspoon salt

1/8 teaspoon pepper

1 teaspoon dried thyme leaves

1 onion, chopped

2 stalks celery, chopped

3 carrots, sliced

8 cups chicken stock

2 tomatoes, peeled and chopped

2 cups egg noodles

1 cup frozen baby peas

Chicken Noodle Soup

- Heat butter and olive oil in soup pot. Add whole chicken breasts and cubed thighs; brown 4–5 minutes.

- Remove chicken, sprinkle with salt, pepper, and thyme, and set aside. Add onion, celery, and carrots to pot; simmer 5 minutes, scraping up pan drippings.

- Return chicken to pot along with stock and tomatoes. Simmer for 15–20 minutes until chicken is done. Remove chicken, shred, and return to soup.

- Add noodles, simmer 7 minutes. Add peas; simmer 2–4 minutes until hot.

Basic Chicken Noodle Soup

Make recipe as directed, except omit zucchini, squash, carrots, and plum tomatoes. Increase the egg noodles to 3½ cups; simmer just until al dente. Add 2 tablespoons lemon juice and serve topped with chopped parsley.

Grandma's Chicken Noodle Soup

Make recipe as directed, except use a whole frying chicken, cut into pieces. Brown the chicken very well, about 10–12 minutes, before adding to soup. Simmer the soup for about 2 hours. Remove chicken; remove meat and return to soup. Add noodles and simmer until done.

Brown Chicken

Add Stock

- Browning the chicken is an important first step. It adds a depth of flavor to the soup, and it also thickens the soup.

- The drippings left in the skillet are made of caramelized fat and meat. They add rich flavor to the soup.

- Let the chicken brown until it releases easily from the pan. Don't tear the skin or force it.

- You can use all boneless, skinless chicken breasts. Simmer 20–30 minutes, then shred chicken and finish the soup.

- To peel tomatoes, drop briefly into boiling water, then into ice water.

- The skins will slip off easily. Their texture can become unpleasant when simmered in liquid.

- When you're ready to serve the soup, taste it. You may need to correct seasonings.

- Add a pinch more salt or pepper, or some more thyme. Add just a little at a time so you don't over season the mixture.

CHICKEN SOUPS

CHICKEN WILD RICE SOUP

Wild rice combines with chicken in a delicious creamy soup

Chicken and wild rice is a wonderful combination. The nutty flavor and chewy texture of wild rice are great complements to tender and mild chicken.

Any combination of vegetables would be delicious in this soup. This recipe uses the classic onions, garlic, carrots, and celery, but you can also use zucchini, mushrooms, and bell peppers.

You can use brown rice in place of the wild rice in this easy soup. It will cook in about the same time frame as the wild rice. White rice really doesn't do well in the slow cooker so it isn't a good substitute, but if you make this dish on the stovetop you can use it.

Serve with a spinach salad and some crisp crackers. *Yield: Serves 6*

Chicken Wild Rice Soup

Ingredients

2 tablespoons olive oil

1 onion, chopped

4 cloves garlic, minced

4 carrots, sliced

2 stalks celery, sliced

1 teaspoon salt

1 teaspoon dried thyme leaves

1 teaspoon dried basil leaves

$^1/_8$ teaspoon white pepper

1 cup wild rice, rinsed

4 boneless, skinless chicken breasts

6 cups chicken stock

$^1/_2$ cup light cream or milk

2 tablespoons cornstarch

2 tablespoons lemon juice

- In saucepan, heat olive oil over medium heat. Add onion and garlic; cook and stir until tender, about 5 minutes.

- Combine all ingredients except cream, cornstarch, and lemon juice in 4- or 5-quart slow cooker.

- Cover and cook on low for 7–8 hours. Remove chicken breasts and shred; return to slow cooker.

- Combine cream, cornstarch, and lemon juice; stir into slow cooker. Cover and cook on high 15–20 minutes until thickened.

Greek Chicken Rice Soup

Make soup as directed, except cook on stovetop. Use 1 cup long-grain basmati rice in place of the wild rice. Cook onion and garlic; add remaining ingredients; simmer 25 minutes. Omit thyme and basil; add 1 teaspoon dried oregano. Add 1 teaspoon lemon zest and $^1/_2$ cup olives; top with $^1/_2$ cup crumbled feta cheese.

Brown Rice Chicken Soup

Make recipe as directed, except use 1 cup long-grain brown rice in place of the wild rice. Start soup by cooking 5 strips bacon until tender; drain, crumble, and refrigerate. Drain bacon fat from pan; continue with recipe. Cook as directed; add bacon when soup is done.

Cook Onion and Garlic

- When vegetables like onion and garlic will be cooked in the slow cooker, cooking them in fat first makes a better texture.

- Not only that, but the onion and garlic flavor will permeate the fat, adding flavor to the whole soup.

- You can cook the onion and garlic just until tender, or cook them longer until they turn brown.

- These caramelized onions will add great flavor to the soup, and will almost dissolve in the finished product.

Add Cream Mixture to Soup

- The mixture of liquid and cornstarch or flour is called a slurry.

- This is the fastest way to thicken soups. Make sure that the cornstarch is dissolved in the liquid before adding it to the soup.

- The soup must simmer for a few minutes after the slurry is added so the raw taste of the cornstarch or flour cooks out.

- Serve this soup with breadsticks made from refrigerated dough, rolled in cheese and herbs and baked.

CHICKEN SOUPS

CHINESE NOODLE SOUP
The flavors of Asia mingle in this hearty soup

Asian soups use wonderful flavors like gingerroot, five-spice powder, onions, garlic, and lemon or lime. Rice flour, which coats the chicken in this recipe, adds a delicate lightness that can't be duplicated with any other ingredient.

Sesame oil is a strongly flavored oil that adds a rich touch to the soup. You can substitute peanut or olive oil, but the taste won't be the same.

If you can find genuine Chinese flat noodles or rice noodles, use them in this soup. Otherwise, generic egg noodles or fine pasta like spaghetti or angel hair will work just fine. If you use the regular pasta, just add it to the soup and simmer until done; there's no need to soak it first. *Yield: Serves 6–8*

Ingredients

2 teaspoons sesame oil

1 onion, chopped

3 cloves garlic, minced

1 tablespoon grated gingerroot

6 boneless, skinless chicken thighs, cubed

2 tablespoons rice flour

$1/2$ teaspoon salt

$1/8$ teaspoon pepper

$1/2$ teaspoon five-spice powder

6 cups chicken broth

16 ounces flat rice noodles or egg noodles

3 green onions, thinly sliced

$1/4$ cup chopped fresh cilantro

2 tablespoons lime juice

Chinese Noodle Soup

- In large pot, heat sesame oil over medium-low heat. Add onion, garlic, and gingerroot; cook 5 minutes.

- Toss chicken in rice flour, salt, pepper, and five-spice powder. Add to pot; cook and stir 3 minutes.

- Add broth; bring to a simmer. Reduce heat to low; simmer, covered, 20–25 minutes until chicken is cooked.

- Soak rice noodles 10 minutes; drain and add to pot. Simmer 6–7 minutes until tender. Add onions, cilantro, and lime juice; stir and serve.

102

Spicy Noodle Soup
Make recipe as directed, except add 2 minced jalapeño peppers with the onions, garlic, and gingerroot. Add 2 tablespoons Asian fish sauce along with the chicken stock. Cook soup as directed. Drizzle with 1 teaspoon red chile oil and serve some at the table.

ZOOM

Five-spice powder is a combination of cinnamon, star anise, gingerroot, cloves, and fennel. If you can't find it, combine an equal amount of these ingredients and mix well. Store in an airtight container and use in Chinese and Asian recipes.

Cook Chicken

- The chicken is cooked in the onion mixture so the onion, garlic, and ginger permeate the chicken meat.

- The flour will thicken the soup as it cooks. It also keeps the chicken moist when it's sautéed in the oil.

- You can use homemade broth or stock, or purchased broth in this easy recipe.

- Boxed stocks and broths are usually higher quality than canned. Look for low-sodium varieties.

Add Noodles

- Flat rice noodles are also called *pho*. They must be soaked in cold water before cooking.

- If you can't find flat rice noodles, just use regular egg noodles. Cook until tender according to package directions.

- Whichever type of noodles you use, cook them just until tender. Overcooked noodles have no place in this soup.

- Serve the soup as soon as it is done. You can top it with thinly sliced lime, chopped peanuts, and Asian sesame oil.

CHICKEN SOUPS

MATZOH BALL SOUP
The Jewish classic, made simple and delicious

Matzoh balls are made from a mixture of matzoh meal, chicken stock, eggs, and seasonings. They are a type of dumpling made without leavening.

You can also make them from a soaked matzoh cracker. These dumplings aren't light, but shouldn't be heavy and dull either. When properly made, they are dense and slightly chewy, but tender enough to cut with a fork.

Surprisingly, sparkling water is the secret ingredient for lighter matzoh balls. The water adds some carbon dioxide to the batter, much like baking powder, without the aftertaste.

Make Chopped Chicken Liver as a traditional appetizer with this soup, served on sturdy whole-wheat crackers. Enjoy this soup for a warming meal on a cold night. *Yield: Serves 6*

Ingredients

1 matzoh cracker

¹/₂ cup water

1 onion, minced

3 tablespoons butter or margarine

2 eggs

10 cups plus 2 tablespoons chicken stock, divided

²/₃ cup matzoh meal

1 teaspoon salt

¹/₄ teaspoon pepper

¹/₄ cup sparkling water

¹/₃ cup chopped green onions

3 cups cooked shredded chicken

2 carrots, sliced

Matzoh Ball Soup

- Break cracker into small pieces; cover with water; let stand 10 minutes. Squeeze cracker to drain.

- Cook onion in butter 6 minutes. Add to cracker along with eggs, 2 tablespoons stock, matzoh meal, salt, and pepper.

- Stir in enough sparkling water to make a stiff batter. Refrigerate 1 hour.

- Bring remaining stock to a boil. Add green onions to matzoh ball mixture; form into balls. Drop into chicken broth; add chicken and carrots. Simmer 15–20 minutes.

Chopped Chicken Liver

Melt 2 tablespoons butter or chicken fat in a saucepan. Add 1 cup chopped onion and 2 minced cloves garlic along with $1/2$ pound trimmed chicken livers. Cook 10 minutes until no longer pink. Add 2 hard cooked eggs and 2 tablespoons sherry; chop mixture until fine or coarse; chill.

Classic Matzoh Ball Soup

Make recipe as directed, except omit cracker and water. Increase the matzoh meal to 1 cup. Mix batter, adding more meal if necessary to make a workable mixture. Chill matzoh mixture for 3–4 hours, then continue with recipe as directed. Top soup with chopped fresh parsley.

Mix Batter

- The combination of matzoh crackers and matzoh meal makes a matzoh ball with interesting texture.

- You can use all crackers or all matzoh meal. The crackers make a heavier matzoh ball; the meal a lighter ball.

- Matzoh crackers and matzoh meal are made of flour, so be careful that you don't overwork the dough.

- Too much gluten development in the matzoh balls will make them heavy and dense.

Make Matzoh Balls

- Rinse your hands with cold water every time you form a matzoh ball; otherwise the batter will stick to your hands.

- Drop the balls into the stock as you work. This recipe should make 8–10 matzoh balls.

- Make sure to cook the balls just until done. To check, cut one open; when cooked through, the texture will be even.

- The matzoh balls should float when they are done; that's another clue to when they are ready to eat.

CHICKEN SOUPS

CAMBODIAN CHICKEN SOUP
Exotic spices combine in this easy and hearty soup

This soup is full of fresh flavors and colors. The ingredients that make it exotic include curry powder, gingerroot, curry paste, fish sauce, jasmine rice, and coconut milk.

If you like a spicy soup that is full of interesting flavors, this is the soup for you. If you go to a farmers' market or Asian or Vietnamese market, you may be able to find more unusual

ingredients to add to the soup, like lily buds or exotic mushrooms. You can make this soup as spicy or as mild as you wish. If your family isn't used to more exotic flavors, just leave them out. That's the great thing about soup—it's so tolerant and easily varied. *Yield: Serves 6*

Ingredients

1 tablespoon olive oil

1 tablespoon butter

1 onion, chopped

3 cloves garlic, minced

1 tablespoon grated gingerroot

2 jalapeño peppers, minced

4 boneless, skinless chicken breasts, cubed

1 tablespoon curry powder

1 teaspoon curry paste

1 tablespoon fish sauce

¹/₂ cup jasmine rice

5 cups chicken broth

2 cups coconut milk

1 cup small raw shrimp

1 tablespoon minced fresh basil

¹/₄ cup minced cilantro

2 tablespoons lime juice

Cambodian Chicken Soup

- Combine olive oil and butter in large pot. Cook onion, garlic, gingerroot, and jalapeño 5 minutes.

- Add chicken, curry powder, curry paste, and fish sauce; cook 2 minutes. Add rice; cook 2 minutes.

- Add broth and coconut milk; bring to a simmer. Cook 15–20 minutes until rice is almost tender.

- Stir in shrimp; cook 4–5 minutes until shrimp curl and turn pink. Add basil, cilantro, and lime juice; serve immediately.

Vietnamese Chicken Soup
Make recipe as directed, except use 2 tablespoons peanut oil in place of the olive oil and butter. Omit curry powder and paste, jasmine rice, coconut milk, and basil. Increase chicken broth to 6 cups. Add 1 ounce soaked cellophane noodles at the last minute.

Cook Chicken and Curry Powder

- The curry powder and curry paste have ingredients with lots of essential oils.

- Heating these ingredients, especially in fats like butter and oil, brings out their flavor and adds richness.

- You can use chicken thighs instead; cook the chicken with the curry powder and paste for 6–7 minutes.

- Make sure that the curry powder and paste don't burn; stir the mixture frequently as it cooks.

Add Coconut Milk and Shrimp

- The broth and coconut milk are added at the same time. Let the mixture simmer; do not let it boil hard.

- The shrimp should be shelled and deveined. If they are not, carefully remove the shells.

- Cut a shallow slit in the back of the shrimp and remove or rinse out the black line; that's the vein.

- Serve the soup as soon as the basil, cilantro, and lime juice are added.

CHICKEN SOUPS

CHICKEN SHEPHERD'S PIE

A lighter version of shepherd's pie is flavored with ketchup and Worcestershire sauce

Shepherd's pie has quite a history. It started out as a "cottage pie," using potatoes, which were an affordable food.

It's a good way to use up leftover chicken, whether light or dark meat. And it's also a good way to use up leftover potatoes, whether russet or sweet.

The pie is traditionally made with lamb or mutton, but can be made with any meat, from chicken to beef to pork.

The potatoes serve as the top "crust" of the pie. There usually isn't a bottom crust, which makes this recipe a good choice for beginning cooks.

Serve with a green salad made with strawberries, almonds, and raspberry vinaigrette. *Yield: Serves 6–8*

Ingredients

4 russet potatoes, peeled and cubed

2 tablespoons butter

$1/2$ cup light cream or milk

2 tablespoons Dijon mustard

1 tablespoon olive oil

1 pound ground chicken

1 onion, chopped

3 cloves garlic, minced

3 carrots, sliced

2 tablespoons flour

1 tablespoon Worcestershire sauce

$1/2$ teaspoon salt

$1/8$ teaspoon pepper

1 teaspoon dried marjoram

3 tablespoons ketchup

1 cup chicken broth

Chicken Shepherd's Pie

- Bring a large pot of salted water to a boil. Add potatoes; boil for 12–16 minutes until tender. Drain, return to pot.

- Add butter; mash. Stir in cream, mustard; set aside.

- In large saucepan, cook chicken, onion, and garlic in olive oil. Add carrots; simmer 5 minutes. Add flour; simmer 2 minutes.

- Add remaining ingredients; simmer until thickened. Pour into 2½-quart casserole; top with potatoes. Bake at 400ºF 25–35 minutes.

Easy Shepherd's Pie
Make recipe as directed, except substitute 6 servings of prepared refrigerated mashed potatoes for the potatoes made from scratch. Stir 2 tablespoons Dijon mustard into the prepared potatoes and heat as directed on package, then continue with the recipe.

Curried Shepherd's Pie
Make recipe as directed, except substitute 3 large sweet potatoes for the russet potatoes. Omit mustard; add 2 teaspoons curry powder. Add 2 teaspoons curry powder to the onion and garlic mixture. Omit Worcestershire sauce and marjoram.

Mash Potatoes

- For the fluffiest mashed potatoes, cook them until just tender.

- Then drain and return to the hot pot; shake over low heat for a few minutes to remove excess moisture from the potatoes.

- Add butter first and mash; this coats the starch granules so the potatoes are fluffy and not sticky.

- Beat in the cream and mustard. You may need to add more to get the correct consistency of mashed potatoes.

Cook Chicken Mixture

- The chicken is almost completely cooked in the saucepan before it's added to the pie.

- You can use precooked chicken in this recipe; just stir it in when the sauce has simmered and thickened.

- The potato mixture has to be added to a hot filling. Spoon it on the filling and spread using the back of a spoon.

- If the filling is chilled, the potatoes act as insulation and will slow down its heating.

CHICKEN SPAGHETTI

Tender ground chicken is cooked with bacon and onions for a delicious pasta meal

Chicken spaghetti is a favorite children's dish. Instead of being made with ground beef or pork, this lighter dish cuts calories and makes a nice change from the traditional recipe.

Bacon is added to contribute some fat and flavor to this recipe. You can use turkey bacon if you'd like for a lighter taste. And use your favorite vegetables. Sliced mushrooms

and chopped zucchini or summer squash add nice flavor, texture, and nutrition.

Some of the water used to cook the pasta is added to the sauce to add flavor and to loosen the sauce. So remember to save some when you drain the pasta. *Yield: Serves 4-6*

Ingredients

3 slices bacon

1 pound ground chicken

1 onion, chopped

4 cloves garlic, minced

1 green bell pepper, chopped

$1/2$ teaspoon salt

$1/8$ teaspoon pepper

1 teaspoon dried basil

$1/2$ teaspoon crushed red pepper flakes

1 (14.5-ounce) can diced tomatoes, undrained

12 ounces spaghetti pasta

$1/2$ cup crumbled feta cheese

1 cup shredded Asiago cheese

Chicken Spaghetti

- Bring a large pot of salted water to a boil. Cook bacon in saucepan until crisp; drain, crumble, and set aside.

- Cook chicken, onion, and garlic in bacon drippings 5 minutes; add bell pepper, salt, pepper, basil, and red pepper flakes.

- Add tomatoes; simmer 12–15 minutes. Add bacon. Cook pasta until al dente.

- Drain pasta, reserving $1/2$ cup cooking water. Add pasta, cooking water, and cheeses to skillet with chicken; toss over medium heat until blended.

Garlic Toast
Broil one side of 8 (1/2-inch-thick) slices French bread until golden. Turn over. In small bowl, combine 1/2 teaspoon salt with 2 minced garlic cloves; mash until a paste forms. Stir in 2 tablespoons each butter and olive oil and 1 pinch of lemon pepper. Spread on toasts and broil until crisp.

Tex-Mex Chicken Spaghetti
Make recipe as directed, except add 1–2 minced jalapeño peppers to the onion mixture as it cooks. Omit basil; add 1 teaspoon dried oregano leaves. Omit feta cheese; use 1/2 cup grated Cotija or Parmesan cheese. Garnish with sliced avocados and sour cream.

Brown Chicken and Onions

- The bacon drippings add great flavor to the chicken and onion as they cook.

- You can drain off the bacon drippings, but don't wipe out the pan. Add a tablespoon of olive oil and continue with the recipe.

- Cook the chicken just until the pink color disappears. Then it's time to add the canned tomatoes.

- You can add sliced mushrooms or other colors of bell pepper to this mixture along with the green bell pepper.

Add Pasta and Pasta Water

- Think about varying the seasonings. A combination of oregano and marjoram would be a good substitute.

- Add just a few tablespoons of pasta water to the chicken mixture, reserving some. Add more if needed for desired consistency.

- Serve this chicken with some grated Parmesan or Romano cheese. Or garnish with chopped parsley or basil.

- Leftovers of this recipe are excellent in a frittata; add to beaten eggs and cook in a skillet until the eggs are set.

GROUND CHICKEN

CHICKEN LASAGNA
Ground chicken adds a new twist to a white lasagna recipe

Lasagna is typically made with beef or pork. This type of lasagna, made without tomatoes, is called a white lasagna.

If you have a favorite lasagna recipe, go ahead and substitute chicken for the beef, pork, or sausage. The recipe will be lighter with a cleaner taste.

Spinach is the traditional addition to this type of lasagna. It adds great color, texture, and flavor to the finished dish. You could also use some sautéed kale or mustard greens for a stronger flavor.

For a faster recipe, you can substitute one 16-ounce and one 10-ounce container of Alfredo sauce for the flour, herbs, broth, and cream.

Serve the lasagna with Garlic Toast and a spinach salad made with mandarin oranges. *Yield: Serves 8*

Ingredients

1 pound ground chicken

1 onion, chopped

3 cloves garlic, minced

^{1}/$_3$ cup butter

^{1}/$_2$ cup flour

Salt and pepper to taste

1 teaspoon dried oregano

1 teaspoon dried basil

2 cups chicken broth

1 cup light cream or milk

1 cup grated Parmesan cheese, divided

1 (16-ounce) container part-skim ricotta cheese

2 eggs

1 (10-ounce) package frozen spinach, thawed and drained

2 cups shredded mozzarella, divided

9 lasagna noodles

Chicken Lasagna

- Bring pot of salted water to a boil. In large saucepan, cook chicken, onion, and garlic in butter.

- Add flour, salt, pepper, oregano, and basil; cook 4 minutes. Add chicken broth and cream; simmer until thick; add ½ cup Parmesan.

- In bowl, combine ½ cup Parmesan, ricotta, eggs, spinach, and ½ cup mozzarella.

- Cook noodles until al dente; drain. Layer noodles, chicken sauce, spinach mixture, and mozzarella in greased 9 x 13-inch dish. Bake at 350°F 45-55 minutes.

Greek Chicken Lasagna

Make recipe as directed, except add another clove of garlic to the chicken mixture. Substitute oregano for basil. Add $1/4$ cup lemon juice with the broth and light cream. And add $1/2$ cup kalamata olives to the spinach mixture. Reduce mozzarella cheese to $1 1/2$ cups and add $1/2$ cup crumbled feta cheese.

Spicy Chicken Lasagna

Make recipe as directed, except add 1 minced jalapeño and 1 minced habanero pepper to the ground chicken mixture, and add 1 tablespoon chili powder. Add 1 teaspoon oregano and $1/4$ teaspoon cayenne pepper to the spinach mixture. And use Pepper Jack cheese in place of the mozzarella.

Simmer Chicken Mixture

Layer Ingredients in Pan

- You need to cook ground chicken in some fat because it is so low in fat. It can be difficult to cook and can stick to the pan on its own.

- The chicken mixture would be dry and slightly tough without that added fat.

- The flour needs to cook with the chicken and onion mixture so it is able to absorb the stock and cream.

- This thick and creamy mixture substitutes for the tomato sauce used in typical lasagna recipes.

- After the lasagna noodles are cooked, drain them and rinse well with cold water until they are easy to handle.

- Make 3 layers of each ingredient for best results. Spread the food evenly in the prepared pan.

- At this point you can refrigerate or freeze the lasagna to cook later. Thaw a frozen lasagna overnight in the fridge before baking.

- If you refrigerate the lasagna, add another 10–15 minutes of baking time. Bake until bubbly and browned.

GROUND CHICKEN

113

BASIL CHICKEN STIR-FRY

Fresh and dried basil add a depth of flavor to this easy stir-fry

Most stir-fry recipes are made with ingredients like soy sauce and gingerroot. This recipe is a bit different, with a slightly Asian twist.

Both dried and fresh basil are used in this recipe. Dried basil has more of a smoky, deep flavor, whereas fresh basil is more minty and lemony. The combination, with quickly cooked chicken and vegetables, is delicious.

To make this dish milder, omit the serrano pepper and reduce the garlic to just three cloves. Omit the chile paste, which is very fiery, but keep the fish sauce as it adds a rich depth of flavor.

Serve this stir-fry over hot cooked rice mixed with some chopped fresh basil leaves and a bit of soy sauce. *Yield: Serves 4*

Ingredients

1 tablespoon sesame oil

1 tablespoon peanut oil

1 pound ground chicken

5 cloves garlic, minced

1 onion, chopped

1 serrano pepper, minced

1 green bell pepper, sliced

1 red bell pepper, sliced

1 teaspoon dried basil

1/4 teaspoon pepper

2 tablespoons soy sauce

1 teaspoon chile paste

1 tablespoon fish sauce

1/2 cup chopped fresh basil

2 tablespoons lime juice

8 whole basil leaves

Basil Chicken Stir-Fry

- Heat sesame and peanut oil over medium-high heat. Add chicken; stir-fry until chicken is cooked. Remove chicken.

- Add garlic and onion; stir-fry 3 minutes. Add peppers, basil, and pepper; stir-fry 4 minutes.

- Return chicken to skillet; add soy sauce, chile paste, fish sauce, and chopped fresh basil.

- Stir-fry for 3–4 minutes until mixture is blended. Add lime juice, garnish with whole basil leaves, and serve over rice.

Herbed Chicken Stir-Fry
Make recipe as directed, except omit serrano pepper. Reduce dried basil to ¹/₂ teaspoon, and add ¹/₂ teaspoon each dried thyme and marjoram. Continue with recipe, except omit whole basil leaves. Add 1 tablespoon each fresh thyme and minced marjoram leaves.

Stir-Fry Peppers

Return Chicken to Skillet

- Make sure you have all of the ingredients prepared and ready to go before you start cooking.

- Cook the chicken first so it will cook evenly. Ground chicken is difficult to stir-fry unless it's cooked alone.

- Remove the chicken to a clean plate and set aside. Cook the garlic and onion next.

- Cook the bell peppers just until they are crisp-tender. They will soften a bit more in the sauce.

- When you return the chicken to the skillet, it only needs to be heated through.

- So the flavors are evenly distributed, mix together the soy sauce, chile paste, and fish sauce before you add them to the pan.

- Serve this meal the second it's done for the best flavor, texture, and aroma.

- The Chinese say that stir-fried food has "the breath of the wok," an ethereal quality that disappears within a few minutes after cooking stops.

115

GROUND CHICKEN

CHICKEN MEATLOAF

Ground chicken makes a tender meatloaf when made with certain ingredients

Most of us have a favorite recipe for meatloaf, made with ground beef, pork, and perhaps veal. Chicken meatloaf is in a whole new dimension.

Because ground chicken is much lower in fat than ground beef or pork, you do have to add more fat to the recipe. Some butter and light cream don't increase calories substantially,

and they make a moist and tender loaf.

As with a beef meatloaf, don't mix the ground chicken mixture too much. A light hand will yield a light meatloaf.

Leftover meatloaf makes a mean sandwich, especially if you grill the sandwich. Use Dijon mustard, bell peppers, and mayonnaise. *Yield: Serves 6–8*

Ingredients

2 tablespoons butter

2 cloves garlic, minced

1 onion, chopped

¹/₃ cup light cream or milk

²/₃ cup dried breadcrumbs

2 eggs, beaten

1 teaspoon salt

¹/₈ teaspoon pepper

1 teaspoon dried Italian seasoning

¹/₄ cup grated Parmesan cheese

2 pounds ground chicken

1 cup shredded provolone cheese

¹/₂ cup tomato sauce

1 teaspoon dried basil

Chicken Meatloaf

- Melt butter in saucepan; add garlic and onion. Cook 5 minutes.

- Remove to bowl with cream, breadcrumbs, eggs, salt, pepper, Italian seasoning, and Parmesan cheese.

- Add chicken and provolone cheese; mix gently but thor-

oughly with hands. Press into 9 x 5-inch loaf pan.

- Mix tomato sauce and basil; spread over loaf. Bake at 400°F 50-60 minutes until meat thermometer registers 160°F. Cover; let stand 10 minutes, remove from pan, and slice.

Turkey Meatloaf

Make recipe as directed, except substitute 2 pounds ground turkey for the ground chicken. You can use all white meat ground turkey, or a combination of light and dark meat. Substitute 1 teaspoon dried oregano for the Italian seasoning, and use mozzarella instead of provolone cheese.

Tex-Mex Chicken Meatloaf

Make recipe as directed, except add 1 minced jalapeño or serrano pepper to the onion mixture. Add $1/3$ cup salsa to the meatloaf mixture; reduce eggs to 1. Add 1 tablespoon chili powder to chicken. Use Pepper Jack cheese instead of mozzarella, and more salsa instead of tomato sauce.

Add Chicken

- The milk, breadcrumbs, and eggs will cool down the garlic and onion mixture so it's easy to handle.

- Mix the breadcrumb mixture well before adding the chicken and the cheese.

- Since you don't want to handle the chicken mixture very much, this is your chance to evenly combine all the ingredients.

- When the chicken is added, work with your hands just until everything is blended. Then press mixture into the loaf pan.

Form Loaf and Top with Sauce

- This meatloaf is very tender, and won't hold its shape well if formed into a free-form loaf.

- The loaf pan also helps protect the chicken from the dry heat of the oven so the result is juicy and moist.

- For best results, meatloaf should always be covered with foil and left to stand for 10–15 minutes after cooking.

- This lets the juices redistribute and the meatloaf set so it will slice evenly into nice thick pieces.

GROUND CHICKEN

CHICKEN PORCUPINES

Small meatballs, filled with chicken, vegetables, and rice, simmer in a savory sauce

Porcupines are little meatballs that contain uncooked rice. As the meatballs cook, the rice cooks and swells, poking through the meat so the balls look (somewhat) like porcupines.

For best results, partially cook the rice before mixing it with the meatball ingredients. This also helps the tender meatballs hold together, since the rice doesn't need to absorb as much liquid to expand. If you want to use white rice in your porcupines, precook the rice for about 12 minutes until it's almost tender.

You can use a nice bottled pasta sauce instead of the tomato sauce, mustard, and chili sauce mixture for an easier recipe. *Yield: Serves 6*

Ingredients

1 onion, chopped

2 cloves garlic, minced

1 tablespoon olive oil

¹/₂ cup uncooked brown rice

1¹/₂ cups chicken broth, divided

¹/₄ cup minced celery leaves

1 teaspoon salt

¹/₈ teaspoon pepper

1 teaspoon dried thyme

¹/₃ cup grated Parmesan cheese

1¹/₂ pounds ground chicken

2 tablespoons butter

1 (8-ounce) can tomato sauce

3 tablespoons Dijon mustard

¹/₂ cup chili sauce

Chicken Porcupines

- In large saucepan, cook onion and garlic in oil 5 minutes. Add rice; cook 2 minutes longer.

- Add 1 cup chicken broth; simmer, covered, for 20 minutes until rice is partially cooked. Remove to large bowl.

- Add celery leaves, salt, pepper, thyme, and cheese. Add chicken; mix well. Form into 24 meatballs. Brown in butter in same saucepan.

- Add ½ cup broth, tomato sauce, mustard, and chili sauce; stir. Cover; simmer 15–20 minutes until 165°F.

···· RECIPE VARIATIONS ····

Curried Chicken Porcupines

Make recipe as directed, except use $1/2$ cup uncooked basmati rice for the brown rice. Add 1 tablespoon curry powder to the onion mixture. Omit thyme and Parmesan cheese. Add $1/4$ cup chutney. Omit mustard and chili sauce; add $1/4$ cup chutney and $1/4$ cup chicken broth to sauce.

Spanish Chicken Porcupines

Make recipe as directed, except use 1 teaspoon oregano in place of the thyme. Omit Parmesan cheese; add $1/4$ cup ground almonds and 5 tablespoons gated Manchego cheese. Add $1/4$ cup olives to the tomato sauce; simmer porcupines as directed.

Simmer Rice

- When the rice is partially done, it will be tender on the outside with an opaque, slightly crunchy center.

- Since rice expands to 3 times its volume when cooked, adding uncooked rice to the porcupines will break them apart.

- You can let the rice mixture cool for 15–20 minutes before adding the chicken so it's easier to handle.

- You can't really make the chicken mixture ahead of time, or the rice will absorb more liquid.

Form into Meatballs

- The meatballs will be very tender and fragile, so handle with care.

- When you start browning the meatballs, don't try to move them until they can be easily dislodged. Shake the pan gently to see if they have released.

- You just want to brown the meatballs, not cook them through, so keep the heat on medium-low.

- Mix the sauce ingredients together well before adding them to the pan with the meatballs.

GROUND CHICKEN

119

CHICKEN & WILD RICE
Wild rice adds nutty flavor and texture to this easy one-pan dish

Skillet meals are so easy to make you can cook them without a kitchen! All you need is an electric skillet and a spoon. And chicken is the perfect choice for these types of meals.

Since all the cooking is usually done in one pan, these recipes are easy to serve and cleanup is a breeze. Choose a heavy skillet for these recipes, with a large surface area and sloping sides. You can use nonstick cookware for these recipes.

This classic dish is simple and straightforward. Cook the wild rice until it's tender but still holds its shape. If you cook it longer than 45 minutes, it will "pop" and become quite tender.

Serve with glazed carrots and a fruit salad. *Yield: Serves 4*

Ingredients

2 tablespoons olive oil

4 boneless, skinless chicken breasts

2 tablespoons flour

$1/2$ teaspoon salt

$1/8$ teaspoon pepper

1 teaspoon dried basil

1 onion, chopped

3 cloves garlic, minced

1 (8-ounce) package cremini mushrooms, sliced

1 cup wild rice

$2^1/2$ cups chicken broth

$1/2$ cup light cream or milk

1 cup frozen peas, thawed

Chicken and Wild Rice

- In large saucepan, heat olive oil. Dredge chicken in flour, salt, pepper, and basil; brown in olive oil; remove from pan.

- Add onion, garlic, and mushrooms; cook and stir 5 minutes. Add wild rice; cook 1 minute.

- Add chicken broth, bring to a simmer, cover, and simmer 15 minutes. Add cream and stir. Top with chicken breasts.

- Cover and simmer for 25–30 minutes until rice is tender and chicken is done. Sprinkle with peas; cover, let stand 5 minutes, then serve.

• • • • RECIPE VARIATIONS • • • •

Chicken and Brown Rice

Make recipe as directed, except substitute brown rice for the wild rice. Omit basil and add 1 teaspoon dried marjoram leaves. Cook the rice for 15 minutes, then stir in 1 cup sliced carrots and top with the chicken. Cook as directed until done.

Curried Chicken and Rice Skillet

Make recipe as directed, except use 2 tablespoons butter in place of the olive oil. Add 2 teaspoons curry powder to the flour mixture used to coat the chicken. Omit basil; add 2 teaspoons curry powder instead. Add $\frac{1}{2}$ cup mango chutney along with the cream.

Brown Chicken

- Once you start making this recipe, don't stop. The chicken is only partially cooked in the first step.

- If you refrigerate the chicken at this point, it will pass through the danger zone of 40°F to 140°F too many times.

- So proceed quickly with the recipe and just let the chicken stand off to the side.

- Have all the ingredients prepared and ready to go before you start, just as in a stir-fried recipe.

Simmer Wild Rice

- Rinse the wild rice before adding to the casserole to remove any dust from processing.

- Don't boil the rice; just simmer it so it cooks evenly and doesn't overcook.

- Wild rice will pop if it's cooked longer than 45–50 minutes. It's not like popcorn; it's just that the outer coat has weakened.

- Popped wild rice will curl and become thicker. This isn't unacceptable; it's just a different look and texture.

STIR-FRIED CHICKEN
Chicken is stir-fried in a flavorful and spicy orange sauce

Chicken is the most popular meat used in stir-fried recipes. It cooks quickly, is easy to prepare, and absorbs the flavors of other ingredients to perfection.

For a velvety texture, stir-fried chicken is sometimes marinated in a mixture of soy sauce and cornstarch. This marinade can be used as the finishing sauce for the dish, with the addition of some liquid like chicken broth.

When you stir-fry it's important that all of the ingredients are completely prepared and ready to go before you start. You can't stop the cooking process to chop or slice mushrooms. Work quickly and keep the food moving and your stir-fry recipes will be perfect.

Serve with hot cooked rice and green tea. *Yield: Serves 4*

Ingredients

¹/₂ cup orange juice

1 teaspoon grated orange zest

2 tablespoons soy sauce

3 cloves garlic, minced

1 tablespoon honey

¹/₈ teaspoon cayenne pepper

4 boneless, skinless chicken breasts, cut into 1-inch cubes

2 tablespoons peanut oil

1 onion, chopped

1 pound broccoli florets

2 tablespoons lemon juice

2 tablespoons cornstarch

¹/₂ cup chicken broth

Stir-Fried Chicken

- In bowl, combine orange juice, zest, soy sauce, garlic, honey, and pepper. Add chicken; cover and refrigerate 4–6 hours.

- Drain chicken, reserving marinade. Heat peanut oil in wok or skillet over medium-high heat.

- Add onion; stir-fry 4 minutes. Add chicken; stir-fry 4 minutes. Add broccoli; stir-fry 4 minutes.

- Add lemon juice, cornstarch, and broth to marinade; stir well. Add to wok or skillet; cook until sauce thickens. Serve over rice.

• • • • RECIPE VARIATIONS • • • •

Kung Pao Chicken
Marinate chicken in mixture of 2 tablespoons each soy sauce, rice wine, and 2 minced jalapeños, and 1 cup chicken broth. Omit broccoli, lemon juice, and cornstarch. For vegetables, add 3 cloves garlic, 2 sliced carrots, and 4 dried red chili peppers. Add cornstarch only to marinade.

Chicken with Almonds
Marinate chicken in mixture of 2 tablespoons each soy sauce and oyster sauce, 1 cup chicken broth, and 1 teaspoon sugar. For vegetables, use 1 (8-ounce) can drained bamboo shoots, 2 cups frozen pea pods, and 1 tablespoon gingerroot. Add 1/3 cup slivered toasted almonds at end.

Stir-Fry Chicken

- You don't need a wok to stir-fry, although it does make the process easier.

- The wok's rounded bottom helps keep the food moving and extends heat evenly up the sides.

- A heavy skillet is fine; just be sure that you move the food around constantly with a long-handled, heavy-duty spatula.

- The chicken will be almost completely cooked in the first step; it will be slightly pink. The chicken will completely cook in the last step.

Add Marinade to Wok

- The food is added in a certain order when stir-frying. Onions and garlic flavor the oil.

- The meat is usually cooked next, so you get some pan drippings and more flavor. Then it's removed so it doesn't overcook.

- Then vegetables are cooked last, before the meat is returned to the wok and the marinade is added.

- Always stir the marinade before adding to the other ingredients so the cornstarch is evenly distributed.

123

CHICKEN PARMESAN

Crisp panfried chicken coated in cheese and breadcrumbs is served with a pasta sauce

Chicken Parmesan is a classic Italian dish that combines tender chicken coated in crisp breadcrumbs, served in a rich tomato sauce topped with cheese.

This dish is traditionally served with spaghetti or linguine to soak up the delicious sauce. You can use a purchased pasta or marinara sauce in place of the homemade sauce; dress it up with some sautéed onions and fresh basil.

The chicken can be deep-fried, but panfrying is a healthier alternative that makes chicken just as crispy.

Panko breadcrumbs are the secret to the crispiest Chicken Parmesan. If you can't find them, regular breadcrumbs are just fine. *Yield: Serves 6*

Ingredients

1 tablespoon olive oil

4 tablespoons butter, divided

1 onion, chopped

3 cloves garlic, minced

1 (14.5-ounce) can diced tomatoes, undrained

1 (8-ounce) can tomato sauce

1 teaspoon dried Italian seasoning

2 eggs

2 tablespoons lemon juice

$^1/_2$ teaspoon salt

$^1/_2$ cup grated Parmesan cheese

$^1/_2$ cup panko breadcrumbs

1 teaspoon dried oregano

6 boneless, skinless chicken breasts

$^1/_2$ teaspoon salt

$^1/_8$ teaspoon cayenne pepper

1$^1/_2$ cups shredded mozzarella cheese

Chicken Parmesan

- Melt olive oil and 1 tablespoon butter in saucepan; cook onion and garlic 5 minutes. Add tomatoes, tomato sauce, and Italian seasoning; simmer on low heat.

- Beat eggs with lemon juice and salt. Combine Parmesan, breadcrumbs, and oregano.

- Sprinkle chicken with salt and pepper. Dip into egg mixture, then into cheese mixture; chill 30 minutes.

- Fry in remaining butter, turning once, 10 minutes. Add to pan with sauce. Sprinkle with mozzarella, and simmer 10–15 minutes until done.

124

• • • • RECIPE VARIATION • • • •

Plain Chicken Parmesan
Make recipe as directed, except omit the entire tomato sauce mixture. Cut chicken breasts into slices. Increase breadcrumbs to 1 cup. Coat chicken as directed, then chill. Fry in butter and 1 tablespoon olive oil 10–12 minutes until chicken is thoroughly cooked; serve immediately.

ZOOM

Panko breadcrumbs are coarsely ground. They look more like flakes than crumbs, with a larger surface area. The crumbs don't press together, but form an open network on the food, which helps create that crunchy coating. White panko is made from crustless bread; tan panko from the whole loaf.

Cook Tomato Sauce

Coat and Cook Chicken

- Tomato sauce is easy to make; all you need are some tomatoes, fresh or canned, and seasonings.

- The longer the sauce simmers, the richer and deeper it will taste.

- You can make the tomato sauce well ahead of time; just refrigerate until you want to make the chicken.

- Then add the chilled sauce to a saucepan. Add a bit of water and heat until it comes to a simmer, then proceed with the recipe.

- The chicken is coated 3 times: with salt and pepper for flavoring, with egg so the breadcrumbs will adhere, and with the breadcrumb mixture.

- This coating keeps the crust on the chicken as it cooks, and makes the coating very crisp.

- It's very important that you don't move the chicken when it's first added to the hot butter.

- Turn the coated chicken only when it releases easily from the pan and is a deep golden brown color.

CHICKEN GUMBO

Delicious gumbo made with sausage and an old-fashioned roux for flavor

Gumbo made from chicken is easy and inexpensive. This recipe can be loaded up with all the vegetables you would like.

Using chicken thighs and breasts makes a richer dish that's less expensive than one made with all chicken breasts. The two meats are cut into different sizes so they will finish cooking at the same time.

The roux in this recipe is made with oil and Andouille sausage drippings for more flavor. Add smoked or thick-cut bacon for even more smoky flavor.

Serve the gumbo in warmed soup plates, with a scoop of hot cooked rice mixed with fresh chopped thyme and parsley, and a fresh fruit salad on the side. *Yield: Serves 6*

Ingredients

1 pound Andouille sausage, sliced

¼ cup peanut oil

⅓ cup flour

1 onion, chopped

3 cloves garlic, minced

1 jalapeño pepper, minced

1 serrano pepper, minced

1 green bell pepper, chopped

3 stalks celery, chopped

4 cups chicken broth

1 (12-ounce) bottle beer

1 bay leaf

3 boneless, skinless chicken breasts

4 boneless, skinless chicken thighs, cubed

1 tablespoon Cajun seasoning

½ teaspoon salt

¼ teaspoon pepper

Chicken Gumbo

- In skillet, cook sausage until some of the fat is rendered. Remove sausage. Add oil and flour to skillet.

- Cook, stirring constantly, until mixture is browned, about 25–30 minutes. Carefully add onion, garlic, peppers, and celery; cook 2 minutes.

- Add chicken broth, beer, and bay leaf; bring to a simmer.

- Sprinkle chicken with seasoning, salt, and pepper; add to gumbo with sausage. Simmer, covered, 20–30 minutes until chicken is tender. Remove chicken, shred, return to pan, and serve.

···· RECIPE VARIATIONS ····

Lighter Chicken Gumbo

Make recipe as directed, except use 4 slices turkey bacon instead of the sausage. Use 2 pounds whole boneless, skinless chicken breasts. Simmer 12–18 minutes until the chicken is tender; remove chicken and shred. Return chicken to the gumbo; let stand, covered, 10 minutes before serving.

Chicken and Bacon Gumbo

Make recipe as directed, except use 1 pound smoked thick-cut bacon in place of the sausage. Slice and brown the sausage. Drain off most of the bacon fat, add the oil, and cook the roux until brown, about 25 minutes. Continue with the recipe, adding the bacon with the chicken.

Cook Roux

- The roux is the essential beginning for any gumbo. The flour is cooked in fat until deep golden brown.

- This adds a rich flavor to the gumbo and helps aid the thickening process.

- If the gumbo burns, evenly slightly, it will ruin the whole dish, so you'll have to start over.

- You can cook your roux until it's just tan colored, or cook until dark brown. Decide if you want a lighter or very intense flavor.

Add Vegetables and Broth

- When you add the vegetables to the roux, it can spatter quite violently, so be careful.

- The vegetables are cold and full of water, and the roux is hot and unstable. Add a batch at a time and stand back.

- When you add the chicken broth and beer, use a wire whisk to help incorporate the liquid into the roux.

- Serve your gumbo with lots of napkins and cold beer. This is a meal for a party!

COQ AU VIN
Literally meaning "rooster in wine," this classic dish is full of flavor

Coq au Vin is a classic French dish that elevates chicken to gourmet status. The chicken is stewed or braised in a wine mixture with fresh herbs and vegetables.

Onions, garlic, and mushrooms are the traditional vegetables used in Coq au Vin, but you can add carrots, green beans, or celery. Salt pork is the classic addition, but bacon is easier to find and easier to work with.

This dish is even better the next day. You can make it completely, then cool and refrigerate. Remove any fat from the top and gently reheat on the stove, adding more wine if necessary.

Serve with a rice pilaf made with chicken stock and thyme leaves. *Yield: Serves 6–8*

Ingredients

¹/₃ cup flour

1 teaspoon poultry seasoning

¹/₂ teaspoon salt

¹/₈ teaspoon pepper

2¹/₂ pounds boneless, skinless chicken thighs, cut into strips

6 slices bacon

2 tablespoons olive oil

1 tablespoon butter

1 onion, chopped

4 cloves garlic, minced

8 ounces cremini mushrooms, sliced

1 cup dry red wine

1 cup chicken broth

1 sprig fresh rosemary

2 sprigs fresh thyme

Coq au Vin

- Mix flour, poultry seasoning, salt, and pepper; dredge chicken.

- Cook bacon until crisp; drain, crumble. Drain skillet; do not wipe. Add olive oil and butter.

- Brown chicken in skillet, turning once, about 6–7

minutes. Remove chicken. Add onion, garlic, and mushrooms to skillet.

- Cook and stir 10–12 minutes. Add wine, broth, rosemary, and thyme; return chicken and bacon to pan.

- Cover; simmer 35–45 minutes until chicken is done.

···· RECIPE VARIATION ····

Whole Chicken Coq au Vin
Make recipe as directed, except use bone-in, skin-on cut-up chicken parts in place of the boneless, skinless thigh strips. Increase the flour to $1/2$ cup and salt to 1 teaspoon. Simmer the mixture, covered, for $1^1/2$–2 hours, adding more wine if necessary, until the chicken is done.

········ GREEN ● LIGHT ········

Always use a wine in cooking that you would drink. Don't think you can use a cheaper wine or one with a sour or off flavor. When the dish cooks, the flavor of the wine will concentrate, and if you have used a poor quality wine, it will ruin your whole dish.

Brown Chicken

- The browning step is very important in this recipe. It distributes the chicken flavor through the dish and adds color.

- The drippings from the chicken are loosened and incorporated into the dish when the onions and garlic are added.

- The chicken is cooked in the bacon fat for even more rich and smoky flavor.

- And the onions, garlic, and mushrooms are cooked until dark brown so their liquid doesn't add too much water.

Add Wine and Herbs

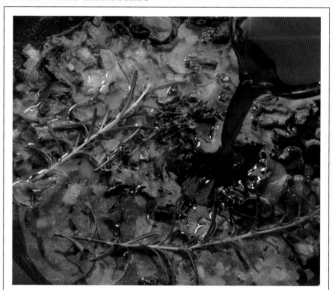

- When you add the wine and broth, the mixture will bubble and steam vigorously.

- Stand back and be careful not to burn your hands or face during this step.

- If the sauce isn't thick enough at the end of cook-

ing time, you can remove the lid and let it simmer for a few minutes.

- Or add 2 tablespoons butter kneaded with 2 tablespoons flour. Add to the sauce in small bits and simmer for 5–6 minutes until thickened.

129

CHICKEN FLORENTINE

Chicken cooked with spinach and cream is tender, juicy, and memorable

Chicken Florentine, or any dish labeled "Florentine," just means it is cooked with spinach. The spinach adds beautiful color, texture, and a mild leafy flavor to the tender chicken.

Frozen spinach is usually used in this dish, but this recipe uses baby spinach for a lighter, more delicate taste.

The cheese is the second most important ingredient in

Chicken Florentine. The chicken and spinach are enveloped in a creamy cheese sauce. Traditionally, Swiss or mozzarella cheeses are used, but Havarti is a rich cheese that adds a slight tartness.

Serve this rich dish with some hot cooked pasta tossed with butter and fresh herbs. *Yield: Serves 6*

Ingredients

6 boneless, skinless chicken breasts

1 teaspoon salt

$1/8$ teaspoon white pepper

1 teaspoon dried basil

3 tablespoons flour

2 tablespoons butter

1 tablespoon olive oil

$1/2$ cup heavy cream

1 cup chicken broth

$3/4$ pound baby spinach leaves

$1/4$ cup basil pesto

$1/4$ cup grated Parmesan cheese

1 cup shredded Havarti cheese

Chicken Florentine

- Sprinkle chicken with salt and pepper. Combine basil and flour; dredge chicken in this mixture.

- Heat butter and olive oil in skillet; add chicken. Brown on both sides, 5–6 minutes; remove from pan.

- Add cream and broth to pan; simmer 3–4 minutes until thickened. Return chicken to pan; simmer 5–7 minutes.

- Add spinach; cook 3 minutes until wilted. Add pesto and cheeses; cover and remove from heat. Let stand 3 minutes, stir, and serve.

···· RECIPE VARIATIONS ····

Slow Cooker Chicken Florentine
Make recipe as directed, except brown chicken on one side 3 minutes. Add 2 chopped onions and 3 cloves minced garlic to drippings; place in 4-quart slow cooker. Add chicken, 1 (16-ounce) jar Alfredo sauce, 1 (10-ounce) package frozen spinach, thawed and drained, and pesto. Cover and cook on low 6–7 hours. Sprinkle with cheeses.

Chicken Florentine Casserole
Cube chicken and dredge in flour mixture; brown in butter; remove. Cook 1 chopped onion in drippings. Add 1 (16-ounce) jar four-cheese Alfredo sauce, $1/2$ cup light cream, 1 (10-ounce) package frozen thawed, drained spinach, and pesto. Pour into 3-quart casserole; top with cheese. Bake at 400ºF 20–30 minutes.

Brown Chicken

- Make sure that the butter and olive oil mixture is hot and sizzling before you add the chicken.

- If the fat is too cold, the chicken will absorb it and be soggy instead of slightly crisp.

- You can add other vegetables to this recipe. When the chicken is removed, add a chopped onion and some garlic.

- Or add mushrooms and green bell peppers; cook until tender, then proceed with the recipe.

Add Spinach and Pesto

- Spinach is always slightly gritty because it is grown in sand. Rinse it thoroughly in a sink of cold water.

- Trim off the tough stems from the spinach and discard, then slice or chop the spinach if desired.

- The basil pesto adds a great flavor to this simple dish, but you don't have to use it.

- You can use a combination of other cheeses; Grùyere and Romano would be delicious.

CHICKEN POT PIE

Topped with puff pastry, this classic pot pie is pure comfort food

Chicken pot pie is a classic recipe that evokes memories of home and mom's cooking. It's made of a rich sauce filled with chicken and vegetables, poured into a casserole and then topped with a pie crust and baked until brown and bubbly.

Using puff pastry to top this recipe is not only easier, but it's more elegant as well. The puff pastry, well, puffs in the oven to create a super flaky top that looks quite fancy.

The traditional vegetables used in this recipe are carrots, celery, onions, and potatoes. A white sauce or gravy is made from the drippings and broth and milk.

Serve this classic recipe with a fruit gelatin salad, a lettuce salad, and chocolate cake for dessert. *Yield: Serves 6–8*

Ingredients

3 cups chicken broth

4 boneless, skinless chicken breasts

4 carrots, sliced

2 russet potatoes, peeled and cubed

3 stalks celery, sliced

3 slices bacon

3 tablespoons butter

1 onion, chopped

4 cloves garlic, minced

$1/2$ cup flour

1 teaspoon celery salt

$1/4$ teaspoon pepper

1 teaspoon dried thyme

$1/2$ cup heavy cream

1 sheet frozen puff pastry, thawed, OR 1 recipe Pie Crust

1 egg, beaten

2 tablespoons water

Chicken Pot Pie

- Simmer broth, chicken, carrots, and potatoes; 15 minutes until chicken is done; remove chicken and vegetables.

- Cube chicken; reserve broth. Cook bacon; drain, crumble, and set aside. Add butter; cook onion and garlic.

- Add flour, salt, pepper, and thyme; cook 3 minutes. Add reserved broth; cook 5 minutes. Add cream.

- Add chicken and vegetables. Pour into 2½-quart dish. Top with puff pastry; brush with beaten egg. Bake at 425ºF 30–35 minutes.

Easy Chicken Pot Pie

Combine 4 cups cubed, cooked chicken with 3 cups thawed hash brown potatoes and 2 cups frozen sliced carrots in saucepan. Add 1 (16-ounce) jar four-cheese Alfredo sauce and 1 cup chicken broth; simmer 15 minutes. Pour into casserole; top with puff pastry. Bake as directed.

Pie Crust

Combine $1/2$ cup butter and 6 tablespoons solid shortening in a bowl. Combine $1/4$ cup water and 1 tablespoon milk in a saucepan; heat until steaming. Add to butter mixture and mix with a fork until fluffy. Add $2 1/3$ cups flour and $1/2$ teaspoon salt; mix until a dough forms. Makes 2 crusts.

Simmer Chicken and Vegetables

- Simmering the chicken in chicken broth makes the broth that much richer, which adds to the pot pie flavor.

- The carrots and potatoes should be tender by the time the chicken is thoroughly cooked.

- Remove the chicken and vegetables from the broth with a slotted spoon or large sieve; place on clean plate.

- Cut the chicken into large cubes, about 1½ inches, so they are very visible in the finished pie.

Assemble Pie

- The gravy is made with bacon fat and butter for even more flavor.

- You can substitute milk for the cream in the gravy; the mixture will just be a bit lighter.

- Drape the puff pastry over the hot filling. Push it onto the sides of the casserole dish to secure.

- Then cut decorative holes or slits in the puff pastry so steam can escape while the pie bakes.

CHICKEN VEGETABLE CASSEROLE

This comforting casserole is topped with a buttery streusel

This recipe is the definition of comfort food. A rich and creamy mixture of chicken and vegetables is topped with a buttery cheese streusel, then baked until golden brown and bubbly.

You can use any combination of vegetables and herbs in this easy recipe. Instead of celery and broccoli, use green beans and sliced carrots. Or use bell peppers and zucchini; the combinations are endless.

You can make the filling mixture ahead of time. Just store it in the refrigerator until you're ready to eat. Reheat the filling in a saucepan, then pour into a casserole and top with the streusel.

Serve this delicious casserole with a spinach salad made with strawberries, and a fruit parfait for dessert. *Yield: Serves 6*

KNACK CHICKEN CLASSICS

Ingredients

3 tablespoons olive oil

4 boneless, skinless chicken breasts

1/2 teaspoon salt

1/4 teaspoon pepper

1 onion, chopped

3 cloves garlic, minced

3 carrots, sliced

1 1/4 cups plus 3 tablespoons flour, divided

1 teaspoon dried thyme

2 cups chicken broth

1 cup light cream or milk

2 stalks celery, sliced

2 cups frozen broccoli, thawed

1 cup shredded Swiss cheese

1/3 cup butter

1 egg, beaten

Chicken Vegetable Casserole

- Heat olive oil in saucepan. Sprinkle chicken with salt and pepper; cook 5–6 minutes per side; remove.

- Add onion, garlic, and carrots; cook 5–6 minutes. Sprinkle with 3 tablespoons flour and thyme; cook 3 minutes.

- Add broth and cream; simmer 4–5 minutes. Shred chicken; add to sauce with celery and broccoli.

- Mix remaining flour, cheese, butter, and egg until crumbly. Pour chicken mixture into 3-quart casserole; top with crumbly mixture. Bake at 375°F 35–45 minutes.

134

Easy Chicken Casserole
Make recipe as directed, except instead of the flour, thyme, broth, and cream, stir in 1 (16-ounce) jar of four-cheese Alfredo sauce. Omit celery; add 2 cups frozen sliced carrots, thawed. Proceed with recipe as directed, using 1 cup shredded cheddar cheese instead of the Swiss cheese in the topping.

Curried Chicken Casserole
Make recipe as directed, except add 1 tablespoon curry powder with the flour; omit thyme. Omit broccoli; add 2 sliced green bell peppers and $1/3$ cup mango chutney to the sauce mixture. Substitute Havarti cheese for the Swiss cheese in the topping.

Add Chicken to Sauce

- The chicken should be cooked until it's done in the first step, but be careful not to overcook it.

- Remove the chicken and let it cool while you cook the onions and garlic and get the sauce started.

- When the chicken is cool enough to handle, shred it by gently pulling it apart with your fingers.

- Shred into large pieces so the chicken is very apparent in the finished casserole.

Mix Crumbly Topping

- To make the topping, first mix together the flour and the cheese.

- Then cut in the butter until fine crumbs form. Beat the egg in a small bowl and drizzle over the crumbs while you toss with a fork.

- When the crumb mixture is evenly mixed, sprinkle over the hot filling.

- You can make the casserole ahead of time; just don't add the crumbly topping until you're ready to bake it.

CHICKEN ENCHILADAS

A creamy, spicy chicken mixture is baked in corn tortillas

This type of enchilada is called a green enchilada because no tomatoes are used. Instead, tomatillos are a featured ingredient.

Lots of peppers of different flavors and heat levels are used in this dish. Jalapeño peppers are quite hot, while poblano peppers are long, thin, and mild. Green bell peppers are sweet and tender.

The cheesy sauce is made from scratch. Part is reserved to stir into the chicken and vegetable mixture that fills the tortillas, and the rest is poured over the tortillas.

You can use flour or corn tortillas to make this recipe. The corn tortillas have a bit more texture and flavor and will stand out more from the creamy sauce. Enjoy this indulgent recipe.
Yield: Serves 6–8

Ingredients

- 4 boneless, skinless chicken breasts
- 1 teaspoon salt
- 1/4 teaspoon pepper
- 1 tablespoon olive oil
- 1 onion, chopped
- 3 cloves garlic, minced
- 2 jalapeño peppers, minced
- 1 poblano pepper, chopped
- 2 green bell peppers, chopped
- 1 cup peeled tomatillos, chopped
- 2 tablespoons butter
- 2 tablespoons flour
- 1 tablespoon chili powder
- 2 cups chicken broth
- 1 cup sour cream
- 1 (8-ounce) package cream cheese, cubed
- 1 cup shredded Pepper Jack cheese
- 12 (6-inch) corn tortillas
- 1/3 cup grated Cotija cheese

Chicken Enchiladas

- Sprinkle chicken with salt and pepper; cook in oil until done; remove. Add onion and garlic; cook 5 minutes.

- Add peppers and tomatillos; cook 5 minutes until tender. Shred chicken; add vegetables.

- Melt butter; add flour and chili powder, cook 3 minutes. Add broth; simmer 3 minutes. Add sour cream, cream cheese, and Jack cheese.

- Stir 1 cup sauce into chicken; fill tortillas. Place in baking dish; add sauce. Sprinkle with Cotija; bake 350°F 35–40 minutes.

Red Chicken Enchiladas
Make recipe as directed, except add 2 chopped red tomatoes to the pepper mixture. Omit the poblano pepper. Make the sauce as directed, except add 1 (14.5-ounce) can diced tomatoes, undrained, in place of the tomatillos. Use cheddar cheese in place of the Pepper Jack.

Tomatillos, also called husk tomato or ground cherry, are related to tomatoes, but they are not tomatoes. The fruit is covered with a papery husk that must be removed before eating. The tomatillos are also covered with a sticky substance that should be rinsed off before chopping.

Cook Vegetables and Chicken

- Cook the chicken until it is completely cooked through in the first step, but not overcooked.

- Place the chicken in a medium bowl as you shred it. When the vegetables are done, add them to the bowl.

- The sauce should be cooked until it thickens and bubbles. The sour cream and cheeses will thicken it further.

- Add just enough sauce to the chicken mixture to add some flavor and hold the filling together.

Fill Tortillas and Assemble Casserole

- To fill the tortillas, place them all on the work surface. Place about ⅓ cup chicken mixture on each, one at a time.

- Make sure that you have some of the sauce in the bottom of the pan before you start assembling the tortillas.

- As you work, add the filled tortillas, seam side down, to the pan.

- Evenly cover the filled tortillas with the sauce, making sure to cover the edges so they don't dry out.

CHICKEN DIVAN

Chicken and broccoli cook together in a creamy curry sauce

Any recipe named "divan" means it's cooked with broccoli in a creamy béchamel sauce. A béchamel sauce is just a white sauce made with chicken broth instead of, or in addition to, milk or cream.

Most modern recipes for this dish call for cream of mushroom or cream of chicken soup. This recipe makes the béchamel sauce from scratch, which reduces the sodium content

and adds sublime flavor. You can use frozen broccoli florets instead of the fresh broccoli in this recipe. Just don't use frozen chopped broccoli; the character of that ingredient, while fine for soups and some casseroles, just isn't appropriate here.

Serve this rich casserole with some glazed carrots. *Yield: Serves 4–6*

Ingredients

2 cups chicken broth

5 boneless, skinless chicken breasts

3 tablespoons butter

1 onion, chopped

3 cloves garlic, minced

1 tablespoon curry powder

3 tablespoons flour

1 teaspoon salt

$1/4$ teaspoon pepper

$1/2$ cup heavy cream

$1 1/2$ pounds fresh broccoli, cut into florets, steamed

1 tablespoon lemon juice

$1/3$ cup grated Parmesan cheese

Chicken Divan

- Combine broth and chicken in saucepan; simmer 12–15 minutes until done. Remove chicken; set aside. Reserve broth.

- In saucepan, melt butter; cook onion, garlic, and curry powder 4–5 minutes. Add flour, salt, and pepper; cook 3 minutes.

- Add broth; simmer until thickened, about 5–6 minutes. Cube chicken; add with cream, broccoli, and lemon juice to sauce.

- Pour into 3-quart casserole; sprinkle with cheese. Bake at 375°F 30–40 minutes until top is browned and bubbly.

Classic Chicken Divan

Make recipe as directed, except add 1 teaspoon dried thyme leaves and $1/2$ teaspoon lemon pepper. Omit curry powder and assemble recipe as directed. For topping, combine 1 cup soft breadcrumbs with 2 tablespoons melted butter and the Parmesan cheese; bake until browned.

Steamed Broccoli

To steam broccoli, cut off the thick end of the stem and separate the head into florets, each about 3 inches long. Rinse well, then place in a steamer basket over simmering water. Cover and steam for 6–7 minutes until broccoli is tender when pierced with a sharp knife.

Cook Chicken and Make Sauce

- Simmering the chicken in chicken broth to cook it makes a super rich sauce that is full of flavor.

- Cut the chicken when it's cool enough to handle. Make cubes at least 1 inch in diameter.

- Steam the broccoli until crisp-tender so it won't overcook in the casserole.

- You can substitute frozen broccoli florets; just cook them until barely tender according to package instructions.

Assemble Casserole

- When you add the chicken and broccoli to the sauce, stir it gently so the large pieces remain intact.

- You can cook the casserole ahead of time to this point. Just cover and refrigerate.

- Sprinkle with cheese just before baking, or use a combination of breadcrumbs and butter.

- If baking from a chilled state, add another 10–15 minutes to the baking time.

SPANISH CHICKEN CASSEROLE

Paprika, bell peppers, and Manchego cheese are used in this fun casserole

Spanish ingredients are those commonly grown in that country. Red bell peppers are a common crop, and when dried and ground they are transformed into paprika.

Almonds are a classic Spanish ingredient in main dishes. If you can find Marcona almonds, which are native to that country, use them in this recipe; they are very rich and buttery.

You can make this recipe with boneless, skinless chicken breasts as well. Bake the casserole for 25–30 minutes until bubbly and hot.

Sweet or smoked paprika will work well in this recipe. Sweet paprika is sweet and spicy, while smoked paprika is smoky and rich. *Yield: Serves 6*

Ingredients

8 boneless, skinless chicken thighs, cut into strips

3 tablespoons flour

1 teaspoon paprika

Salt and pepper to taste

2 tablespoons butter

1 onion, chopped

5 cloves garlic, minced

1 cup uncooked long-grain rice

2 red bell peppers, chopped

1 (4-ounce) jar pimentos, drained

1 teaspoon dried thyme leaves

1/8 teaspoon cinnamon

3 cups chicken stock

2 tomatoes, peeled, seeded, and chopped

1/3 cup ground almonds

1 cup shredded Manchego cheese, divided

1/3 cup sliced black olives

Spanish Chicken Casserole

- Dredge chicken in flour, paprika, salt, and pepper. Melt butter in saucepan. Add chicken; brown on all sides; remove.

- Add onion and garlic to pan; stir to remove drippings. Add rice; cook 3–4 minutes. Add bell peppers and pimentos; cook 3–4 minutes.

- Add thyme, cinnamon, and stock; simmer, covered, for 15 minutes. Add chicken, tomatoes, almonds, and ½ cup cheese.

- Pour into 2½-quart casserole. Top with remaining cheese and olives. Bake, covered, at 375°F 35–40 minutes.

· · · · RECIPE VARIATIONS · · · ·

Slow Cooker Spanish Chicken Casserole
Make recipe as directed, except use long-grain brown rice in place of the white rice. When the rice has been sautéed, combine all ingredients in a 4-quart slow cooker. Cover and cook on low for 7–9 hours until chicken is tender and thoroughly cooked.

Spicy Spanish Chicken Casserole
Make recipe as directed, except add 1 chipotle pepper in adobo sauce, minced, along with the onion and garlic. Use smoked paprika, and add 1 tablespoon chili powder along with the rice. Continue with recipe. Use $1/2$ cup sliced kalamata olives in place of the black olives.

Cook Chicken and Vegetables

Assemble Casserole

- Just brown the chicken; don't cook it all the way through in the first step.

- The drippings will be incorporated into the casserole because the onions and garlic will loosen them.

- Cooking the rice in the onion-scented oil adds to the flavor and also keeps the rice grains separate and discrete.

- Be sure to stir the rice constantly as it cooks, because it can burn easily, which will ruin the dish.

- The cinnamon is added to highlight the taste of the paprika; you really don't taste cinnamon in this dish.

- To grind the almonds, use slivered plain almonds or shelled and skinned Marcona almonds.

- Place them in a food processor and pulse several times, until the nuts are ground into even and fine pieces.

- For a nice crunchy finish to this casserole, combine more ground almonds and breadcrumbs with butter and sprinkle on top.

KING RANCH CASSEROLE
This classic casserole is rich and spicy

There really is a King Ranch, and it exists to this day! Richard King came from Manhattan and became a steamboat captain. He bought a 15,000-acre Mexican land grant in the 1840s. Today the King Ranch is involved in farming and ranching. The casserole named after the ranch most probably developed from chilaquilas, a casserole made with tortillas, chicken, cheese, and tomatoes.

This dish is typically made with lots of condensed cream soups, which may be convenient, but don't have the best taste. Making your own white sauce instead makes this dish more sophisticated.

Serve this rich casserole with a simple green salad made from mixed lettuces and baby spinach, and some glazed baby carrots. *Yield: Serves 6–8*

Ingredients

12 (6-inch) corn tortillas

2 tablespoons olive oil

2 tablespoons chili powder, divided

2 cups chicken broth

4 boneless, skinless chicken breasts, cubed

1 onion, chopped

3 jalapeño peppers, minced

5 cloves garlic, minced

3 tablespoons butter

1 red bell pepper, chopped

1/4 cup flour

1/2 teaspoon salt

1/4 teaspoon pepper

1 cup light cream or milk

2 cups shredded cheddar cheese

King Ranch Casserole

- Cut tortillas into 1-inch strips. Toss with oil and 1 tablespoon chili powder. Bake at 400ºF 10–12 minutes until crisp.

- Combine broth and chicken; simmer 8–9 minutes until cooked. Remove chicken, reserving broth.

- Cook onion, jalapeños, and garlic in butter 5 minutes. Add bell pepper, flour, salt, pepper, and remaining chili powder; cook 3 minutes.

- Add broth and cream; simmer until thick. Add cheese, chicken, and tortillas. Pour into 9 x 13-inch dish. Bake 30–40 minutes.

····· RECIPE VARIATION ·····

Slow Cooker King Ranch Casserole

Make recipe as directed, but instead of the light cream or milk, add 1 (10-ounce) refrigerated container of Alfredo sauce. Layer tortillas, cheese, and sauce in a greased 4-quart slow cooker. Cover and cook on low for 7–9 hours until casserole is bubbly.

······· GREEN ● LIGHT ·······

This casserole, like most casseroles, freezes quite well. Pour into the casserole dish, then chill in the refrigerator. Cover with freezer wrap, seal, and label with the date and recipe name along with reheating instructions; freeze up to 3 months. Defrost in fridge overnight; bake for 55–65 minutes.

Bake Tortilla Chips

- You don't have to bake the tortilla chips, but this does help them keep their texture in the creamy sauce.

- For a shortcut, just use tortilla chips instead of baking the chips yourself.

- Let the chips cool before you add them to the sauce with the remaining ingredients.

- The chicken must be thoroughly cooked in the broth because it won't cook any more in the casserole.

Assemble Casserole

- You can make this casserole as mild or spicy as you'd like. Use serrano or habanero peppers for more heat.

- Add more vegetables, like sliced mushrooms, more bell peppers, or sliced zucchini and yellow summer squash.

- There are several ways to make this casserole. You can combine all of the ingredients in the pan.

- Or layer the ingredients for a fancier look. Layer tortillas, then the sauce with chicken, then cheese; repeat.

CHICKEN HERB STEW

Lots of fresh and dried herbs add depth of flavor to this classic stew

Stews are thicker and heartier than soups. They are thickened with a roux, a flour or cornstarch slurry, or with pureed vegetables.

If the only stew you've ever tried has been out of a can, you're in for a treat. Nothing compares to a homemade stew. The blend of flavors, colors, and textures is just gorgeous.

Using fresh and dried herbs together really contributes to the flavor of this or any recipe. Dried herbs taste slightly different from the fresh, with a sharper and smokier edge.

You can use any vegetable combination you like in this easy recipe. Carrots, peas, and celery would be a natural combination, and bell peppers add color and a fresh flavor. *Yield: Serves 6*

Ingredients

6 boneless, skinless chicken thighs, cut into strips

¹/₄ cup flour

1 teaspoon paprika

1 teaspoon salt

¹/₈ teaspoon pepper

2 tablespoons olive oil

1 onion, chopped

4 cloves garlic, minced

1 tablespoon fresh thyme

1 teaspoon dried thyme

1 teaspoon dried basil

¹/₂ teaspoon dried oregano

3 carrots, sliced

5 cups chicken stock

1 (14.5-ounce) can diced tomatoes, undrained

1¹/₂ cups frozen corn

¹/₄ cup chopped parsley

¹/₄ cup minced fresh basil

Chicken Herb Stew

- Dredge chicken in mixture of flour, paprika, salt, and pepper. In large pot, brown chicken in olive oil.

- Add onion and garlic; cook and stir 4–5 minutes until crisp-tender. Add fresh and dried thyme, dried basil, oregano, and carrots; cook 3 minutes.

- Stir in stock and tomatoes; bring to a simmer. Cover and simmer over low heat 30–35 minutes until chicken is done.

- Add corn, parsley, and basil; simmer 10–12 minutes until hot and blended.

Slow Cooker Chicken Herb Stew
Make recipe as directed, except after cooking the onion, garlic, and carrots in the drippings from the chicken, combine all ingredients in a 4-quart slow cooker. Cover and cook on low for 8–9 hours. If the stew isn't thick enough, cook with the lid off 1 hour.

Tex-Mex Chicken Stew
Make recipe as directed, except add 1 minced jalapeño and 1 minced serrano pepper with the onions and garlic. Omit thyme and basil; add 1 teaspoon chili powder and 1 teaspoon cumin. Stir in 1 1/4 cups shredded Pepper Jack cheese tossed with 1 tablespoon cornstarch during the last 5 minutes.

Cook Chicken

- After dredging the chicken, shake off the excess flour mixture. If there is leftover flour mixture, just discard it; don't save it for another use.

- The flour coats the chicken, protecting it from the heat so the meat stays moist, while thickening the stew.

- Add the dredged chicken to the fat in the pot and don't move it for several minutes.

- The heat not only caramelizes the chicken, adding flavor, but it helps the flour combine with the liquid.

Add Corn and Fresh Herbs

- You can use fresh corn if you'd like. Cut it off the cob using a sharp knife. Don't precook the corn before you cut it.

- Any combination of fresh and dried herbs can be used in this easy recipe.

- Try a combination of basil and marjoram, or thyme and oregano along with some cilantro.

- This soup can be made ahead of time and reheated; in fact, the flavor will get even better.

CHICKEN DUMPLING STEW

Tender, fluffy dumplings add great character to this simple stew

Dumplings are an old-fashioned food that isn't made often today. They are really like a big noodle, but were originally made to help fill people up during lean times.

The secrets to the best dumplings are to use a light hand with the dough, to drop the dumplings onto simmering stock or soup, and to leave the lid on until the dumplings are completely cooked through.

You can make dumplings from scratch, as in this recipe, or use a baking mix. There are even dumpling mixes available on the market. Ethnic names for dumplings include gnocchi and spaetzle; look for those mixes in the supermarket.

Serve this rich stew with some Garlic Toast or breadsticks and a fruit salad. *Yield: Serves 6–8*

Ingredients

6 slices bacon

8 boneless, skinless chicken thighs, cubed

1/4 cup flour

1 teaspoon paprika

1 teaspoon salt

1/8 teaspoon pepper

1 teaspoon dried thyme

2 tablespoons butter

1 onion, chopped

4 cloves garlic, minced

4 carrots, sliced

3 stalks celery, sliced

6 cups chicken stock

1 cup frozen peas

1 1/2 cups flour

1 teaspoon baking powder

1 teaspoon baking soda

1/2 teaspoon salt

1/4 cup butter

3/4 cup buttermilk

1/4 cup minced parsley

3 tablespoons minced basil

Chicken Dumpling Stew

- Cook bacon until crisp; drain, crumble, and refrigerate. Drain pot; do not wipe.

- Dredge chicken in flour, paprika, salt, pepper, and thyme. Add butter to pot; brown chicken. Add onion and garlic; cook 4 minutes.

- Add carrots, celery, and stock; simmer 35–40 minutes. Add peas and bacon; bring to a simmer.

- For dumplings, mix flour, baking powder, soda, and salt; cut in butter. Add buttermilk, parsley, and basil; drop into stew. Simmer, covered, 17–21 minutes.

146

• • • • RECIPE VARIATION • • • •

Slow Cooker Chicken Dumpling Stew

Make recipe as directed, except when the onions and garlic are cooked, transfer everything except the peas and the dumplings to a 4-quart slow cooker. Cover and cook on low for 8–9 hours until chicken is tender. Drop dumplings onto bubbling stew; cover and cook on high 25 minutes.

GREEN ● LIGHT

To test for dumpling doneness, there are a few rules. If you cut a dumpling in half, the texture will be even and fluffy all the way through. The dough will be very hot; internal temperature should be around 180 degrees. And the dumplings will float when they are properly cooked.

Add Carrots and Stock

- The chicken won't be completely cooked in the first step; just brown it to add flavor.

- You can use any combination of vegetables in this easy stew. Add mushrooms; omit the peas, or add some chopped red and green bell peppers.

- Other herbs would also be nice in this recipe; use basil and marjoram, or just add some oregano.

- Add the bacon along with the peas, or you can reserve it to sprinkle on top of the stew.

Drop Dumplings into Stew

- The dumplings should be fairly small when you drop them into the simmering stew.

- Use a soup spoon and drop a rounded mound onto the stew.

- Keep the dumplings the same size so they cook evenly. And remember to space them evenly around the pot.

- The dumplings will double in size when they are done. To serve, ladle the stew into a bowl and top each serving with 2–3 dumplings.

CHICKEN TORTILLA STEW

Tortilla strips are added to chicken stew to add texture and flavor

Tortillas are used as the thickener in this stew. Even when they are baked until crisp, as in this recipe, they will soften in the stew as they simmer and thicken it.

You can use unbaked tortilla strips, either made from corn or flour, in this easy recipe. Try flavored flour tortillas for a nice change of pace. Green tortillas are colored with spinach, while red tortillas are seasoned with peppers, and blue tortillas are made from blue corn. Try adding herbs to this recipe in addition to the chili powder. Oregano is always a classic addition, and thyme will add a slightly lemony and minty flavor.

Serve this stew with warmed tortillas or cornbread straight from the oven. *Yield: Serves 6*

Ingredients

5 corn tortillas

2 tablespoons olive oil

2 tablespoons chili powder, divided

6 cups chicken broth

4 boneless, skinless chicken breasts

2 tablespoons butter

1 onion, chopped

3 cloves garlic, minced

2 serrano peppers, minced

2 tablespoons masa harina

3 tomatoes, peeled, seeded, and chopped

1 cup salsa

2 cups frozen corn

2 tablespoons lime juice

1/2 teaspoon grated lime zest

Chicken Tortilla Stew

- Cut tortillas into strips. Drizzle with olive oil; toss with 1 tablespoon chili powder. Bake at 400°F 10–12 minutes.

- Simmer broth and chicken 15–20 minutes until chicken is done. Shred chicken; reserve broth.

- Melt butter in large pot. Add onion, garlic, and peppers; cook 5 minutes. Add masa harina; cook 2 minutes.

- Add broth, tomatoes, tortillas, and salsa; simmer 15 minutes. Add chicken and corn; simmer 10 minutes. Add lime juice and zest.

Cornbread

Mix ³/₄ cup flour, ¹/₄ cup whole wheat flour, 1 cup yellow cornmeal, ¹/₂ cup sugar, ¹/₂ teaspoon salt, 2 teaspoons baking powder and 1 teaspoon baking soda. Add ¹/₂ cup each buttermilk and heavy cream, 1 egg, and ¹/₃ cup melted butter. Bake in 9 x 9-inch pan at 400ºF 20–30 minutes.

Slow Cooker Tortilla Stew

Make recipe as directed, except after you bake the tortillas, combine all ingredients except the tortillas, lime juice, and zest in a 4-quart slow cooker. Cover and cook on low 7–8 hours. Shred chicken and return to soup with tortillas, lime juice, and zest. Cover and cook on low for 1 hour longer.

Bake Tortilla Strips

- The tortilla strips are baked to add more texture and a slight smoky and spicy flavor to the stew.

- For a shortcut, you can substitute prepared tortilla chips, or even seasoned chips.

- You can make the tortilla strips ahead of time. Store them, tightly covered, in an airtight container.

- If you want to use unbaked tortilla strips in the stew, add them at the same time in the recipe.

Add Masa Harina

- Masa harina is ground corn flour. It is not the same as cornmeal, so don't try to substitute one for the other.

- If you can't find masa harina, combine 2 tablespoons flour with ½ cup chicken broth and add that along with the broth.

- If you want to make this stew ahead of time, don't add the tortilla strips.

- Chill the stew. To reheat, pour into a pan and start simmering. Add the tortilla strips and simmer for 10–15 minutes until softened.

JAMBALAYA

Classic jambalaya is updated with lots of vegetables

Jambalaya is one of the treasures of Cajun cuisine. It can be made with chicken, seafood, and sausage, or a combination of chicken and shrimp.

This stew can be made as mild or spicy as you'd like. You can add jalapeño, chipotle, or habanero peppers along with the onions, or keep it mild to let the flavor of the chicken shine through.

The classic way to serve this jambalaya is to cook some medium-grain white rice until tender. Spoon the jambalaya into warmed deep soup bowls, then top with a scoop of the rice.

Serve this jambalaya with some ice cold beer and a fresh fruit salad piled onto chilled plates. *Yield: Serves 4–6*

Ingredients

$^1/_2$ pound chorizo sausage, sliced

$^1/_2$ pound kielbasa, sliced

2 tablespoons olive oil

4 boneless, skinless chicken breasts

1 onion, chopped

4 cloves garlic, minced

2 green bell peppers, chopped

3 stalks celery, sliced

8 cups chicken stock

1 (14.5-ounce) can diced tomatoes, undrained

2 bay leaves

2 teaspoons Creole seasoning

$^1/_2$ teaspoon salt

$^1/_4$ teaspoon pepper

$^1/_4$ teaspoon hot pepper sauce

1 cup long-grain white rice

1 pound small raw shrimp

Jambalaya

- In large pot, cook chorizo and kielbasa until some of the fat is rendered. Add olive oil and chicken; brown chicken 5–6 minutes.

- Add onion, garlic, green peppers, and celery; cook 5–6 minutes. Add stock and tomatoes; bring to a simmer.

- Add bay leaves, Creole seasoning, salt, and pepper; simmer 10 minutes until chicken is tender. Shred chicken; return to pot.

- Add pepper sauce and rice; simmer 15 minutes. Add shrimp; simmer 5 minutes until rice is done and shrimp pink; remove bay leaves.

All-Chicken Jambalaya

Make recipe as directed, except use 1 pound spicy chicken or turkey sausage in place of the chorizo and kielbasa. Use a combination of chicken breasts and thighs; cube thighs before adding to recipe. Omit shrimp, or you can add it if desired.

Slow Cooker Jambalaya

Make recipe as directed, except after cooking the onions, garlic, bell pepper, and celery, put all ingredients except rice and shrimp into a 4-quart slow cooker. Cover and cook on low 7–8 hours. Add rice; cook on low 40 minutes. Add shrimp; cook on low 20–30 minutes.

Add Onion and Vegetables

- Make sure that the onion, celery, and bell pepper are cut to about the same size.

- You want the vegetables to melt into the stew; it's important that they be even and soft.

- Other vegetables to try include sliced or chopped mushrooms and chopped zucchini. Corn would be a nice, if unorthodox, addition.

- For a spicier jambalaya, add some minced jalapeño or serrano peppers, or choose Anaheim or Cascabel peppers.

Add Rice

- You can use brown rice instead of white; simmer the soup for 35–45 minutes until the rice is tender.

- Exotic flavored rice is appropriate in this recipe. Basmati, jasmine, or Texmati rice would all be delicious.

- Even though rice is cooked in the jambalaya, you can still serve it with more rice to soak up the sauce.

- Always remove bay leaves when they are used in any recipe. The sharp spine of the leaf never softens in cooking and can hurt you if you eat it.

MULLIGATAWNY STEW

Literally meaning "pepper water," this is a classic English-Indian stew

Mulligatawny stew is a combination of flavors and ingredients from India, via England. When the English occupied India, they were introduced to the recipe. It may be that the original soup was invented for the soup course traditionally served in English dinners, which had no place in Indian meals. British employees of the East India Company brought the recipe home to England with them.

The soup was originally made with lots of peppers, but now is more commonly made with chicken, curry, onion, and apples.

The Indian flavors in this soup are emphasized with the addition of curry powder, ginger, and cream. *Yield: Serves 6*

Ingredients

2 tablespoons butter

1 tablespoon olive oil

1 onion, chopped

3 cloves garlic, minced

1 tablespoon grated gingerroot

3 stalks celery, chopped

3 tablespoons flour

1 tablespoon curry powder

$1/2$ teaspoon cayenne pepper

1 teaspoon dried thyme

4 boneless, skinless chicken breasts, cubed

$1/2$ teaspoon paprika

$1/2$ teaspoon salt

$1/8$ teaspoon pepper

6 cups chicken broth

$3/4$ cup uncooked long-grain white rice

1 apple, peeled and chopped

$1/2$ cup heavy cream

Mulligatawny Stew

- In large pot, melt butter and oil over medium heat. Add onion and garlic; cook 6 minutes.

- Add ginger, celery, flour, curry powder, cayenne pepper, and thyme; cook 3 minutes until bubbly.

- Toss chicken with paprika, salt, and pepper; add to pot; cook and stir 3 minutes. Add broth; bring to simmer.

- Simmer 20 minutes, then add rice and apple. Simmer 20–25 minutes until rice is tender. Stir in cream and serve.

Herbed Breadsticks

In bowl, combine ¹/₂ cup grated Parmesan cheese, 2 tablespoons fresh oregano leaves, 2 teaspoons minced fresh thyme, and 2 tablespoons ground almonds. Unroll 1 refrigerated breadstick package. Dip breadsticks in cheese mixture to coat. Bake at 350ºF 15–18 minutes.

Dark Meat Mulligatawny Stew

Make recipe as directed, except use 8 boneless, skinless chicken thighs instead of the breasts. Add 2 green bell peppers, chopped, and omit the celery. Omit apple; add another onion and 2 cloves garlic. Simmer as directed and continue with the recipe.

Add Chicken to Pot

- You can use bone-in, skin-on chicken breasts in this recipe. Simmer for 30–40 minutes, then remove chicken, shred meat, and return to pot.

- Curry powder is found in many variations; use your favorite type, or make your own blend.

- You can substitute chicken thighs for the breasts in this easy recipe; just simmer the soup for 30–40 minutes.

- Then add the rice and apple and simmer until the rice is tender.

Add Rice and Apple

- The best apple to use in this recipe is a tart cooking apple like Granny Smith or McIntosh.

- You don't have to peel the apple. Leaving the skin on will add more color and texture to the finished soup.

- If you want to make the soup ahead of time, don't add the apple and rice.

- Reheat the soup and bring it to a simmer, then add the apple and rice and cook until rice is tender.

PORTUGUESE CHICKEN STEW
Black beans, olives, and tomatoes add flavor and color to this stew

Portuguese stew is made with ingredients like paprika, lots of garlic, tomatoes, and olives. The flavors are similar to flavors from Spain, but most Portuguese recipes in this country come from the East coast, where settlers from Portugal fished the seas.

This recipe can be made as mild or spicy as you'd like. The paprika adds a bit of spice, but adding some chili powder,

cumin, chile paste, or chopped hot chile peppers will make the stew spicy and rich.

The rice helps thicken the stew, but it still needs some help, so a cornstarch slurry is added at the end of cooking time.

Serve this stew with some chewy breadsticks and a chopped fruit salad with a yogurt dressing. *Yield: Serves 6*

Ingredients

2 tablespoons olive oil

1 onion, chopped

6 cloves garlic, minced

4 boneless, skinless chicken breasts, sliced

1 teaspoon paprika

$^1/_2$ teaspoon salt

$^1/_8$ teaspoon pepper

1 bay leaf

$^1/_2$ cup dry white wine

3 tomatoes, peeled, seeded, and chopped

1 yellow bell pepper, chopped

6 cups chicken broth

$^1/_2$ cup long-grain white rice

$^1/_3$ cup kalamata olives

1 cup frozen peas

2 tablespoons lemon juice

2 tablespoons cornstarch

$^1/_3$ cup chopped cilantro

$^1/_3$ cup grated Parmesan cheese

Portuguese Chicken Stew

- In large pot, heat olive oil. Add onion and garlic; cook and stir until onions start to brown, about 9 minutes.

- Add chicken; sauté briefly. Add paprika, salt, pepper, and bay leaf; simmer 2 minutes. Add wine; simmer 3 minutes.

- Add tomatoes, peppers, broth, and rice; bring to a simmer. Simmer 15–20 minutes until chicken is tender.

- Add olives and peas. Combine lemon juice and cornstarch; add to stew. Simmer 10 minutes; top with cilantro and cheese and serve.

Slow Cooker Portuguese Stew

Make recipe as directed, except after the chicken is browned, combine all ingredients except rice, olives, peas, lemon juice, cornstarch, cilantro and cheese in a 4-quart slow cooker. Cover and cook on low 7–8 hours. Add rice and olives; cook 40 minutes. Add remaining ingredients; cook 10 minutes.

Spicy Portuguese Chicken Stew

Make recipe as directed, except use 8 boneless, skinless chicken thighs in place of the chicken breasts. Cut them into slices and toss with paprika, salt, and pepper. Continue with recipe; simmer soup for 35–40 minutes until chicken is tender, then add rice and continue.

Sauté Chicken

Add Olives and Peas

- The onions and garlic can be cooked until crisp-tender, until they just start to brown, or until they are quite brown.

- Caramelizing the onions and garlic adds a nice, complex depth of flavor to the stew.

- You can substitute 1 (14.5-ounce) can of diced undrained tomatoes in place of the chopped ripe tomatoes.

- The broth is quite important in this stew, so try to use a homemade broth, or a boxed one at the minimum.

- Kalamata olives have a complicated flavor and are very rich.

- You can also use Manzanilla olives, which are packed in salt and an acidic brine.

- Liguria olives are an Italian black olive, which are deep burgundy in color with a rich and fruity flavor.

- You can use other varieties of cheese instead of Parmesan. Romano is slightly more tangy, and Manchego is authentic.

MARINATED GRILLED CHICKEN

Chicken marinates in a spicy sweet sauce, then is grilled to perfection

Grilling is a quick cooking method that adds great smoky flavor to any cut of chicken. You can use a charcoal or gas grill to cook outdoors, an electric dual contact grill indoors, or a grill on a stovetop.

You can use just about anything for a marinade, as long as it has an acidic ingredient like vinegar or lemon juice and some type of oil. Herbs and spices add flavor to marinades but aren't necessary.

Chicken should always be marinated in the refrigerator, even if it's only for 30 minutes, for food safety reasons. Marinate chicken breasts no longer than 24 hours; thighs, wings, and drumsticks can marinate up to 48 hours. *Yield: Serves 6*

Ingredients

1 tablespoon olive oil

1 onion, chopped

4 cloves garlic, minced

2 tablespoons honey

2 tablespoons cider vinegar

1/2 cup chili sauce

2 tablespoons lemon juice

1/2 teaspoon salt

1/4 teaspoon pepper

1 teaspoon grill seasoning

6 boneless, skinless chicken breasts

Marinated Grilled Chicken

- Heat olive oil in pan; add onion and garlic. Cook and stir 6–7 minutes. Add remaining ingredients except chicken; simmer 5 minutes.

- Let marinade cool 20 minutes, then add chicken. Cover and chill 8–24 hours in refrigerator.

- When ready to cook, prepare and preheat grill. Remove chicken from marinade; reserve marinade.

- Grill chicken 6 inches from medium coals for 17–22 minutes, turning and brushing with marinade, until done. Discard remaining marinade.

Grilled Chicken Thighs
Make recipe as directed, except use bone-in, skin-on chicken thighs. Marinate the chicken for 24–36 hours in the refrigerator. Remove and cut 3 slashes into the chicken skin, not going through to the meat. Grill on indirect coals for 25–35 minutes, turning once, until temperature registers 170ºF.

Simmer Marinade

Grill Chicken

GRILLED CHICKEN

- You can substitute any purchased good quality barbecue sauce for the homemade sauce for a shortcut.

- Make the marinade as mild or spicy as you'd like. If you are using a purchased marinade, add more fresh herbs or spices.

- You can make the marinade ahead of time; refrigerate it until you're ready to marinate and cook the chicken.

- If you'd like to use the marinade as a sauce at the table, double it and simmer it while the chicken grills.

- To grill the chicken more quickly, flatten the chicken with a rolling pin before marinating.

- Pounded chicken breasts will cook for 5–6 minutes per side. Pounded chicken thighs will cook for 7–9 minutes per side.

- Grill an extra chicken breast or two to use in sandwiches or salads the next day.

- Let the chicken rest, covered, for 5–10 minutes after grilling to let the juices redistribute.

CHICKEN KEBABS

Chicken marinates in a sweet and salty mixture, then is grilled with vegetables on skewers

Kebabs are an easy and elegant way to grill chicken. They are especially good for company, because you can double and triple the recipe and still have the same cooking times as long as your grill is large enough.

Kebabs are easy for a buffet party; just set out all the food and let your guests assemble their own. You can use grill charms to mark the individual skewers so the kebabs are easily identified on the grill.

If you want to use chicken thighs instead of breasts, cook the chicken all on one skewer and the vegetables on another. The thighs take a longer time to grill than most of the vegetables. *Yield: Serves 8*

KNACK CHICKEN CLASSICS

Ingredients

3 tablespoons olive oil

$1/4$ cup soy sauce

3 tablespoons hoisin sauce

$1/4$ cup brown sugar

3 minced garlic cloves

$1/4$ teaspoon pepper

$1/4$ cup chicken broth

8 boneless, skinless chicken breasts, cut into $1^1/_2$-inch cubes

1 zucchini, sliced $1/2$ inch thick

2 red bell peppers, sliced

8 ounces whole mushrooms

Chicken Kebabs

- In bowl, combine olive oil, soy sauce, hoisin sauce, brown sugar, garlic, pepper, and broth; mix well.

- Add chicken, zucchini, and bell peppers; stir to coat. Cover and refrigerate for 8–24 hours.

- Thread chicken, zucchini, bell peppers, and mushrooms on skewers; reserve marinade.

- Preheat grill. Place kebabs on clean grate; grill, turning and brushing with marinade, until chicken is done, 12–16 minutes. Discard any remaining marinade.

Tex-Mex Chicken Kebabs
Make recipe as directed, except use ¹/₂ cup salsa, 2 tablespoons lime juice, and 2 tablespoons olive oil for the marinade. Marinate chicken, green onion pieces, and bell peppers overnight in refrigerator. Thread onto skewers along with mushrooms; grill as directed.

Hawaiian Chicken Kebabs
Make recipe as directed, except for marinade combine ¹/₂ cup pineapple juice, 1 teaspoon gingerroot, soy sauce, ¹/₄ cup sugar, garlic, and pepper. Marinate the chicken with bell peppers and onion wedges overnight in fridge. Make kebabs with chicken, vegetables, and pineapple cubes.

Mix Marinade

- The marinade can be made with any proportion and any combination of ingredients you'd like.

- You can substitute oyster sauce for the hoisin sauce.

- A substitute for this marinade would include an Asian dressing or a red wine vinaigrette.

- You can make the marinade ahead of time; just keep it covered in the fridge. Make a large quantity if you like it, and spoon out the amount you need each time.

Thread Food on Skewers

- When you thread the food on the skewers, be sure to leave a small space in between the pieces of food.

- This will let the heat circulate around the food and cook everything evenly.

- Turn the kebabs frequently on the grill, but only when they release easily from the grill rack.

- Cook until the chicken registers 160°F. The vegetables will be tender by the time the chicken is done.

GRILLED CHICKEN

159

CHICKEN BURGERS

Tender and juicy chicken burgers are easy to make with a few additions

Chicken burgers are a nice change of pace from beef burgers. The ground chicken makes delicate burgers that are well suited to many flavors and cuisines.

You can usually find ground chicken in the supermarket. Use a combination of dark and white meat for moister and juicier burgers. Burgers made from all dark meat chicken will have just as much fat as beef burgers.

A grill mat will help keep the tender burgers together and prevent them from sticking to the grill rack. A sprayed and perforated piece of heavy-duty foil is a good substitute. *Yield: Serves 6*

Chicken Burgers

Ingredients

2 tablespoons olive oil

1 onion, finely chopped

3 cloves garlic, minced

$1/2$ cup shredded carrots

1 red bell pepper, minced

1 cup mushrooms, minced

1 teaspoon salt

1 tablespoon fresh thyme

2 tablespoons chopped parsley

1 egg

2 tablespoons Dijon mustard

1 tablespoon lemon juice

1 cup soft fresh breadcrumbs

$1^1/2$ pounds ground chicken

2 tablespoons butter

6 onion buns, split

6 slices Muenster cheese

6 thick slices tomato

6 leaves butter lettuce

- Heat oil in pan. Add onion, garlic, carrots, bell pepper, and mushrooms; cook 3 minutes. Sprinkle with salt; cook about 6 minutes.

- Place in bowl; add thyme and parsley; cool 30 minutes. Add egg, mustard, lemon juice, and breadcrumbs; mix well.

- Add chicken; mix gently but thoroughly. Form into 6 patties. Grill on grill mat 6 inches from medium coals.

- Butter onion buns and grill, then make into sandwiches using burgers, cheese, tomato, and lettuce.

Spicy Chicken Burgers
Make recipe as directed, except omit bell pepper and mushrooms. Add 1 minced jalapeño and 1 minced poblano pepper to the onion mixture. Substitute ¼ cup salsa for the mustard and lemon juice. Top burgers with Pepper Jack cheese, tomato, and avocado slices.

Greek Chicken Burgers
Make recipe as directed, except omit red bell pepper and mushrooms. Substitute 1 minced green bell pepper. Omit thyme; use 1 teaspoon dried oregano. Add ½ cup crumbled feta cheese along with the ground chicken. Grill burgers, then serve in pita breads with cucumber and yogurt.

Cook Vegetables

Form and Cook Burgers

- Cook the vegetables until the liquid evaporates and they are very tender.

- If the vegetables are cooked only until crisp-tender, they will add too much water to the burgers and the burgers will fall apart.

- You can make the vegetable mixture ahead of time; just cover and refrigerate, then add the egg, mustard, breadcrumbs, and chicken.

- If you let the vegetable and breadcrumb mixture cool completely, you can form the burgers ahead of time.

- Ground chicken is very perishable; use it within 1–2 days of purchase.

- If you can't find ground chicken, make your own by pulsing dark and light meat chicken in a food processor until ground.

- Handle the meat gently but firmly. Shape into round patties, and press a spoon into the center.

- This indentation stops the burgers from puffing up as they cook, so they are easier to layer on the bun.

GRILLED CHICKEN

161

CHICKEN WITH SALSA
Tender, smoky grilled chicken is topped with a spicy fruit salsa

Salsa is the perfect topping for grilled chicken. The contrast in flavor, texture, color, and temperature is really beautiful.

Salsa can be made with fruit, vegetables, or even beans and nuts. It can be as spicy or as mild as you like; vary the flavor with the peppers and spices that you add.

Match the marinade to the salsa. In fact, you can drain the salsa and use the liquid to marinate the chicken. Be sure that you don't let any part of the raw chicken touch the fresh salsa.

For entertaining, marinate chicken in several marinades and serve with a selection of salsas and let your guests mix and match. Serve with a mixed green salad. *Yield: Serves 8*

Ingredients

1 teaspoon grill seasoning

1 teaspoon salt, divided

$1/4$ teaspoon pepper

1 teaspoon dried thyme

1 teaspoon dried basil

2 tablespoons olive oil

8 boneless, skinless chicken breasts

1 red onion, chopped

1 clove garlic, minced

1 jalapeño pepper, minced

1 mango, peeled and chopped

2 tablespoons lime juice

$1/8$ teaspoon cayenne pepper

1 avocado, peeled and chopped

1 cup fresh raspberries

Chicken with Salsa

- In bowl, combine grill seasoning, ½ teaspoon salt, pepper, thyme, basil, and olive oil; brush over chicken. Refrigerate 2–3 hours.

- Meanwhile, combine red onion, garlic, jalapeño, mango, lime juice, remaining salt, and cayenne pepper and mix gently. Cover and chill 2–3 hours.

- When ready to eat, prepare and preheat grill. Place chicken on grill; cook, covered, 6 inches from medium heat 15–18 minutes.

- Add avocado and raspberries to salsa; mix gently and serve with chicken.

Grilled Dark Chicken with Salsa

Make recipe as directed, except use 6 bone-in, skin-on chicken thighs and 6 drumsticks. Marinate as directed, except add 1 tablespoon chili powder to the marinade. For salsa, combine 1 cup each chopped strawberries, blueberries, and raspberries.

Apricot Glazed Chicken and Salsa

Make recipe as directed, except omit basil from marinade and add $1/2$ cup apricot nectar and $1/4$ cup apricot preserves. Marinate chicken as directed. For salsa, combine 1 cup chopped fresh apricots, $1/2$ cup chopped dried apricots, 1 cup raspberries, and $1/4$ cup apricot preserves.

Mix Salsa

Grill Chicken

- Some delicate fruits and vegetables shouldn't be added to the salsa until it's ready to serve.

- Raspberries, avocado, blackberries, and mushrooms should be added later. Other produce benefits from marinating.

- Other spices that can be added to the salsa include chili powder, cumin, dry mustard, curry powder, or cinnamon.

- You can keep the salsa and the chicken in the refrigerator up to 24 hours before grilling.

- Boneless, skinless chicken breasts cook in about 15 minutes. If you pound the breasts, they'll cook in about 8–9 minutes.

- Boneless, skinless chicken thighs will grill in 20–30 minutes; bone-in in about 35–45 minutes.

- Move the chicken around on the grill once it releases easily from the rack. Make sure you have cool and hot parts on your grill.

- Let the chicken stand, covered, for 5–10 minutes after it comes off the grill to let the juices redistribute.

GRILLED CHICKEN

TERIYAKI CAN CHICKEN

Teriyaki is a sweet and salty sauce that is a perfect match with chicken

Chicken cooked on a can was invented in the 1990s. The chicken is literally impaled on a can of beer, cola, or other liquid and grilled upright on a closed grill.

The liquid in the can will boil and steam while the chicken grills, seasoning it and cooking it from the inside out. Beer makes a savory chicken, while cola makes a sweet chicken,

and chicken broth adds more chicken flavor.

Put some of the marinade that coats the chicken in the can to add more flavor. Be sure to pour off at least 1/3 of the liquid from the can so it won't boil over on the grill.

Serve this chicken with a chopped vegetable salad and some crusty bread heated on the grill. *Yield: Serves 4*

Ingredients

1 whole chicken

1/3 cup brown sugar

2 tablespoons sugar

2 tablespoons honey

1/4 cup pineapple juice

1/4 cup soy sauce

2 tablespoons lemon juice

3 cloves garlic, minced

1/2 cup minced onion

2 tablespoons grated gingerroot

1/4 teaspoon white pepper

1 (12-ounce) can cola

Teriyaki Can Chicken

- Pat chicken dry and place in large casserole dish. In bowl, combine remaining ingredients except cola and mix.

- Pour over chicken; turn to coat. Cover and marinate in refrigerator 8–24 hours.

- Drain chicken; discard marinade. Prepare and preheat grill. Pour off 1/3 of the cola. Push chicken onto can, leg side down.

- Balance the chicken on the grill, using the can and legs. Cover and grill on medium indirect heat for 75–85 minutes until done.

Beer Can Chicken
Rub the chicken with a mixture of chili powder, salt, pepper, sugar, cumin, and dried oregano. Drain off $1/3$ of the beer from a 12-ounce can. Place the chicken on the can, wedging the can into the chicken between the legs. Grill, covered, for 70–80 minutes.

ZOOM

You can balance the chicken on its legs and the can, or you can purchase a rack made just for this purpose, if you make this recipe often. The metal rack has a space for the can and spikes for the chicken. Look for the rack in kitchen specialty stores, in grilling catalogs, or online.

Marinate Chicken

Balance Chicken on Grill

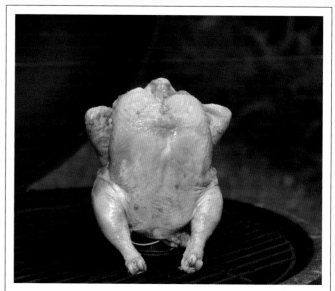

- You can marinate the chicken in any mixture you'd like. A sweet purchased marinade is a good substitute.

- Vary the proportions of the ingredients to your taste. For a hot chicken, add minced hot chile peppers.

- For milder chicken, reduce the garlic, onion, and gingerroot.

- You can simmer the marinade for 2 minutes, then pour it over the finished chicken for a sticky glaze.

- The can that you use should be all metal; don't use any can with a paper cover.

- Even if you remove the paper cover, there will still be glue on the can that isn't edible.

- You may have to work a bit to get the chicken and can properly balanced on the grill.

- Once you've started grilling, don't open the cover to check the chicken until an hour has passed, or you'll release too much heat.

GRILLED CHICKEN

MARGARITA CHICKEN

Chicken is marinated in a lime and tequila sauce, then grilled to perfection

A marinade that uses alcohol makes the chicken very tender and flavorful. Based on the drink, this chicken is sweet and sour with quite a kick.

You can substitute bottled margarita mix or a frozen concentrate for the homemade marinade for a shortcut. You may want to taste the mix before you add the chicken, and add lime juice or honey to balance the flavor to your taste.

Balance the flavors in the homemade marinade as well. Taste it before you add the chicken to make sure it has a good sweet and sour balance.

Serve this tender and juicy chicken with a fruit salsa and some toasted garlic bread. *Yield: Serves 6*

Ingredients

2 cloves garlic, minced

1 teaspoon salt

¹/₄ cup lime juice

¹/₂ teaspoon grated lime zest

¹/₄ cup tequila

¹/₄ cup honey

¹/₄ cup chicken broth

¹/₄ teaspoon white pepper

¹/₄ cup minced cilantro

6 boneless, skinless chicken breasts

Margarita Chicken

- In bowl, place garlic; add salt and mash until a paste forms. Add lime juice, zest, and tequila and mix well.

- Add honey, broth, pepper, and cilantro and mix. Add chicken; cover and refrigerate for 8–24 hours.

- Prepare and preheat grill. Drain chicken, reserving marinade. Grill chicken 6 inches from medium coals.

- Cook for 7–8 minutes per side, brushing occasionally with marinade, until chicken registers 160ºF. Discard remaining marinade.

Daiquiri Chicken

Make recipe as directed, except substitute $^1/_3$ cup light or dark rum instead of the tequila. Add 2 tablespoons of sugar to the marinade and stir until dissolved. Marinate the chicken and grill as directed. If you want to use chicken thighs, grill them for 12–14 minutes per side, turning once.

ZOOM

Tequila is a liqueur made from the agave plant. It was originally produced in the city of Tequila, Mexico. It comes in several categories: silver is aged less than two months. Gold tequila can have caramel coloring added. Aged or extra-aged tequila is aged for three years in oak barrels.

Marinate Chicken

Grill Chicken

- Make the marinade ahead of time. If you like it, make a big batch and remove about 1 cup each time you want to make the recipe.

- The longer the chicken marinates, the more intense its flavor will be.

- For even more flavor, pierce the chicken with a fork several times before you add it to the marinade.

- You can marinate boneless, skinless chicken thighs longer than the breasts.

- Always discard leftover marinade when you cook chicken.

- If you want to serve the marinade as a sauce, you need to boil the marinade for at least 2 minutes.

- If you want a sauce with this dish, double the marinade. Never dip the basting brush in the marinade while it's simmering.

- Make extra chicken breasts; the leftovers are wonderful in a chicken salad.

GRILLED CHICKEN

CLASSIC CHICKEN SALAD

Large chunks of tender chicken are mixed with grapes and celery in this classic salad

Chicken salad comes in so many varieties that it's hard to choose just six. There's no question about what makes the best chicken salad, though: it's perfectly cooked chicken.

A meat thermometer is a real necessity when you're cooking chicken for salads. In this recipe, the chicken is simmered until tender; its temperature when you take it off the heat should be just barely 160ºF. Cut the chicken into large chunks when it's the centerpiece of the salad. Pieces that are 2 inches in diameter are appropriate for the nicest presentation.

Let the chicken chill in the refrigerator for several hours to blend the flavors. Then serve it with some muffins hot from the oven and a glass of iced tea. *Yield: Serves 6*

Ingredients

6 boneless, skinless chicken breasts

3 cups water

1 lemon, sliced

6 slices bacon

$^{1}/_{2}$ cup mayonnaise

1 cup yogurt

2 tablespoons lemon juice

$^{1}/_{2}$ teaspoon paprika

$^{1}/_{2}$ teaspoon salt

$^{1}/_{8}$ teaspoon pepper

2 cups green grapes

3 stalks celery, sliced

$^{1}/_{2}$ cup chopped red onion

$^{1}/_{2}$ cup toasted slivered almonds

$^{1}/_{2}$ cup dried cherries

$^{1}/_{2}$ cup heavy whipping cream

Classic Chicken Salad

- Combine chicken, water, and lemon in pot. Simmer 10 minutes.

- Remove chicken from heat, cover, and let stand 10 minutes. Cube chicken.

- Cook bacon until crisp; drain, crumble, and set aside. In bowl, mix mayon-naise, yogurt, lemon juice, paprika, salt, and pepper.

- Add chicken, grapes, celery, red onion, almonds, cherries, and bacon; mix. Cover and chill 3–4 hours.

- When ready to eat, whip cream until stiff; fold into salad and serve.

Chicken Pasta Salad
Make recipe as directed, except use 1¹/₂ cups mayon-naise and 1¹/₂ cups yogurt. Cook 3 cups farfalle pasta in boiling salted water until tender, drain well, and fold into the salad along with the chicken. Cover and chill as directed.

Chicken Vegetable Salad
Make recipe as directed, except omit the grapes and dried cherries. Add 1 red bell pepper and 1 yellow bell pepper, chopped, and 1 cup sliced cremini mushrooms. Omit the whipped cream. Cover and chill salad before serving.

Cook Chicken

- This chicken isn't technically poached since the water is simmering.

- But make sure that the water is just at a simmer, and never let it boil, or the chicken will be tough.

- For more flavor, you can simmer the chicken in chicken broth. After you've removed the chicken, save the broth for another use.

- Thick-cut bacon will stand up better in this salad and keep some of its crunch, but plain bacon works just fine.

Mix Salad

- Adding the chicken to the dressing while its warm will help the chicken absorb the dressing's flavors.

- In fact, it's a good idea to make the dressing while the chicken is cooking, and add the chicken to the dressing as it's cut into cubes.

- The cut sides of the chicken will absorb some of the liquid from the dressing and make it very moist.

- Use any combination of fruits and vegetables in this easy and delicious salad.

CHICKEN SALADS

ASIAN CHICKEN NOODLE SALAD

Crisp fried noodles provide crunch and a fun appearance in this easy salad

Asian flavors and foods blend beautifully in this salad to complement tender and juicy chicken. Five-spice powder adds a complex sweet and sour note, bok choy and napa cabbage are crisp and mild, and radishes are spicy and peppery.

The type of noodles you want for this recipe is the brown, curly, thin noodles that are deep fried. They are very crisp and come in cellophane packages in the international foods aisle of the supermarket. They're often served with chow mein and are called chow mein noodles.

You could add other Asian ingredients to this salad like water chestnuts, lotus root, enoki mushrooms, or eggplant. *Yield: Serves 6*

Ingredients

4 boneless, skinless chicken breasts

3 cups water

1 lemon, sliced

2 tablespoons sesame oil

3 tablespoons peanut oil

1/4 cup rice wine vinegar

2 tablespoons soy sauce

2 tablespoons sugar

2 tablespoons lemon juice

2 tablespoons chicken broth

1/2 teaspoon five-spice powder

1/8 teaspoon pepper

2 cups shredded bok choy

2 cups shredded napa cabbage

1/2 cup sliced radishes

2 cups snow peas

4 cups fried crisp chow mein noodles

Asian Chicken Noodle Salad

- Combine chicken, water, and lemon in pan; bring to a simmer. Cover and simmer 10 minutes; remove from heat and let stand 10 minutes. Cube chicken.

- Mix sesame oil, peanut oil, vinegar, soy sauce, sugar, lemon juice, broth, five-spice powder, and pepper in bowl; add chicken.

- Add bok choy, cabbage, radishes, and snow peas; toss well. Cover and chill 3-4 hours.

- When ready to eat, toss salad. Serve on top of the crisp chow mein noodles.

Peanut Chicken Salad

Make recipe as directed, except omit sesame oil dressing. For dressing, combine $1/3$ cup peanut butter, 2 tablespoons soy sauce, 2 tablespoons hoisin sauce, 1 tablespoon sugar, 2 tablespoons rice vinegar, and $1/3$ cup chicken broth in bowl. Use this to dress the chicken and vegetables.

Ramen Noodle Chicken Salad

Make recipe as directed, except substitute 2 (3-ounce) packages ramen noodles, slightly crushed, for the chow mein noodles. Discard seasoning packet. Omit the napa cabbage and add 1 (5-ounce) can of drained water chestnuts along with 2 cups of blanched snow peas.

Mix Dressing

- You can substitute any Asian or Chinese salad dressing for this homemade dressing if you'd like.

- Change the proportion of the ingredients in the dressing to suit your taste.

- You can add more pepper and hoisin sauce or oyster sauce to the dressing for more spice and flavor.

- You can make the dressing ahead of time. Store it in the refrigerator in a tightly covered container, and whisk or shake before use.

Toss Ingredients

- Add the chicken to the dressing as soon as it's cooked, so it can absorb some of the flavors.

- To prepare bok choy, rinse it thoroughly, cut off the ends, and chop it into rough pieces.

- Napa cabbage is prepared just like romaine lettuce. Rinse the leaves and chop them into pieces.

- The snow peas can be added raw, or blanched for a few seconds in boiling salted water.

CURRIED CHICKEN SALAD

Curry powder and fruit add great flavor to this chicken salad

The ingredients for a curry include curry powder, which is a blend of spices, mango chutney, and hot peppers. These ingredients blend beautifully with mild, tender, and juicy chicken to make a perfect salad.

If you use a sweet chutney, like mango chutney, this salad is best made with fruits like grapes and cherries. There are many varieties and flavors of chutney available, including tomato,

apple, and coconut. You can make your own chutney to add your touch to the recipe.

Curry powder has a more intense flavor if it's heated. Toss it with raw chicken and cook in olive oil for a wonderfully flavored and tender chicken.

Serve this salad on chilled salad plates on a warm summer day on the porch. *Yield: Serves 6*

Ingredients

¹/₄ cup plus 2 tablespoons olive oil, divided

2 cloves garlic, minced

5 boneless, skinless chicken breasts, cut into cubes

1 teaspoon salt, divided

1 tablespoon plus 2 teaspoons curry powder, divided

³/₄ cup mayonnaise

¹/₄ cup milk

¹/₄ cup mango chutney OR Apple Chutney

2 tablespoons lemon juice

¹/₈ teaspoon pepper

4 stalks celery, sliced

4 green onions, sliced

2 cups red grapes

¹/₂ cup dried cherries

1 cup chopped toasted pecans

Curried Chicken Salad

- Heat 2 tablespoons olive oil in pan. Add garlic, then toss chicken with ½ teaspoon salt and 1 tablespoon curry powder. Cook chicken until done, about 6 minutes; remove.

- In bowl, combine remaining olive oil, mayonnaise, milk, chutney, lemon juice, remaining curry powder, remaining salt, and pepper; mix well.

- Add chicken and remaining ingredients and stir to mix.

- Cover and chill for 5–6 hours before serving. Serve chicken on bed of lettuce, topped with more chutney.

Curried Chicken Pasta Salad

Make recipe as directed, except add $1/2$ cup vanilla yogurt to the dressing and increase the chutney to $1/2$ cup. Cook 2 cups orzo or small shell pasta until tender, drain, and add to the salad with the chicken. Continue with the recipe; chill until serving time.

Apple Chutney

In large saucepan, combine 5 Granny Smith apples, peeled and cubed, with 1 chopped onion, 2 cloves minced garlic, and 1 tablespoon grated gingerroot. Add $1/3$ cup red wine vinegar, $1/3$ cup sugar, and $1/4$ teaspoon each salt, cinnamon, and nutmeg. Simmer 30 minutes until blended.

Cook Chicken

Mix Salad

- You can toss the chicken with the curry powder, but not the salt, ahead of time and let it marinate in the refrigerator.

- This will tenderize the chicken and give it more flavor, as it has time to absorb the powder.

- Don't add the salt ahead of time or it will leach moisture from the chicken.

- Cook the chicken just until it isn't pink in the center. Don't overcook the chicken or it will be tough.

- Add the chicken to the salad dressing as soon as it comes out of the pan so it stays tender and juicy.

- The hot chicken will absorb flavors from the dressing as it cools.

- Mix the salad using two large spoons gently but

thoroughly, being careful not to tear the chicken or bruise the fruits and vegetables.

- If you're using tomato chutney, use grape tomatoes, chopped bell peppers, and mushrooms instead of the fruit.

CHICKEN SALADS

SOUTHWEST CHICKEN SALAD
Spicy flavors of the southwest make this salad special

Spicy ingredients from the Southwest and tender, moist chicken make a wonderful salad that's perfect for entertaining.

The flavorful dressing is a delicious combination of creamy sour cream; fresh, chunky, and spicy salsa; and spices. It complements the mild chicken and fresh, crisp vegetables.

Baby corn is only found canned, unless you're lucky enough to find it at a farmers' market. Rinse the corn very well to help reduce sodium content. It's edible, cob and all. You can use plain, blue corn, or flavored tortilla chips in this fun salad, or offer an assortment and let your guests pick and choose.

Serve the salad with some cold iced tea and fruit parfaits for dessert; that's all it needs. *Yield: Serves 8*

Ingredients

- ¼ cup cider vinegar
- 1 cup sour cream
- 1 cup salsa
- 2 tablespoons honey
- 1 tablespoon chili powder
- 1 chipotle pepper, minced
- 1 tablespoon adobo sauce
- ½ teaspoon salt
- ⅛ teaspoon pepper
- 5 boneless, skinless chicken breasts, cubed
- 2 tablespoons olive oil
- 1 red bell pepper, chopped
- 1 (15-ounce) can baby corn, drained
- 3 tomatoes, chopped
- 1 red onion, chopped
- 6 cups baby spinach
- 1 cup diced sharp cheddar cheese
- 2 avocados, peeled and cubed
- 2 cups crushed tortilla chips

Southwest Chicken Salad

- In large bowl, combine vinegar, sour cream, salsa, honey, chili powder, chipotle, adobo, salt, and pepper.

- Cook chicken in olive oil until tender, about 6 minutes; add to dressing and mix.

- Add bell pepper, baby corn, tomatoes, and red onion; mix gently; cover and refrigerate 2–3 hours.

- When ready to serve, combine spinach, cheese, and avocados; place on serving platter. Top with chicken mixture and tortilla chips; serve.

Grilled Southwest Chicken Salad

Make recipe as directed, except grill the chicken over medium coals until done, turning once, about 8–10 minutes. Cube and add to dressing. Omit baby corn; grill 3 ears fresh corn for 3–4 minutes until tender; cut corn off cob and add to salad. Omit cheddar cheese; use Pepper Jack cheese.

ZOOM

Chipotle peppers are dried jalapeño peppers. They have a mild heat and a wonderful smoky flavor. Look for them packed in adobo sauce, which is a thick and spicy tomato mixture. Wipe off the peppers and mince finely. You can use the adobo sauce in recipes too.

Add Chicken to Dressing

- You can use boneless, skinless chicken thighs instead of the breasts in this recipe.

- Cook the cubed thighs for 9–12 minutes until they are just done, then add to the dressing.

- Make sure to stir the chicken in the dressing so it is completely coated before you add the rest of the ingredients.

- You want the chicken to be coated so it stays moist and absorbs the dressing's flavors.

Assemble Salad

- The combination of the marinated ingredients and fresh ingredients adds great texture and flavor.

- Don't prepare the spinach, cheese, and avocado until you're ready to serve the salad.

- You can use lettuces other than spinach. A combination of romaine and butter lettuce would be nice.

- This salad can be topped with sour cream and salsa, or some guacamole if you'd like.

COBB SALAD

A classic Cobb salad, packed with vegetables and chicken, is a treat

The original Cobb Salad was served at the Brown Derby restaurant in Los Angeles in the 1930s. It was invented by the manager, Bob Cobb, who needed to use up leftovers. What an invention!

This salad has the perfect combination of textures, colors, and flavors. It can be served two ways: as a composed salad, with separate strips of the individual ingredients, or as a tossed salad.

The crisp and smoky bacon, the tender and velvety chicken, creamy and buttery avocado, sweet tomatoes, and hard cooked eggs with a tangy dressing are really delicious. *Yield: Serves 6*

Ingredients

8 slices bacon

$^1/_4$ cup plus 1 tablespoon olive oil

6 boneless, skinless chicken breasts, cubed

1 teaspoon paprika

$^1/_2$ teaspoon salt

$^1/_8$ teaspoon pepper

$^1/_3$ cup red wine vinegar

3 tablespoons Dijon mustard

2 tablespoons honey

$^1/_2$ cup crumbled blue cheese

2 tablespoons minced chives

6 cups chopped romaine lettuce

4 hard cooked eggs, chopped

4 tomatoes, chopped

2 avocados, peeled and diced

Cobb Salad

- Cook bacon until crisp; drain, crumble, and set aside. Drain fat from pan; don't wipe. Add 1 tablespoon olive oil.

- Sprinkle chicken with paprika, salt, and pepper; cook in pan until tender, about 6 minutes; remove from pan.

- In bowl, combine vinegar, remaining olive oil, mustard, honey, blue cheese, and chives; mix well.

- Layer lettuce, chicken, bacon, eggs, tomatoes, and avocados on serving plate; drizzle with dressing and serve immediately.

Hard Cooked Eggs

Place 8–10 large eggs in large saucepan. Cover with cold water. Bring to a boil. Boil hard for 1 minute, then remove pan from heat, cover, and let stand 15 minutes. Place pan in sink; run cold water into pan until eggs are cold. Crack eggs under water; peel.

Classic Cobb Salad Dressing

In a clean jar with a tight lid, combine $1/4$ cup red wine vinegar, $1/2$ teaspoon sugar, 1 tablespoon lemon juice, $1/2$ teaspoon salt, $1/4$ teaspoon pepper, $1/2$ teaspoon Worcestershire sauce, 1 tablespoon Dijon mustard, and 1 small clove garlic, finely minced. Add $2/3$ cup olive oil and shake well.

Cook Chicken in Bacon Drippings

Mix Dressing

- It's important to leave some of the bacon fat in the pan because it adds a lot of flavor to the chicken.

- You can use boneless, skinless chicken thighs in this recipe, but chicken breasts are the classic Cobb Salad ingredient.

- You can cook the chicken ahead of time. Mix it with a bit of the dressing after it's cooked and refrigerate until serving time.

- This step helps keep the chicken moist and adds even more flavor.

- To easily mix the dressing, use a wire whisk, or combine the ingredients in a small jar.

- The jar should have a tight-fitting screw-top lid so the dressing doesn't fly around the kitchen as you shake it.

- The dressing can be made ahead of time; store it tightly covered in the refrigerator.

- Assemble the salad just before serving so the ingredients stay whole and separate.

CHICKEN SALADS

CHICKEN POTATO SALAD

Chicken and roasted potatoes make a hearty and traditional salad

Potato salad is the classic summer salad, and everyone has their own favorite recipe. But add chicken and some fresh vegetables, and you can turn potato salad into a delicious main dish. Potato salad is usually made with red potatoes. These are waxier than russet potatoes, and hold their shape better when mixed with a dressing. The potatoes are boiled so they stay nice and moist.

A creamy mustard dressing is the perfect complement to the chicken and potatoes. You can use a creamy honey mustard salad dressing instead of the scratch recipe; just add some sour cream or mayonnaise and mix well.

This is the perfect salad to take on a picnic; all you need is some fresh fruit. *Yield: Serves 6–8*

Ingredients

4 boneless, skinless chicken breasts

2 cups water

2 tablespoons lemon juice

1 cup mayonnaise

$1/2$ cup yogurt

$1/3$ cup mustard

$1/4$ cup milk

$1/2$ teaspoon salt

$1/8$ teaspoon pepper

2 tablespoons fresh thyme

3 pounds red potatoes

$1/3$ cup chopped green onion

3 stalks celery, sliced

1 red bell pepper, chopped

Chicken Potato Salad

- Simmer chicken in water and lemon juice 10 minutes. Remove chicken from heat, cover, and let stand 10 minutes.

- While chicken cooks, mix mayonnaise, yogurt, mustard, milk, salt, pepper, and thyme. Cube chicken and add to dressing; refrigerate.

- Cover potatoes with water; boil until tender, about 18–23 minutes. Cool 20 minutes; peel and cube.

- Add potatoes to the salad as you work. Add green onion, celery, and bell pepper; cover and chill 3–4 hours.

Roasted Potato Chicken Salad

Make recipe as directed, except omit the red potatoes. Scrub and cube 3 pounds russet potatoes. Place in roasting pan; drizzle with 2 tablespoons olive oil. Roast potatoes at 400ºF for 55–65 minutes until tender. Add to salad along with vegetables.

Slow Cooker Chicken Potato Salad

Place 6 cubed russet potatoes and 1 chopped onion in a 4-quart slow cooker; top with 4 boneless, skinless chicken breasts. Add 1 cup chicken broth; cover and cook on low 7–8 hours. Make dressing as directed; drain potatoes and chicken and add along with vegetables. Cover and chill.

Mix Dressing

- The creamy dressing should be about the consistency of pancake batter or cake batter.

- Add more milk or more mayonnaise to reach the desired consistency; it shouldn't be too thick.

- It's a good idea to make more dressing and reserve it, well covered, in the refrigerator.

- You can add it at serving time if the salad seems a bit dry; the chicken and potatoes absorb the dressing as they cool.

Mix Salad

- Gently mix the hot potatoes into the salad. The potatoes will break up a bit, but should remain mostly intact.

- You can add other vegetables to this fresh-tasting salad. Try adding corn just cut off the cob and grape tomatoes.

- Sliced mushrooms, yellow summer squash, or more bell peppers are great additions.

- This salad should be made ahead of time so the flavors have a chance to blend and develop.

CHICKEN SALADS

CHICKEN MARSALA

Chicken braised in Marsala wine and mushrooms is an elegant dish

Chicken Marsala is a classic Italian recipe that combines chicken with Marsala wine for a rich and delicious dish.

Chicken cooked in wine is exceptionally tender and rich tasting. The acids in the wine help break down the fibers in the meat as it cooks.

Not all of the alcohol cooks off in this dish, so be warned if you are serving those who do not or cannot imbibe.

The classic recipe adds mushrooms to the dish. The mushrooms soak up the flavor of the wine and add an earthy, smoky flavor. You can use any variety of mushrooms you'd like.

Serve this dish with hot cooked egg noodles tossed with butter and some fresh chopped oregano to soak up all the delicious sauce. *Yield: Serves 4–6*

Ingredients

4 slices bacon

8 boneless, skinless chicken thighs, cut into strips

$1/4$ cup flour

$1/2$ teaspoon salt

$1/8$ teaspoon pepper

1 teaspoon dried oregano

2 onions, chopped

3 cloves garlic, minced

1 (8-ounce) package cremini mushrooms, sliced

1 cup sliced shiitake mushrooms

1 cup Marsala wine

2 tablespoons cornstarch

$1/2$ cup chicken broth

Chicken Marsala

- Cook bacon until crisp; drain, crumble, and set aside. Drain pan; do not wipe out.

- Dredge chicken in flour, salt, pepper, and oregano; brown 5–6 minutes; remove from pan.

- Add onions and garlic to pan; cook. Place in 4-quart slow cooker with mushrooms.

- Top with chicken and bacon; pour wine over. Cover and cook on low 7–9 hours until chicken is tender. Add cornstarch mixed with broth; cook on high 10 minutes.

•••••••••• *GREEN* ● *LIGHT* ••••••••••

Marsala wine is a fortified wine. That means that hard liquor, usually some type of brandy, is added to the wine. This makes the wine richer and also makes it last longer. You can buy sweet or dry Marsala in wine shops; either is good in this recipe.

Brown Chicken

- It's important to brown the chicken before cooking it in the slow cooker to develop the flavor.

- The flour needs to be cooked too, so it will readily absorb the liquid in the slow cooker.

- Don't cook the chicken completely; just let it brown until it has some color.

- Use thick-cut bacon if you want it to be prominent in the stew; thin-cut if you want it to dissolve in the stew.

Layer Ingredients in Slow Cooker

- The vegetables go in the bottom of the slow cooker because they take longer to cook than the chicken.

- The mushrooms and onions will give off liquid as they cook.

- Remember, there's no evaporation when slow cooking, so don't add more liquid.

- To check on the doneness, twirl the lid of the slow cooker to remove condensation rather than lifting the lid.

BRUNSWICK STEW
This classic southern dish is rich with vegetables and herbs

Brunswick Stew originated in the southern United States, particularly in Georgia and Virginia, but no one is sure who created it first. It is made with lima beans, onion, corn, and other vegetables. One thing historians do agree on: the original stew used ingredients like rabbit or squirrel. In these areas of the country in the nineteenth century, many people relied on hunted meats to feed their family.

The stew is very rich and thick with vegetables. You can add other vegetables if you'd like. Okra is a natural addition, as are sliced mushrooms.

Chicken thighs, with their rich taste, are the natural meat to use in this stew, but you can use chicken breasts if you'd like. *Yield: Serves 6–8*

Ingredients

2 tablespoons butter

1 tablespoon olive oil

3 pounds bone-in, skin-on chicken thighs

$1/3$ cup flour

1 teaspoon salt

$1/4$ teaspoon cayenne pepper

2 onions, chopped

3 cloves garlic, minced

1 green bell pepper, chopped

3 stalks celery, sliced

2 (14.5-ounce) cans diced tomatoes, undrained

3 cups chicken broth

$1/2$ cup chili sauce

2 cups frozen corn

2 cups frozen lima beans

Brunswick Stew

- Melt butter and olive oil in large pan. Dredge chicken in flour, salt, and pepper; brown in pan; remove.

- Add onions to pan; cook and stir 4–5 minutes. Place in 4-quart slow cooker with chicken, garlic, bell pepper, celery, tomatoes, broth, and chili sauce.

- Cover and cook on low for 7 hours. Remove chicken and shred. Return to slow cooker with corn and lima beans.

- Cover and cook on low 1–2 hours longer until stew is hot and blended.

•••• RECIPE VARIATIONS ••••

Stovetop Brunswick Stew

Make recipe as directed, except when the onions are browned, don't remove from the pan. Add the chicken and all of the remaining ingredients. Bring to a simmer, then cover pan, reduce heat to low, and simmer for 75–80 minutes until chicken is tender and stew is thickened.

Cheese Drop Biscuits

In bowl, combine $1\frac{1}{2}$ cups all-purpose flour, $\frac{1}{2}$ cup whole wheat flour, 1 cup shredded cheddar cheese, $\frac{1}{4}$ cup grated Parmesan cheese, 2 teaspoons baking powder, and $\frac{1}{2}$ teaspoon baking soda. Cut in $\frac{1}{2}$ cup butter, then add 1 cup buttermilk. Drop onto greased baking sheet. Bake 450°F 12–17 minutes until golden. Serve warm.

Layer Ingredients in Slow Cooker

- Trim excess fat from the chicken before you dredge it in the flour.

- The chicken is browned to add flavor, and the onions are cooked to help remove the drippings from the pan.

- The onions also need a head-start in order to become soft and mellow in the stew.

- Be sure to layer the ingredients in the slow cooker in the order provided.

Shred Chicken

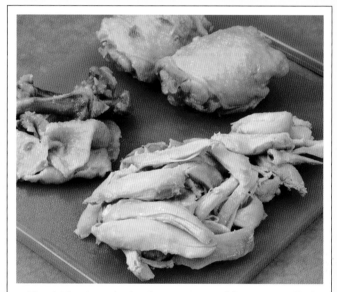

- The chicken is cooked with the bone in and skin on to add more flavor to the stew.

- This also helps keep the meat very moist as it cooks, since the skin adds fat.

- Be careful to remove all of the bones from the chicken. Shred the chicken using 2 forks or your hands.

- The chicken will be very tender. If it seems a little dry to you, drizzle with 1-2 tablespoons broth before returning it to the slow cooker.

SLOW COOKER POSOLE

Usually made with pork, this version with chicken is just as rich and flavorful

Posole is a soup or stew from Mexico, typically made with a pork roast. Chicken makes a nice change, resulting in a lighter dish.

The recipe always includes hominy, or processed corn, chile peppers, and some type of beans. Refried beans add a richness, thickness, and depth of flavor to the stew.

The slow cooker is a great way to cook posole, because it can cook unattended for hours to develop the flavor.

Posole (also known as Pozole) is quite spicy, but you can make a milder dish by reducing or eliminating the jalapeños, using a mild salsa, and reducing the cayenne pepper. *Yield: Serves 6*

Ingredients

2 onions, chopped

4 cloves garlic, minced

2 tablespoons olive oil

2 jalapeño peppers, minced

2 pounds boneless, skinless chicken thighs

1 tablespoon chili powder

1 teaspoon cumin

1 teaspoon paprika

1/4 teaspoon cayenne pepper

1 teaspoon salt

2 (15-ounce) cans hominy, drained

1 cup salsa

2 cups chicken broth

1 (8-ounce) can tomato sauce

1 (15-ounce) can refried beans

1/3 cup chopped cilantro

1 cup sour cream

2 avocados, peeled and chopped

2 tomatoes, chopped

Slow Cooker Posole

- In pan, cook onion and garlic in olive oil 4–5 minutes. Place in 4-quart slow cooker with jalapeños.

- Cut chicken into strips and toss with chili powder, cumin, paprika, cayenne pepper, and salt; add to slow cooker.

- Top with hominy, salsa, tomato sauce, and refried beans. Cover and cook on low 7–8 hours until chicken is done.

- Stir well, sprinkle with cilantro, and serve with sour cream, chopped avocados, and chopped tomatoes, if desired.

ZOOM

Hominy is made from corn that has had its hull, or bran and germ, removed. The hard kernels of corn are soaked in a weak lye solution to separate the hull from the rest of the grain. Hominy is quite soft and the lye treatment makes some of the corn nutrients more available for digestion.

Prepare Ingredients

- You can cook the onions and garlic until they start to turn brown for a richer flavor.

- Trim excess fat from the chicken thighs before you cut them into strips and toss with the spice mixture.

- Hominy just needs to be drained. Don't rinse it or you'll rinse away some of the flavor.

- The salsa you choose can be purchased or home-made, mild, medium, or spicy in heat.

Add Ingredients to Slow Cooker

- You can find hominy in the canned foods aisle of the supermarket. You may have to look for it in the international foods aisle.

- White hominy is made from white corn, and yellow hominy from yellow. Yellow hominy is sweeter.

- It may be helpful to combine the tomato sauce and refried beans in a small bowl with some of the broth.

- Mix together until smooth, then stir into the remaining ingredients in the slow cooker.

185

CHICKEN ADOBO

The national dish of the Philippines, this recipe is easy to make in the slow cooker

Adobo is the Spanish word for "marinade" or "sauce." There are many varieties of this recipe in the Spanish cultures.

Adobo is a stew made with chiles, meat, and rice. It's also a condiment made with chile peppers, vinegar, and garlic. Chipotle peppers in adobo are one variation of the condiment.

Adobo has a rich and deep flavor from long cooking time and a complex combination of ingredients.

Adobo can also refer to chicken cooked with vinegar and lots of garlic. In this recipe, the chicken is cooked in a slow cooker until very tender, and then the juices are used to cook rice to serve with the chicken. *Yield: Serves 4*

Ingredients

1 (3-pound) frying chicken, cut into serving pieces

$1/4$ cup soy sauce

$1/4$ cup white vinegar

$1/4$ cup red wine vinegar

2 tablespoons brown sugar

$1/3$ cup coconut milk

2 cups chicken broth

10 cloves garlic, minced

2 onions, chopped

2 bay leaves

$1/8$ teaspoon cayenne pepper

$1/8$ teaspoon pepper

$1\,1/2$ cups long-grain white rice

Chicken Adobo

- Place chicken in 4- or 5-quart slow cooker. In bowl, mix soy sauce, white vinegar, red wine vinegar, and brown sugar.

- Add remaining ingredients except rice and mix well. Pour vinegar mixture over the chicken.

- Cover and cook on low for 7–9 hours until chicken is very tender. Remove chicken to 375ºF oven; bake to crisp skin while preparing rice.

- Pour 3 cups liquid into pan; add rice. Simmer 15–20 minutes until rice is tender; serve with chicken.

• • • • RECIPE VARIATIONS • • • •

Slow Cooker Adobo Stew
Make recipe as directed, except use 1¹/₂ pounds bone-less, skinless chicken thighs. Add 2 cups frozen sweet corn, 1 (14.5-ounce) can of diced tomatoes, undrained, and 1 cup chopped celery. Cover and cook on low 8–9 hours. Add ¹/₂ cup white rice; cover and cook on high 20–30 minute until tender.

Grilled Chicken Adobo
Substitute 3 pounds of bone-in, skin-on chicken thighs. Combine all other ingredients except rice; simmer for 50 minutes; let cool. Add chicken; marinate overnight in refrigerator. Remove bay leaves and start simmering sauce. Grill chicken 30–40 minutes over medium coals until done; serve with sauce.

Cook Chicken in Slow Cooker

- This recipe can be made with any combination of bone-in, skin-on chicken parts.

- Lots of garlic is essential to this recipe. If you don't like garlic, you can leave it out but the dish won't be the same.

- Other vegetables like chopped green bell pepper or chopped mushrooms can be added.

- When you remove the chicken from the slow cooker, use a sieve to remove any small pieces.

Cook Rice with Juices

- Strain the liquid before adding the rice so there are no small bones in the mixture.

- Cooking rice using the juice the chicken was cooked in is a wonderful way to use all of the flavors in this dish.

- You can also simmer the juices in a saucepan until thickened and serve with the chicken as a sauce.

- Any liquid left over after cooking the rice can be reduced and spooned over the chicken as a glaze.

187

MOROCCAN CHICKEN
Chicken slow cooked with lots of spices and squash makes an excellent meal

The spices of Morocco add wonderful flavor and color to slow-cooked chicken. This recipe is really more of a stew than chicken with sauce and vegetables.

Morocco and other North African nations use spices liberally in their cooking. Lots of turmeric, cinnamon, curry powder, and peppers make this style of cooking distinct.

This recipe is similar to a tagine, which is named after the clay pot in which it is cooked. The pot has low sides and is wide and flat. This shape holds steam in as the food cooks, concentrating the flavors. *Yield: Serves 6*

Ingredients

2 pounds boneless, skinless chicken thighs

2 tablespoons lemon juice

1 teaspoon cinnamon

1/2 teaspoon turmeric

1 teaspoon cumin

2 teaspoons curry powder

1 teaspoon salt

1/4 teaspoon cayenne pepper

2 tablespoons butter

1 onion, chopped

4 cloves garlic, minced

1 butternut squash, peeled and cubed

1 cup chopped dried apricots

1 (14.5-ounce) can diced tomatoes, undrained

1 cup chicken broth

2 tablespoons cornstarch

1/3 cup coconut milk

1/3 cup chopped cilantro

Moroccan Chicken

- Cut chicken into strips. Sprinkle with lemon juice. Mix cinnamon, turmeric, cumin, curry powder, salt, and pepper; toss with chicken.

- Melt butter in pan; cook onion and garlic 5 minutes. Place in 4-quart slow cooker with squash and apricots.

- Place chicken on top of squash. Pour tomatoes and broth over. Cover and cook on low 7–8 hours until chicken is tender.

- Mix cornstarch and coconut milk; add to slow cooker. Cover; cook on high 15 minutes. Sprinkle with cilantro.

• • • • RECIPE VARIATION • • • •

Cilantro Rice

Cook 1 chopped onion in 2 tablespoons olive oil. Add 1 teaspoon cumin, $\frac{1}{4}$ teaspoon cayenne pepper, and 2 cups long-grain white rice; cook 2 minutes. Add 4 cups chicken broth; cover and simmer until tender, 20 minutes. Add $\frac{1}{2}$ cup chopped fresh cilantro and serve.

• • • • • • • • • • *GREEN ● LIGHT* • • • • • • • • • •

Turmeric is proving to be a very healthy spice. This bright yellow powder is made from the root of a plant similar to ginger. Curcumin, a component of the powder, has been found to have strong anti-cancer properties and may help reduce the risk of Alzheimer's disease.

Toss Chicken with Spices

- You can vary the combination and types of spices you use in this recipe to your own taste.

- Other spices to use include saffron, ground ginger, paprika, and other types of peppers.

- You can also add golden raisins, chopped apples or pears, prunes, or dates in addition to or instead of the other fruits.

- For more flavor, you can marinate the chicken in the spice mixture, in the refrigerator, for several hours.

Layer Ingredients in Slow Cooker

- The onion, garlic, squash, and apricots have to be placed in the bottom of the slow cooker.

- These foods cook more slowly than the chicken, so they turn out better if placed right next to the heat source.

- The liquid in this recipe, which will cover the vegetables, will also help them cook until tender.

- The apricots and other dried fruits, if you use them, will plump during the long slow cooking time and become very tender.

189

BARBECUED CHICKEN

Chicken slow cooked in a spicy barbecue sauce is fall-apart tender

Barbecued chicken cooked in the slow cooker may seem like a contradiction in terms. Barbecued meats are typically cooked over charcoal or wood for long periods of time, basting with a spicy sauce.

But barbecue can be cooked in the oven or in the slow cooker. It's the long, slow cooking time that's most important for the development of flavors.

Many people have their own favorite barbecue sauce; by all means, use that in this recipe. About 2 cups of the sauce will cook and glaze the chicken nicely.

As always, season the sauce to your taste. Use more or less chili powder, more chile peppers, more mustard, or more lemon juice to make the recipe your own. *Yield: Serves 6*

Ingredients

1 tablespoon olive oil

1 onion, chopped

4 cloves garlic, minced

2 jalapeño peppers, minced

1 tablespoon chili powder

1 teaspoon curry powder

1 teaspoon dry mustard

$^1/_3$ cup cider vinegar

1 (8-ounce) can no-salt-added tomato sauce

$^1/_4$ cup brown sugar

2 tablespoons lemon juice

12 boneless, skinless chicken thighs

Barbecued Chicken

- In saucepan, heat olive oil. Cook onion, garlic, and jalapeño peppers 5–6 minutes until tender.

- Add chili powder and curry powder; cook 2–3 minutes longer. Add remaining ingredients except chicken; simmer 15 minutes.

- Put chicken in 3½-quart slow cooker; pour sauce over.

- Cover and cook on low 7–9 hours until chicken is very tender. Cook, uncovered, on high 20 minutes until sauce is thickened.

···· RECIPE VARIATIONS ····

BBQ Chicken Breasts
Make recipe as directed, except use 6–8 bone-in, skin-on chicken breasts. Brown the chicken breasts, skin side down, in the oil before placing in the slow cooker. Cover and cook on low for 7–8 hours until chicken is tender and thoroughly cooked.

Slow Cooker Grilled Chicken
Cook vegetables in oil. Add remaining ingredients except chicken and simmer for 1 hour until thickened. Refrigerate sauce. Place chicken in slow cooker with 1 cup broth; cover and cook on low 7 hours. Drain chicken and cook on grill, brushing with sauce, until glazed, about 10–15 minutes.

Simmer Sauce

- You can simmer the barbecue sauce for hours, adding more chicken broth as necessary.

- But since the sauce cooks in the slow cooker along with the chicken, this classic step isn't really necessary.

- If you want to use a purchased barbecue sauce, add fresh herbs like oregano and parsley to jazz up the flavor.

- You can add as many chicken thighs as you'd like to the slow cooker as long as there is enough sauce.

Place Chicken in Slow Cooker

- Fill the slow cooker ½ to ¾ full for best results. If it is less than ½ full, the food can burn.

- If the appliance is more than ¾ full of food, the food may not get hot enough to cook through in the specified time.

- You also run the risk of the slow cooker overflowing. Remember, there is no evaporation in this appliance.

- The food will release water and juices into the slow cooker, adding to the liquid level.

ROASTED GARLIC CORNISH HENS

Tender little game hens, roasted with garlic and wine, are perfect for a party

Cornish hens are not a game bird, but are simply smaller chickens. The name comes from the original cross-breeding between Cornish hens and White Rock hens. The small birds are no larger than two pounds.

The hens first appeared in the market in the 1960s, most probably to appeal to the growing interest in gourmet cuisine. The little hens do have gourmet status and are usually only served for entertaining.

Cornish Hens can be flavored in many ways. Because their meat is so mild, they pair well with everything from herbs and garlic to exotic spices and fruit. *Yield: Serves 6*

Ingredients

3 tablespoons butter

6 cloves garlic, minced

1¹/₂ teaspoons salt, divided

6 Cornish game hens

2 tablespoons olive oil

¹/₄ teaspoon pepper

1 teaspoon paprika

1 teaspoon dried thyme leaves

2 lemons, sliced, divided

12 cloves garlic, whole

6 sprigs thyme

1 cup dry white wine

Roasted Garlic Cornish Hens

- Melt butter in pan; add minced garlic; cook 3 minutes.

- Remove from heat and add ¾ teaspoon salt. Loosen skin from hens; rub mixture under skin; smooth skin back over flesh.

- Drizzle hens with olive oil; sprinkle with remaining salt, pepper, paprika, and dried thyme.

- Place half of lemon slices, whole garlic, and thyme in cavity. Place remaining lemons on hens; pour wine over. Roast at 350ºF 55–65 minutes.

• • • • RECIPE VARIATIONS • • • •

Caramelized Onion Game Hens

Make recipe as directed, except add 1 chopped onion to the minced garlic; cook until the onion mixture is browned, about 15 minutes. Rub this mixture under the skin of the hens. Stuff the hens with quartered onions, lemon, and thyme and proceed with recipe as directed.

Roast Cornish Hens

Make recipe as directed, except omit garlic. Don't rub anything in between the skin and the flesh of the birds. Cover the hens with the lemon and pour wine over; roast as directed. You can use the lemon and thyme to stuff the birds, or use oranges and oregano.

Stuff Hens

Baste Hens

- Most Cornish hens are sold frozen. Defrost according to the package directions, or thaw in the refrigerator for 24 hours.

- If you find fresh hens, use or freeze them within 1 day, as they are very perishable.

- You can stuff the hens with other ingredients too. Try orange slices and fresh marjoram, or apple slices and fresh basil.

- Or just stuff them with lemon slices, which will add plenty of flavor with less work.

- Baste the hens at least once during cooking time. Work quickly so the hens don't cool down.

- You can use a baster or a spoon to drizzle liquid over the chicken.

- A baster is made of a bulb that is squeezed to pull liquid up into the cylinder.

- When the hens come out of the oven, cover to keep warm and let stand for 10–15 minutes to let the juices redistribute.

193

TEX-MEX CORNISH HENS
The spices of the Southwest flavor tender game hens

Tex-Mex ingredients include chile peppers, chili powder, cumin, dried chiles, corn, masa harina, and adobo. Mild little Cornish hens soak up these flavorings for an excellent result.

Since the meat is so mild, it takes lots of spices to add significant flavor, but adjust the spice amounts and flavoring ingredients to your own taste level.

You can marinate the chicken after it's rubbed with the spices for a more intense flavor. Cover and refrigerate for 8–24 hours. Make sure the spice mixture is cool before you rub it on the hens.

Serve these spicy little birds with rice cooked with tomatoes and herbs, a green salad made with avocados, and ice cream sundaes for dessert. *Yield: Serves 4*

Ingredients

4 Cornish game hens

2 onions, peeled and sliced

1/4 cup minced onion

4 cloves garlic, minced

2 tablespoons olive oil

2 tablespoons lemon juice

2 chipotle chiles, minced

2 tablespoons adobo sauce

1 tablespoon chili powder

1/2 teaspoon cumin

1 teaspoon salt

1/4 teaspoon pepper

1 cup chicken broth

Tex-Mex Cornish Hens

- Place hens in roasting pan on top of sliced onions. In separate pan, cook minced onion and garlic in olive oil until tender, about 7 minutes.

- Remove from heat; add lemon juice, chipotle chiles, adobo sauce, chili powder, cumin, salt, and pepper.

- Rub half of this mixture under skin of hens; smooth skin back over flesh. Rub remaining mixture into skins.

- Pour broth into pan, then roast hens at 375ºF 55–65 minutes until hens are done.

•••• RECIPE VARIATION ••••

Chili Cornish Hens
Make recipe as directed, except omit chili powder and cumin. Add 1 minced jalapeño pepper, 1 minced habanero pepper, and ¼ teaspoon crushed red pepper flakes to the minced onion mixture. Serve the hens with ½ cup salsa mixed with ½ cup sour cream.

ZOOM

A Cornish hen usually serves one person, since the meat to bone ratio is fairly low. But you can cut the hens in half if they are larger. The bones are fairly soft, so it's easy to cut them in half, starting at the center of the breast and working through the bird.

Rub Onion Mixture on Hens

- It can be difficult to loosen the skin from the hens. Work slowly and be careful not to tear the skin.

- You can vary the rub as much as you'd like. Omit the onions, increase the garlic, or use lime juice instead of lemon juice.

- Use fresh jalapeño peppers instead of the chipotle peppers, and use 1 teaspoon chile paste for the adobo.

- Rub the mixture into the skin gently but firmly. It will add color as well as flavor to the birds.

Roast Hens

- Roast the hens until a meat thermometer inserted into the thigh registers 170°F.

- It can be difficult to insert the meat thermometer without hitting a bone; insert it about ½ inch.

- When the hens are done, cover with foil to keep warm and let stand for 10 minutes.

- This will let the juices redistribute so every bite is moist and tender.

SPATCHCOCKED HENS

Hens, split in half and grilled with a lemon mustard marinade, are delicious

Spatchcocking is a preparation technique that describes cutting chickens in half and flattening them so they cook evenly on the grill. The term probably began in Ireland. Another word for this technique is "butterflying."

Other chickens are more difficult to prepare, but the little hens cut easily and flatten easily, so this recipe is a good choice for beginning cooks. Because the hens are flat, they will grill more quickly than whole hens, and the meat will be tender and juicy.

The birds are also easier to eat, since they will sit flat on the plate. You can also stuff the hens by placing any stuffing mixture between the skin and the flesh. *Yield: Serves 4*

Ingredients

4 Cornish game hens

4 cloves garlic, minced

1 teaspoons salt

1/4 teaspoon pepper

1 teaspoon paprika

2 tablespoons olive oil

2 tablespoons lemon juice

1 teaspoon lemon zest

1/4 cup Dijon mustard

Spatchcocked Hens

- Place hens, breast side down, on work surface. Using shears, cut along both sides of backbone; reserve for stock.

- Place hens breast side up on work surface. Flatten chicken with hands.

- Mash garlic with salt and pepper until a paste forms. Add paprika, olive oil, lemon juice, zest, and mustard; mix well.

- Rub into both sides of hens; cover and chill 3–4 hours. Grill hens, skin side down, 15 minutes. Turn and grill 15–20 minutes longer until done.

Curried Spatchcocked Hens

Make recipe as directed, except omit mustard and paprika from rub. Add 1 tablespoon curry powder and 1 teaspoon brown sugar. Marinate hens in the refrigerator and then grill as directed. Serve with mango or blueberry chutney.

Stuffed Spatchcocked Hens

Make any of your favorite stuffing recipes, allowing about ³/₄ cup per bird. After the hens are flattened, loosen the skin from the flesh. Spoon the stuffing under the skin, then smooth the skin back over the meat. Grill as directed, moving hens to cooler part of grill as necessary.

Flatten Hens

- A good pair of sturdy kitchen shears or poultry shears is needed for this procedure.

- You don't need to press very hard to flatten the chicken, but you do need to break the breastbone.

- When you have succeeded, you'll hear a snapping sound and the bird will flatten.

- You can save the backbones in the freezer and use them to make stock, along with other chicken trimmings.

Grill Chicken

- You have to watch the hens closely when they are on the grill. If they start turning dark, move them to a cooler spot.

- The skin will be much crispier, since more of it is exposed directly to the heat of the grill.

- Be careful to not overcook the birds. Use a meat thermometer and check the temperature frequently.

- Because these birds look bigger than whole Cornish hens, you can cut them in half and serve two people apiece.

STUFFED CORNISH HENS

Cornish hens stuffed with a savory wild rice mixture are fit for company

Stuffed Cornish Hens are a special recipe perfect for entertaining. You can stuff them with any sweet or savory mixture, using bread, rice, or sausage.

There isn't a lot of room for stuffing in these little birds, but you can usually fit about a cup of stuffing into the cavity of each, which makes a good serving.

Just as with turkey, stuff the hens just before you put them in the oven. For food safety reasons, never stuff the birds ahead of time.

You can substitute brown rice for the wild rice, or use two cups of stuffing mix or dried bread cubes. *Yield: Serves 4*

Ingredients

¹/₄ cup butter, divided

¹/₂ cup chopped onion

4 cloves garlic, minced, divided

1 stalk celery, sliced

²/₃ cup uncooked wild rice

2¹/₂ cups chicken broth, divided

¹/₂ teaspoon salt

¹/₈ teaspoon pepper

¹/₃ cup dried cranberries

2 tablespoons Dijon mustard

1 tablespoon fresh thyme

4 Cornish game hens

¹/₂ teaspoon paprika

¹/₂ teaspoon poultry seasoning

Stuffed Cornish Hens

- Melt 2 tablespoons butter; cook onion and half the garlic until tender. Add celery, wild rice, 1½ cups broth, salt, and pepper.

- Simmer for 40–45 minutes until rice is tender. Remove from heat; add cranberries, mustard, and thyme.

- Stuff hens with the rice mixture. Place on rack in roasting pan.

- Cook remaining garlic in remaining butter; add paprika and poultry seasoning and brush on hens. Pour remaining broth into pan. Roast at 375ºF 70–80 minutes, basting often.

Greek Stuffed Hens

Make recipe as directed, except substitute long-grain brown rice for the wild rice. Omit cranberries and thyme; add 2 teaspoons fresh oregano leaves and $^1/_3$ cup chopped kalamata olives along with $^1/_4$ cup crumbled feta cheese. Add 2 tablespoons lemon juice to the basting mixture.

Fruit-Stuffed Hens

Make recipe as directed, except use $1^1/_2$ cups dried stuffing cubes in place of the rice. Add $^1/_3$ cup chopped dried apricots and $^1/_3$ cup dried currants. Moisten the stuffing mixture with about $^1/_3$ cup apricot nectar. Stuff hens and roast as directed.

Mix Stuffing

- You can make the stuffing ahead of time, but don't stuff the hens until you're ready to bake them.

- Rinse the hens and pat dry before adding the stuffing. Make sure that the interior is dry.

- Spoon the stuffing lightly into the cavity of each hen; don't pack.

- The stuffing will expand as it cooks, and if there's too much in the birds, they will split.

Roast Hens

- Brush the butter mixture evenly on the hens just before they go into the oven.

- There should be some left over; save in the refrigerator until it's time to baste the hens.

- These hens are a nice change from stuffed turkey during the holidays.

- Allow 1 hen per person for a holiday meal. Set the table with sharp knives so your guests can carve the birds easily.

199

LEMON GRILLED HENS
Little hens are grilled until smoky and tender

Lemon is a natural partner for grilled chicken. Lemon juice and zest are both used, for different reasons. Lemon juice is more astringent and spreads the flavor around. And zest contains aromatic oils, which intensify the flavor.

When you're preparing the grill to cook whole Cornish hens, make sure to build a graduated fire, or prepare an indirect fire with a drip pan in place of some of the coals. The hens will probably need to be moved around on the grill so they don't overcook or burn.

Stuff the hens with some quartered lemons for even more flavor.

Serve these hens with potato salad, some grilled corn on the cob, and an ice cream pie for dessert. *Yield: Serves 4*

Ingredients

1 onion, chopped

3 cloves garlic, minced

$1/4$ cup olive oil

$1/3$ cup lemon juice

2 teaspoons grated lemon zest

2 tablespoons honey

1 teaspoon salt

$1/4$ teaspoon pepper

1 teaspoon dried basil

1 teaspoon dried oregano

4 Cornish game hens

Lemon Grilled Hens

- In saucepan, cook onion and garlic in olive oil until tender. Let cool 15 minutes, then place in food processor.

- Add lemon juice, zest, honey, salt, pepper, basil, and oregano and process until smooth; pour into large pan or bowl.

- Add hens; turn to coat. Cover and marinate in fridge 8–24 hours.

- Drain hens; reserve marinade. Grill over medium heat 55–65 minutes, brushing with remaining marinade, until 170°F. Let stand 10 minutes; discard remaining marinade.

Citrus Grilled Hens

Make recipe as directed, except use a combination of orange juice, lemon juice, and grapefruit juice to equal $1/2$ cup. Use 1 teaspoon each of the grated zest. Omit the onion and increase garlic to 5 cloves. Stuff hens with orange slices and grill as directed.

• • • • • • • • • • GREEN ● LIGHT • • • • • • • • • • •

Choose lemons that are heavy for their size, with thin skins for the most juice and flavor. The lemons should be firm, not puffy, with no soft spots or bruises. Wash the lemons before you remove the skin, and remove only the bright yellow part of the skin.

Make Marinade

- Process the onion and garlic mixture until smooth, because otherwise the bits of onion would burn on the grill.

- The onions and garlic can be cooked until tender, or caramelize them for additional flavor.

- When the onions are caramelized, they will be golden brown. Don't let them burn.

- You can make the marinade ahead of time and refrigerate it; add to the hens and marinate, then grill.

Grill Hens

- Let the hens stand on the grill rack until they release easily. Then turn and brown on the second side.

- Turn the hens frequently after that, and check their temperature after 50 minutes.

- As soon as the temperature reaches 170ºF, remove the hens and cover with foil.

- Let stand to let the juices redistribute. This also makes the hens easier to carve.

APRICOT CORNISH HENS
Apricots add a sweet and tart note to the tender hens

Apricots add an elegant touch to these special little birds. The fruit is sweet and tart, with a honey perfume. The mixture, which is high in sugar, glazes the birds and creates a shiny crust.

Both apricot nectar, found in the juice aisle of the supermarket, and apricot preserves are used in this easy recipe. The nectar creates the marinade, and the preserves thicken the glaze so it coats the hens. Since the apricots have an excellent balance of sweet and tart, the finished product isn't overly sweet.

Serve this dish with a spinach salad made with sliced canned apricots, raspberries, toasted almonds, and a raspberry vinaigrette, and glazed baby carrots. A chocolate cake is the perfect dessert. *Yield: Serves 4*

KNACK CHICKEN CLASSICS

Ingredients

1 cup apricot nectar

2 tablespoons honey

2 tablespoons cider vinegar

2 tablespoons grated onion

1 clove garlic, minced

1 teaspoon salt

$^1/_4$ teaspoon pepper

4 Cornish game hens

$^1/_2$ cup apricot preserves

2 tablespoons mustard

2 tablespoons butter, melted

1 tablespoon fresh thyme

Apricot Cornish Hens

- In large casserole, combine nectar, honey, vinegar, onion, garlic, salt, and pepper. Add hens; turn to coat.

- Cover and refrigerate for 8–24 hours. When ready to cook, remove hens; reserve marinade.

- Combine preserves, mustard, butter, and thyme. Place hens in roasting pan; add 1 cup marinade.

- Bake at 350°F 30 minutes, then baste with half of the preserves mixture. Bake 20 minutes longer; baste with remaining mixture. Bake 15–20 minutes longer.

····· RECIPE VARIATIONS ·····

Orange Glazed Cornish Hens

Make recipe as directed, except substitute 1 cup orange juice for the apricot nectar and ½ cup orange marmalade for the apricot preserves. Use Dijon mustard in place of the regular mustard, and add 1 teaspoon dried thyme leaves to the marinade.

Plum Glazed Cornish Hens

Make recipe as directed, except use 1 cup plum nectar in place of the apricot nectar, and ½ cup plum preserves or jam in place of the apricot preserves. Use Dijon mustard and add 1 teaspoon dried marjoram leaves to the marinade.

Marinate Hens

- The marinade can be made ahead of time and stored in the refrigerator up to 2 days.

- You can marinate the hens longer than 24 hours, but don't marinate longer than 48 hours.

- Turn the hens several times in the marinade so the birds don't dry out.

- You can bake the hens directly on a roasting pan, or put them on a wire rack in the pan.

Baste Hens

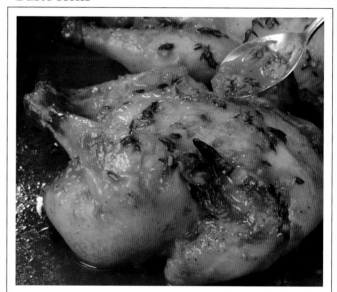

- If the pan starts to look dry halfway through the roasting time, add more marinade to the bottom of the pan.

- You can use any kind of mustard in the preserves glaze mixture.

- Coarse grained or brown mustard will make the mixture spicier, while Dijon mustard adds a sharp and tart flavor.

- Add some apricot halves to the pan during the last 30 minutes of cooking and serve them with the hens as an edible garnish.

STUFFED ROAST TURKEY

A turkey stuffed with a delicious mixture is traditional at Thanksgiving

A beautifully bronzed, stuffed roast turkey is on almost every American table the third Thursday in November.

Many cooks are intimidated by this large bird, but it's as easy to cook as a chicken. It doesn't take all day to cook, either; a maximum of five hours will ensure a juicy and well-done bird.

Some food safety experts recommend not stuffing the turkey. The stuffing does have to reach 165ºF, so don't pack it into the cavity; add loosely until the cavity is full. You can cook the stuffing in a slow cooker or in the oven; it's then called dressing.

Thaw the turkey in the refrigerator, never at room temperature. *Yield: Serves 10–12*

Ingredients

1 pound sweet Italian sausage

1/2 cup butter, divided

1 onion, chopped

3 cloves garlic, minced

3 stalks celery, sliced

1 apple, chopped

2 eggs

2 teaspoons salt, divided

1/4 teaspoon pepper

2 tablespoons chopped fresh sage

1 tablespoon minced fresh rosemary

1 teaspoon dried marjoram

2 tablespoons chopped parsley

5 cups cubed oatmeal bread

1/2 cup chicken broth

1 (13–15-pound) turkey, thawed

2 teaspoons paprika

Stuffed Roast Turkey

- Remove sausage from casings; cook, stirring to break up meat, until brown. Remove meat; drain pan; do not wipe.

- Add ¼ cup butter, onion, and garlic; cook 5 minutes. Add to sausage with celery, apple, eggs, 1 teaspoon salt, pepper, sage, rosemary, marjoram, and parsley.

- Add bread; add enough broth to moisten. Stuff neck and body cavity of turkey; place in roasting pan.

- Melt remaining butter; add remaining salt and paprika; pour over turkey. Roast 325ºF 4½–5½ hours.

Turkey from Frozen

Make recipe as directed, except cook the turkey frozen solid. Unwrap, rub with butter, and roast at 325ºF 4 hours. Remove from oven, remove giblets, stuff, and return turkey to the oven. Roast 3–4 hours longer until thermometer registers 180ºF.

Roast Turkey with Dressing

Make recipe as directed, except place the stuffing mixture in a 3- or 4-quart slow cooker. Stuff turkey with a lemon and onion, each cut in half. Place on roasting pan, baste with butter mixture, and roast at 325ºF for 3¹/₂–4¹/₂ hours until meat thermometer registers 175ºF.

Mix Stuffing

Stuff Turkey

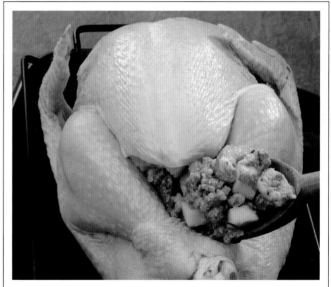

- Use your own favorite stuffing recipe if you have one. Stuffings can be savory or sweet.

- The stuffing mixture should be moist but not wet. The turkey interior is a very moist environment, and the turkey will release juices as it cooks.

- If the stuffing is too wet when you put it in the turkey, it will be gluey when it's cooked through.

- Never stuff the turkey ahead of time; stuff it only when you are ready to put it in the oven.

- If the bird is still frozen, even after days of thawing in the refrigerator, you can place it under cold running water.

- Don't turn off the water and don't use warm or hot water. The bird should thaw in 20–30 minutes.

- You can place the stuffing in the neck cavity and the body cavity of the turkey. Remove giblets and the turkey neck first.

- You can sew the cavities shut using cotton string, or place a slice of bread in the opening to seal.

TURKEY POT PIE

For leftover Thanksgiving turkey, this recipe is hearty and delicious

Turkey Pot Pie is pure comfort food. A flavorful mixture of moist and juicy turkey, tender vegetables, and a creamy sauce is topped with a flaky pastry and baked until bubbly.

You can use puff pastry to top the pie or use homemade Pie Crust or your own favorite pie pastry. It's important to cut slits in whichever pastry you use to top the pie so the steam can escape while the pie cooks.

Traditionally, pot pie has only a top crust, so it's easier for beginning cooks to make. You can use a top and bottom crust, but you'll need to use a 10-inch-diameter, deep-dish pie pan. Top the filling with the second crust, flute, and bake. *Yield: Serves 6*

Ingredients

- **2 tablespoons butter**
- **1 tablespoon olive oil**
- **1 onion, chopped**
- **3 cloves garlic, minced**
- **1 (8-ounce) package cremini mushrooms, sliced**
- **2 potatoes, peeled and cubed**
- **3 carrots, sliced**
- **2 stalks celery, sliced**
- **2 cups chicken broth**
- **3 tablespoons flour**
- **1/2 cup heavy cream**
- **1 teaspoon salt**
- **1/4 teaspoon pepper**
- **1 teaspoon dried basil**
- **2 tablespoons Dijon mustard**
- **3 cups cooked cubed turkey**
- **1 puff pastry sheet, thawed**

Turkey Pot Pie

- Melt butter and olive oil in saucepan; add onion and garlic; cook 5 minutes. Add mushrooms; cook 5–6 minutes.

- Add potatoes, carrots, and celery; cook 4 minutes, then add broth. Simmer 12–16 minutes until potatoes are tender.

- Combine flour, cream, salt, pepper, basil, and mustard; add to pan with turkey. Simmer until thickened.

- Pour mixture into 2½-quart casserole. Top with puff pastry, sealing edges. Bake at 375ºF 35–45 minutes until pie is bubbly and crust is golden brown.

Double Crust Turkey Pot Pie
Make recipe as directed, except cook mixture with mushrooms until liquid evaporates and mushrooms are deep brown. Line a 10-inch, deep-dish pie plate with 1 crust. Let filling cool for 45 minutes, then add to crust. Top with second crust, seal and flute edges, and cut vent holes.

Cheesy Turkey Pot Pie
Make recipe as directed, except add 1½ cups shredded Swiss cheese to the hot turkey mixture. Pour into casserole and top with puff pastry. Brush pastry with 1 egg beaten with 1 tablespoon water, and sprinkle with ¼ cup grated Parmesan cheese. Bake as directed.

Simmer Filling

Assemble Pie

- Cut the mushrooms, potatoes, carrots, and celery to about the same size.

- They will cook evenly and be easier to eat, and the finished pie will have a better appearance.

- For a rustic look, cut them into larger pieces or chunks. The larger pieces should simmer for 14–18 minutes until tender.

- Stir the mixture frequently as it simmers so the vegetables and the sauce don't burn.

- If you are using plain, or short, pastry, let the filling cool for 30–40 minutes before assembling the pie.

- Otherwise, the pie crust can melt and disappear into the pie as it cooks.

- You can fill and top the pie immediately if you are using puff pastry.

- Gently roll out the pastry on a floured surface, drape it over the casserole, and press to the sides to seal.

GRILLED TURKEY BREAST

A boneless turkey breast, cut in half, is grilled to juicy perfection

A turkey breast is easy to cook on the grill. This flavorful dish is a good choice for an alternative Thanksgiving or holiday menu.

Boneless breasts can be found in the supermarket, or you can remove the bone yourself. Just follow along against the bone with a sharp knife, cutting the meat away. Save the bone and skin for broth.

A boneless breast cooks in about 30 minutes on a medium grill, while a bone-in breast takes about 1½ hours.

Marinating or brining the turkey before cooking makes the turkey very juicy and flavorful. Brining is like marinating, except the mixture consists mostly of water, sugar, and salt. The brine literally makes the meat pull water into its cells, resulting in a juicy bird. *Yield: Serves 6–8*

Ingredients

- 3 tablespoons butter
- 1 tablespoon olive oil
- 1 tablespoon grated gingerroot
- 3 cloves garlic, minced
- 2 tablespoons lemon juice
- 2 tablespoons soy sauce
- 2 tablespoons honey
- 1 tablespoon fresh thyme
- ¼ teaspoon salt
- ¼ teaspoon pepper
- ½ teaspoon curry powder
- 1 boneless skin-on turkey breast

Grilled Turkey Breast

- Heat butter and olive oil in small pan. Add gingerroot and garlic; cook 2–3 minutes until fragrant.

- Pour into bowl; add lemon juice, soy sauce, honey, thyme, salt, pepper, and curry powder.

- Cut turkey breast in half through the center; add to marinade. Cover and refrigerate 8–24 hours.

- Prepare grill. Drain turkey, reserving marinade. Grill turkey, covered, skin side down, 15 minutes. Turn; brush with marinade; grill 15 minutes longer until 160°F.

Grilled Brined Bone-in Turkey Breast

Make brine by mixing 4 cups water, $1/3$ cup salt, and $1/4$ cup sugar until dissolved. Add turkey breast; refrigerate 12 hours. Remove breast, rinse, and pat dry. Rub with butter and olive oil and grill turkey over medium indirect coals 15–18 minutes per pound until temperature registers 160ºF.

Grilled BBQ Turkey Breast

Make your own barbecue sauce or use a favorite sauce. Use 1 cup to cover the turkey breast. Cover and marinate for 12–24 hours. When ready to cook, prepare grill for medium coals. Add the turkey and grill for 30–40 minutes, brushing occasionally with more barbecue sauce, until done.

Marinate Turkey

- Use your favorite flavors to marinate your turkey. You can use spicy Tex-Mex ingredients or curry powder.

- Greek ingredients like oregano, lemon juice, and olive oil make a nice marinade.

- When you remove the turkey from the marinade, be careful to drain out the cavity.

- Pat the turkey dry before adding it to the grill. And be sure that the grill rack is clean and lightly oiled.

Grill Turkey

- If you are using charcoal and grilling the turkey longer than 1 hour, you'll need to add 8–10 more briquettes after 1 hour to maintain heat.

- For indirect cooking, place a drip pan in the center of the grate; add coals around the edges. Place the turkey over the drip pan.

- This turkey is grilled with the skin on, but you can grill a skinless breast too.

- The skinless breast may cook for 5–10 minutes shorter cooking time. Be sure it doesn't burn.

TURKEY

GREEK STUFFED TENDERLOINS
Turkey tenderloins are stuffed with a rice and lemon mixture

Turkey tenderloins are easy to stuff. The meat is very tender and easy to work with and is boneless.

A small, tough piece of white tendon often runs through the tenderloin. This should cook down to nothing, but you can cut it out and discard it before preparing the tenderloin.

There are a couple of ways to stuff the tenderloins. First, cut each one in half crosswise. You can then cut them in half and open up like a book, or cut a pocket in the wide side of each tenderloin.

This elegant, easy-to-make recipe should be served with a wild rice pilaf, a fruited spinach salad, some breadsticks, and a fruit pie for dessert. *Yield: Serves 6*

Ingredients

¹/₂ cup chopped onion

2 cloves garlic, minced

1 tablespoon olive oil

¹/₃ cup long-grain rice

¹/₄ teaspoon salt

1 cup chicken broth

¹/₂ cup baby spinach leaves

1 teaspoon dried oregano

3 tablespoons lemon juice

¹/₂ teaspoon grated lemon zest

¹/₂ cup crumbled feta cheese

4 turkey tenderloins

1 cup dried breadcrumbs

3 tablespoons flour

¹/₄ cup grated Parmesan cheese

¹/₂ teaspoon salt

¹/₈ teaspoon pepper

2 eggs, beaten

Greek Stuffed Tenderloins

- Cook onion and garlic in olive oil 5 minutes. Add rice and salt; cook 2 minutes; add broth; simmer 20 minutes.

- Add spinach; cook 2 minutes. Add oregano, lemon juice, zest, and feta cheese.

- Cut tenderloins in half crosswise; cut each in half lengthwise to ½ inch of opposite side; open.

- Stuff with rice mixture; close tenderloins; secure with toothpick. Mix crumbs, flour, cheese, salt, and pepper. Dip turkey in eggs, then crumbs. Bake at 325ºF 40–45 minutes, turning once, until done.

210

Bacon Stuffed Tenderloins

Make recipe as directed, except start stuffing with 6 slices bacon, crisply cooked. Drain and crumble bacon; drain pan. Increase onion to 1 cup; omit rice, chicken broth, oregano, lemon juice, zest, spinach, and feta cheese. Add 1 (10-ounce) package frozen thawed drained spinach and 2 cups shredded Swiss cheese.

Cordon Bleu Tenderloins

Make recipe as directed, except omit rice, lemon, spinach, and feta. Increase onion to 1 cup. When onion is cooked, add $1^1/_2$ cups cubed cooked smoked ham and 1 cup cubed Havarti cheese. Stuff tenderloins with this mixture and proceed with the recipe.

Make Filling

Stuff Tenderloins

TURKEY

- Rice is a very good base for any stuffing. It is tender and moist and holds together well.

- The filling can be made ahead of time and refrigerated until you're ready to cook the turkey.

- In fact, chilling can make the filling easier to handle and the tenderloins easier to stuff.

- Add herbs to the filling for more flavor. Some fresh thyme or chopped basil would be nice additions.

- You can pound the tenderloins after they have been cut in half to make them easier to roll around the filling.

- Spread the filling over the tenderloins and gently roll the meat around the filling to enclose.

- Use a toothpick threaded parallel to the length of the tenderloin to hold the opening closed.

- Be sure to remove the toothpicks before you serve the tenderloin for the nicest presentation.

PEACH TURKEY TENDERLOINS

Marinated tenderloins are grilled and glazed with a spicy peach mixture

Turkey tenderloins are very easy to grill. Because they are boneless and low in fat, they do need to be marinated before grilling.

Like a brine, a marinade helps force liquid into the meat to make it juicier. A marinade is just a more concentrated brine, usually made with more flavoring ingredients.

Fruit and meat are a natural combination. The sweet and tart fruit complements the rich and mild flavor of the turkey, and the fruit's acidity is a natural marinade. Any fruit, from raspberries to cranberries to peaches and pears, will work well as a marinade for this mild meat. *Yield: Serves 4–6*

Ingredients

2 tablespoons butter

2 shallots, minced

2 cloves garlic, minced

2 tablespoons soy sauce

2 tablespoons balsamic vinegar

1 cup peach nectar

1 teaspoon salt

$1/2$ teaspoon pepper

1 teaspoon dried thyme leaves

2 tablespoons honey mustard

2 ($1 1/2$-pound) turkey tenderloins

$1/3$ cup peach preserves

1 tablespoon lemon juice

2 tablespoons brown sugar

Peach Turkey Tenderloins

- Melt butter in pan; cook shallots and garlic 4 minutes until tender. Remove from heat.

- Add soy sauce, vinegar, nectar, salt, pepper, thyme, and honey mustard. Add tenderloins; cover and marinate in fridge 8–12 hours.

- Drain turkey. Mix ½ cup marinade, preserves, lemon juice, and sugar in pan.

- Simmer sauce 5 minutes. Put turkey on grill over medium coals. Grill, covered, 8 minutes. Brush with sauce, turn, brush again with sauce, and grill 8–10 minutes until done.

Marinate Turkey

- The turkey can be marinated up to 24 hours in the refrigerator, but no longer or it can become mushy.

- You can vary the marinade ingredients to your taste. Use lemon or lime juice instead of vinegar, or Dijon mustard instead of honey mustard.

- Make the marinade ahead of time and store it in the refrigerator up to 2 days before adding the turkey.

- You can use the leftover marinade that isn't combined with the preserves to baste the turkey.

Grill Turkey

- Grill the turkey over medium coals. The turkey should be wet with the marinade when added to the grill.

- Be sure that the grill rack is cleaned and well oiled before you add the tenderloins.

- Let the tenderloins sit for 10 minutes, then slice into 1-inch slices and arrange on serving platter.

- Grill an extra tenderloin or two to use in turkey salad or sandwiches over the next couple of days.

UPSIDE DOWN TURKEY

An unstuffed turkey cooked upside down stays moist and tender

It makes sense when you think about it. Since the major problem with roast turkey is breast meat that is dried out, if the turkey is cooked upside down, the fat will run down into the breast and keep it moist as it roasts.

This approach may look funny, but the result is a beautifully even turkey, with moist dark and white meat.

The turkey is turned over toward the end of cooking time to brown the breast and crisp the skin. It's a good idea to have a large pair of heatproof gloves to aid you in this process, because the hot turkey is quite unwieldy.

Make the stuffing (now called dressing) in the slow cooker while the turkey roasts. *Yield: Serves 10*

Ingredients

¹/₃ cup butter

3 cloves garlic

2 tablespoons chopped fresh sage leaves

1 teaspoon salt

¹/₂ teaspoon pepper

1 teaspoon poultry seasoning

1 (12–14-pound) turkey

1 lemon, cut in half

1 onion, quartered

1¹/₂ cups chicken broth

Upside Down Turkey

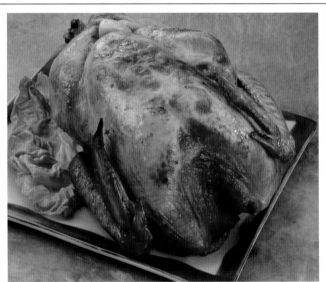

- Melt butter in pan; cook garlic 2–3 minutes until fragrant. Remove from heat; add sage, salt, pepper, and poultry seasoning.

- Divide mixture in half; rub half under skin. Place lemon and onion in cavity; truss turkey.

- Place turkey upside down in roasting pan. Pour remaining butter mixture on top. Pour broth around turkey.

- Cover and roast at 350°F 3 hours, basting occasionally. Uncover, carefully turn turkey over, and roast 30–40 minutes longer until turkey is done.

• • • • RECIPE VARIATION • • • •

Grilled Turkey
Prepare recipe as directed, except reserve half of the butter mixture. Brush remaining butter mixture over the turkey. Prepare and preheat grill for indirect medium heat. Place turkey over the drip pan, cover, and cook 12–14 minutes per pound. Add briquettes if necessary every hour.

• • • • • • RED ● LIGHT • • • • • • • • • • •

Deep-frying turkeys has become popular in recent years. Only attempt this if you are very skilled at deep-frying. Underwriter Laboratories has issued warnings about turkey fryers, since homes and garages have caught fire using this method. Deep-fry your turkey well away from any structures or flammable materials.

Place Turkey in Pan

- The turkey can be difficult to balance in the pan. A rack made for turkey can help hold it securely.

- You can also prop the turkey up with some russet potatoes and onions. This also adds flavor to the drippings.

- There are also turkey holders available on the market that will make turning the turkey easier.

- Make sure your oven rack is low enough so the turkey fits easily into the oven and is at least 6 inches away from the top burner.

Baste Turkey

- It's important to baste the turkey as it cooks. This will keep the meat moist and helps the skin become crisp.

- Use a turkey baster to suck the juices from the bottom of the pan; then squeeze them over the bird.

- You can also spoon the liquid from the pan over the bird. Use a hot pad to protect your hand.

- Make pan gravy or giblet gravy using the drippings while the turkey rests after it's thoroughly cooked.

CHICKEN FAJITAS

Leftover chicken marinates in a spicy lime mixture, then is combined with veggies

Fajita is a Mexican term, used in Tex-Mex cooking, that means grilled meat that's served on a tortilla. This recipe became popular in restaurants in the 1990s. It was originally made with skirt steak, but is now made with chicken, pork, and even seafood.

Fajitas are a fun way to use up leftover chicken. Since the meat is already cooked, this recipe just seasons the meat in a spicy marinade, then heats it until tender and soft.

The dish that was originally all meat now includes vegetables. Onions and bell peppers are traditionally used. Their fresh taste and crisp texture are perfect wrapped in the soft tortillas. *Yield: Serves 4*

Ingredients

3 tablespoons cider vinegar

2 tablespoons honey

1 teaspoon cumin

1 tablespoon chili powder

1 tablespoon lime juice

$1/2$ teaspoon salt

3 cups cooked sliced or cubed chicken breast

2 tablespoons olive oil

2 red bell peppers

1 green bell pepper

1 red onion, chopped

8 (8-inch) flour tortillas

1 cup salsa

1 cup sour cream

2 avocados, peeled and sliced

1 cup shredded Pepper Jack cheese

Chicken Fajitas

- In bowl, combine vinegar, honey, cumin, chili powder, lime juice, and salt; add chicken and stir.

- Cover and marinate in refrigerator 30 minutes. Then heat olive oil; add bell peppers and onion; cook 5–6 minutes until tender.

- Add chicken mixture to bell peppers; cook and stir 3–4 minutes until heated. Meanwhile, wrap tortillas in foil; warm in 350°F oven 8–10 minutes.

- Make fajitas with flour tortillas, chicken mixture, salsa, sour cream, avocados, and cheese.

Chicken Tacos

Make recipe as directed, except chop bell peppers and chicken. Substitute 12 crisp formed tortilla shells for the soft flour tortillas. Heat the taco shells in a 350ºF oven 8–9 minutes until crisp, then fill with the chicken mixture and top with sour cream, salsa, avocados, and cheese.

Add Chicken to Peppers

- You can use any spicy salad dressing to marinate the chicken instead of this homemade combination.

- You're adding flavor to the chicken as well as helping to keep it moist as it is reheated.

- Only heat the chicken for a few minutes until it's soft and hot.

- Other vegetables you can use in fajitas include mushrooms and corn, along with shredded lettuce.

Assemble Fajitas

- The tortillas are usually fairly stiff, so warming them is essential so they don't split or tear when folded.

- You can buy a tortilla warmer from a kitchen supply store if you make a lot of tortillas.

- There are also baskets to put on the table that will keep the tortillas warm and pliable while you eat.

- For a party, place the tortillas and several types of filling on a warming tray, then let everyone assemble their own.

CHICKEN MANICOTTI
Chicken and cheese are stuffed into manicotti shells for this rich and elegant dish

Manicotti and cannelloni are Italian terms that mean the same thing: a pasta shaped into a tube and filled with a spicy mixture. Cannelloni are traditionally made from crepes, while manicotti are preformed tubes.

Manicotti pasta is sold in every grocery store. The tubes are nestled into plastic containers made to hold them so they don't crack or break during shipping. Some recipes call for cooking the manicotti shells before filling them; other recipes call for you to fill the shells, then cook them in the sauce.
Yield: Serves 8–10

Ingredients

1 cup part-skim ricotta cheese

1 (3-ounce) package cream cheese, softened

1/2 cup sour cream

1/3 cup sliced green onions

1/2 cup grated Parmesan cheese

1 teaspoon dried basil

1 teaspoon dried thyme

1/2 teaspoon salt

1/4 teaspoon pepper

2 eggs, beaten

1 1/2 cups shredded part-skim mozzarella cheese, divided

3 cups cubed cooked chicken

12 manicotti shells

1 (26-ounce) jar spaghetti sauce

1/4 cup grated Romano cheese

Chicken Manicotti

- Bring a large pot of water to a boil. In bowl, beat ricotta and cream cheese.

- Add sour cream, green onions, Parmesan, basil, thyme, salt, pepper, eggs, 1 cup mozzarella, and chicken.

- Cook manicotti according to directions until al dente.

Drain; rinse with cold water. Fill with chicken mixture.

- Place ½ cup spaghetti sauce in 9 x 13-inch pan; top with manicotti. Pour remaining sauce over; sprinkle with remaining mozzarella and Romano cheeses. Bake at 375ºF 35–45 minutes.

Tex-Mex Chicken Manicotti

Make recipe as directed, except omit sour cream; add ½ cup salsa. Add 1 minced chipotle pepper in adobo, 1 tablespoon chili powder, and 2 teaspoons adobo sauce to the chicken filling. Use Pepper Jack cheese in place of the mozzarella, and add 4 ounces chopped green chiles to the pasta sauce.

Greek Chicken Manicotti

Make recipe as directed, except use thick Greek yogurt in place of the sour cream. Add 2 tablespoons lemon juice to the cream cheese mixture, along with 1 cup sliced black olives and 1 teaspoon dried oregano. Omit Romano cheese; use ½ cup crumbled feta cheese.

Mix Filling

- You can make the filling ahead of time; cover it and store in the refrigerator up to 2 days.

- Don't completely cook the manicotti; it should be slightly undercooked.

- It will continue cooking in the pasta sauce while the dish bakes in the oven.

- Use a small soup spoon or a long handled teaspoon to fill the manicotti shells. Or you can pipe the filling into the shells using a pastry bag without a tip.

Assemble Dish

- Arrange the shells in a single layer on the pasta sauce in the baking dish.

- If necessary, you can stack one or two of the filled shells on top of the others.

- Make sure that the pasta sauce covers the pasta completely, but it doesn't have to be drowning in sauce.

- Any exposed pasta will become slightly crisp as it bakes in the oven.

LEFTOVER POULTRY

CHICKEN WELLINGTON
Chicken and shrimp are surrounded with puff pastry in this elegant recipe

Wellington is a fancy dish that encloses meat, usually filet mignon, in puff pastry. The meat is topped with a pâté mixture and decorated with cut-outs of the pastry.

This recipe can be made with any meat, and chicken is a good choice. Since the chicken is rather bland, it should be dressed up with flavorful foods like shrimp, vegetables, and cheeses.

Puff pastry can be found in the frozen foods aisle of any supermarket, near the frozen desserts. Each package has two sheets. For best results, thaw overnight in the refrigerator, although there are directions for thawing the pastry at room temperature on the package. *Yield: Serves 6*

Ingredients

2 tablespoons butter

1 onion, chopped

3 cloves garlic, minced

1 cup small raw shrimp

3 cups cubed cooked chicken

$1/2$ cup sour cream

2 tablespoons mustard

1 egg

1 cup frozen spinach, thawed and drained

1 cup shredded Havarti cheese

Pinch nutmeg

1 teaspoon dried tarragon

$1/2$ teaspoon salt

$1/4$ teaspoon pepper

2 sheets frozen puff pastry, thawed

Chicken Wellington

- Melt butter in pan; add onion and garlic; cook 5 minutes. Add shrimp; cook and stir 2–3 minutes until pink.

- Place in bowl. Add chicken, sour cream, mustard, egg, spinach, cheese, nutmeg, tarragon, salt, and pepper; mix well.

- Cut each pastry sheet into 3 rectangles on fold lines. Divide chicken mixture onto one half of each pastry piece.

- Fold over; seal edges. Place on cookie sheet. Bake at 400°F 25–35 minutes until golden brown.

Pesto Chicken Wellington

Make recipe as directed, except omit shrimp and mustard. Add 1 (7-ounce) package of prepared basil pesto to the chicken mixture. Place this mixture on the puff pastry rectangles, fold and seal as directed, and bake until puffed and golden brown.

Spicy Chicken Wellington

Make recipe as directed, except omit shrimp and mustard. Add 2 minced jalapeño peppers with the onions and garlic, and add 2 teaspoons chili powder, 1 teaspoon cumin, and ¼ teaspoon cayenne pepper to the chicken filling. Fill, shape, and bake the pastries as directed.

Make Filling

- Puff pastry, while flaky and buttery, is quite bland, so the filling should be well flavored.

- In beef Wellington, the beef provides most of the flavor. In this recipe, other ingredients flavor the mild chicken.

- You can make the filling ahead of time; cover it and refrigerate up to 2 days.

- This makes this recipe a great make-ahead dish, perfect for entertaining. Just fill the pastry and bake when your guests arrive.

Form Pastry

- Working with puff pastry is easy; just make sure it stays cold and don't handle it too much.

- It's made of hundreds of layers of butter encased in a flour dough. When the dough bakes, the butter melts and creates steam, which makes crisp and flaky layers.

- To seal the edges, you can press them with your fingers or with the tines of a fork.

- Make sure the edges are well sealed so the pastries don't pop open in the oven.

GRILLED CHICKEN SANDWICHES

Grilled sandwiches, with melty cheese and tender chicken, are fun and easy to make

Grilled sandwiches are the classic way to use up leftover chicken. But you don't have to be reduced to just slapping some chicken and mayonnaise between slices of bread! Sandwiches can be elegant and creative.

Grilling sandwiches, whether on a skillet or a dual contact indoor grill, automatically elevates sandwiches from a snack to a main dish. Keep a selection of chicken sandwich fillings in the refrigerator, so hungry teenagers or weekend guests can make a meal any time they want. Grill until the filling is hot and the bread crisp and golden brown. *Yield: Serves 5*

Ingredients

3 cups cubed cooked chicken

¹/₂ cup mayonnaise

3 tablespoons yogurt

¹/₂ teaspoon salt

¹/₈ teaspoon pepper

2 teaspoons fresh dill weed

¹/₂ cup crumbled feta cheese

1 cup shredded Swiss cheese

1 cup arugula leaves

10 slices French bread

2 tablespoons butter

Grilled Chicken Sandwiches

- In bowl, combine chicken, mayonnaise, yogurt, salt, pepper, dill, feta, and Swiss cheeses; mix well.

- You can make this mixture up to 8 hours ahead of time; store covered in fridge.

- Divide arugula among 5 slices French bread; top with chicken mixture and another piece of bread.

- Spread outsides of sandwiches with butter. Grill, pressing down with spatula, 4–6 minutes per side until golden.

222

Grilled Chicken Bacon Sandwiches
Make recipe as directed, except add 6 slices crisply cooked, crumbled bacon to the filling. Omit yogurt, dill, and feta; increase mayonnaise to ³/₄ cup. Add 1 cup shredded cheddar cheese, and use cracked wheat bread to make the sandwiches.

······ *GREEN ● LIGHT* ······

A dual contact indoor grill, most famously made by George Foreman, is a great tool for grilling sandwiches. Because the sandwiches cook on both sides at the same time, they cook in half the time. You can also use a panini maker; they work on the same principle.

Mix Filling

- You can use any combination of herbs and cheeses in this mild filling.

- Try shredded cheddar cheese with caramelized onions, or use blue cheese and Havarti cheese with sliced green onions.

- Substitute mascarpone cheese or softened cream cheese for the mayonnaise and yogurt mixture.

- You can use light or dark meat chicken, leftovers from a rotisserie chicken, or canned chicken.

Assemble Sandwiches

- Don't assemble the sandwiches ahead of time. To make ahead, make the filling and refrigerate it.

- Then assemble the sandwiches and spread them with butter just before grilling.

- If you aren't using a dual contact or panini grill, cover the sandwiches with the pan lid while they grill.

- Gently press down on the sandwiches occasionally to help them hold together and so the cheese melts.

LEFTOVER POULTRY

TURKEY TETRAZZINI
Turkey in a cheesy cream sauce is mixed with spaghetti in a bubbly casserole

Turkey Tetrazzini is an Italian-American dish that combines cooked chicken or turkey with pasta and vegetables in a creamy cheese sauce. The whole concoction is baked until it's bubbly and golden brown.

This recipe is a great way to use up leftover Thanksgiving turkey or grilled chicken. In fact, it's a good excuse for cooking extra grilled chicken—tetrazzini the next day!

Mushrooms, onions, and garlic are the classic vegetables used in this dish, but you can add everything from green bell peppers to peas to tomatoes. *Yield: Serves 6–8*

Ingredients

1 onion, chopped

3 cloves garlic, minced

1 (8-ounce) package mushrooms, sliced

1/4 cup butter

1/4 cup flour

1 teaspoon salt

1/4 teaspoon pepper

1 teaspoon dried basil

1 teaspoon dried oregano

1 1/2 cups chicken broth

1 1/2 cups light cream or milk

12 ounces spaghetti pasta

1 cup grated Parmesan cheese, divided

4 cups cubed cooked turkey

3 tomatoes, chopped

Turkey Tetrazzini

- Cook onion, garlic, and mushrooms in butter 8–9 minutes until mushrooms are browned.

- Add flour, salt, pepper, basil, and oregano; cook 4 minutes. Add broth and cream; cook and stir until thickened.

- Cook pasta until al dente; drain well. Add ¾ cup cheese, turkey, and tomatoes to sauce; stir in pasta.

- Pour into 3-quart baking dish; top with remaining cheese. Bake at 350°F 50–60 minutes until browned and bubbly.

• • • • RECIPE VARIATIONS • • • •

Herbed Turkey Tetrazzini
Make recipe as directed, except substitute 2 tablespoons chopped fresh basil and 1 tablespoon fresh oregano for the dried in the sauce. Add 1/2 cup chopped flat-leaf parsley and 1 teaspoon grated lemon zest when you add the turkey. Bake recipe as directed.

Spicy Turkey Tetrazzini
Make recipe as directed, except add 1 minced habanero pepper and 1 chipotle pepper in adobo, drained and rinsed, to the onion mixture as it cooks. Add 1 tablespoon chili powder, 1 teaspoon cumin, and 1/2 teaspoon dried oregano to the turkey mixture.

Make Cream Sauce

- Make sure that you cook the flour in the onion mixture for several minutes. This gets rid of the raw flour taste.

- It also helps open up the flour so it will absorb the liquid and make a smooth sauce with the broth and cream.

- Cook the pasta until it's just shy of al dente. It will continue cooking in the sauce as the dish bakes.

- You can use any type of cheese that you'd like. Parmesan is traditional, or use 2 cups of Swiss, provolone, or mozzarella.

Mix All Ingredients

- Mix all of the ingredients gently but thoroughly to coat everything with the sauce.

- Spread the ingredients evenly in the baking dish so it bakes evenly and completely.

- To make ahead of time, prepare the whole dish, cover, and refrigerate up to 3 days, or freeze up to 3 months.

- For the frozen casserole, defrost overnight in the refrigerator. Add 10–20 minutes to the total baking time.

LEFTOVER POULTRY

225

TURKEY CRANBERRY PIZZA

Pizza made with turkey is an unconventional and delicious change of pace

And finally, pizza is the perfect recipe to use leftover poultry. If you have a pizza crust on hand, you can have a delicious gourmet pizza on the table in about 30 minutes.

Prebaked thick crusts that are seasoned with cheese and herbs are available in the grocery store. There are also refrigerated pizza crusts, and pizza dough available.

Or you can make your own crusts. Make a few and keep them in the freezer for pizza that's faster (and better) than takeout.

Use your imagination when topping your pizzas. Use your favorite pizza ingredients or go wild and use anything from bacon to pistachio nuts to cream cheese and herbs. *Yield: Serves 4–6*

Ingredients

1 onion, chopped

3 cloves garlic, minced

1 tablespoon grated gingerroot

1 tablespoon olive oil

3 cups cubed cooked turkey

1 cup sour cream

1/2 cup dried cranberries

1 (12-inch) prebaked thick pizza crust (such as Boboli)

1 cup whole-berry cranberry sauce

1 tablespoon fresh thyme leaves

1 cup shredded Havarti cheese

1 cup shredded part-skim mozzarella cheese

Turkey Cranberry Pizza

- Cook onion, garlic, and gingerroot in olive oil until tender, about 6–7 minutes. Add turkey; remove from heat.

- Add sour cream and dried cranberries. Spread on pizza crust. Drop cranberry sauce by spoonfuls over turkey mixture.

- Sprinkle with thyme leaves, then Havarti and mozzarella cheeses.

- Bake at 425°F 15–20 minutes until crust is crisp and cheeses are melted and browned in spots. Let cool 10 minutes; slice to serve.

Turkey Club Pizza

Make recipe as directed, except omit gingerroot, dried cranberries, and cranberry sauce. Use mayonnaise instead of the sour cream. Add 6 slices crisply cooked, crumbled bacon and ¹/₂ cup sliced green onions, and use Swiss cheese in place of the Havarti cheese. Bake as directed until golden brown and crisp.

Turkey Artichoke Pizza

Make recipe as directed, except omit gingerroot, dried cranberries, and cranberry sauce. Add 1 (14-ounce) can artichoke hearts, drained and chopped, 2 chopped tomatoes, and ¹/₂ cup sliced black olives to the pizza. Use cheddar cheese in place of the Havarti; bake until crisp and golden brown.

Cook Onion and Garlic

- The gingerroot adds a nice snap of flavor to this recipe and contrasts well with the tart cranberries.

- The onions and garlic must be cooked ahead of time because the pizza doesn't bake long enough to cook them.

- Use other types of herbs in this easy recipe. Fresh chopped basil or sage would be delicious.

- Also, use your favorite cheeses. Provolone, Asiago, Romano, or Colby are good choices.

Assemble Pizza

- Make sure that you drop small spoonfuls of the cranberry sauce onto the pizza so it is evenly distributed.

- Stir the cranberry sauce before adding it to the pizza so it's easier to spoon out small portions.

- Either light or dark meat turkey will work well on this pizza, as long as the pieces are cut to an equal size.

- Have a pizza party—offer a selection of prebaked crusts and different toppings and let your guests assemble their own.

WEB SITES, TV SHOWS, & VIDEOS
Information on cooking chicken

Chicken is ubiquitous around the world, and recipes for the bird are found in nearly every cooking television show, Web site, and video. Online, there are lots of videos, recipes, and tips and hints to help you make the perfect chicken.

Product manufacturers, books, magazines, and catalogs can also help. You'll be able to find information about products, many recipes, chicken cooking tips, and where to find special ingredients, tools, and equipment.

Online message boards and forums are wonderful resources as well. On popular boards, you will get answers to your questions very quickly. Don't be afraid to ask for help!

Chicken Web sites

AllRecipes.com
http://allrecipes.com/Recipes

- AllRecipes, which features reader-submitted recipes that are rated by members, is a reliable source of hundreds of chicken recipes.

BH&G
www.bhg.com/recipes

- *Better Homes and Gardens* offers hundreds of simple and interesting chicken recipes, all tested in their test kitchens.

Busy Cooks at About.com
http://busycooks.about.com

- This time-tested site is full of information and recipes for everything from five-ingredient chicken to a whole roasted turkey.

Crockpot@CDKitchen.com
http://crockpot.cdkitchen.com

- This Web site features recipes submitted by bloggers. More than 4,200 old-fashioned and updated recipes are reliable and delicious.

Eat Chicken
www.eatchicken.com

- This site, run by the National Chicken Council, has lots of soup recipes for chicken, along with nutrition info and cooking tips.

RecipeZaar
www.recipezaar.com

- Thousands of chicken recipes are submitted by readers and rated by viewers.

Chicken-preparation videos

About.com
http://video.about.com/food.htm

- Thousands of videos will teach you how to make lots of chicken recipes.

AllRecipes Videos
http://allrecipes.com/Search/Recipes.aspx?WithTerm=chicken

- AllRecipes.com has a lot of excellent videos showing how to make chicken in their test kitchen.

Expert Village
www.expertvillage.com

- You'll learn how to make everything from chicken Parmesan to chicken soup in these videos.

Group Recipes
www.grouprecipes.com/videotag/chicken

- Video shows you exactly how to make easy and delicious chicken dishes.

iFoods.tv
http://ifoods.tv/all-recipes/Chicken-Breast-Presentation/204

- iFoods TV offers lots of informative videos that will teach you how to prepare every chicken recipe in the world.

TV cooking shows

America's Test Kitchen
- *Cook's Illustrated* is responsible for this show on PBS that teaches you how to cook. Lots of excellent chicken recipes.

Quick Fix Meals with Robin Miller on the Food Network
- On her show "Quick Fix Meals," Robin Miller uses chicken, turkey, and Cornish hens in primary recipes and as leftovers.

Semi-Homemade Cooking with Sandra Lee on the Food Network
- Sandra Lee developed the concept of "30 percent fresh food, 70 percent prepared food." She makes chicken.

BOOKS & MAGAZINES

Hundreds of chicken recipe books and magazines are here to help

Chicken books

Amster, Linda. *The New York Times Chicken Cookbook,* St. Martin's Press, 2005.
- Delicious, classic chicken recipes include family favorites and information about grilling, broiling, frying, poaching, and stir-frying chicken.

Better Homes & Gardens. Biggest Book of Chicken Recipes, BH&G, 2007.
- Kitchen-tested recipes for the best chicken, including lots of kid-friendly recipes.

Betty Crocker. *Betty Crocker Chicken Tonight,* Betty Crocker, 2007.
- Excellent collection of triple-tested chicken recipes from the giant of cooking.

Betty Crocker. *Betty Crocker's Best Chicken Cookbook,* Betty Crocker, 1999.
- Excellent collection of triple-tested chicken recipes with nutrition information and preparation and cooking times.

Editors of *Cook's Illustrated. The Best Chicken Recipes,* Boston Common Press, 2008.
- Three hundred recipes for "perfect chicken," from the people who created America's Test Kitchen.

Editors of *Good Housekeeping. Good Housekeeping's 100 Best Chicken Recipes,* Hearst, 2005
- This book offers one hundred recipes for chicken, including Chicken Cordon Bleu and Arroz con Pollo.

Chicken magazines

Better Homes & Gardens
- This magazine has tons of chicken recipes that follow the seasons.

Family Circle
- This magazine offers lots of chicken recipes and menus, seasonal recipes, and tips.

Taste of Home
- This venerable magazine focuses on reader-submitted recipes, tested in their test kitchens.

Woman's Day
- This magazine has chicken recipes in each issue, along with cooking lessons and tips.

EQUIPMENT RESOURCES
Find equipment through these resources to stock your kitchen

Catalogs for cooking equipment

Brylane Home
- This catalog has lots of kitchen equipment, including specialty tools, utensils, and dishware.

Solutions
- Lots of new equipment and tools to make cooking quick and easy.

Sur la Table
- Catalog offers lots of kitchen equipment along with dishes, serving utensils, and flatware.

Williams-Sonoma
- Top of the line equipment, along with cookbooks and many appliances, tools, and accessories.

Web sites for chicken cooking equipment

Chefsresource.com
www.chefsresource.com

- Cutlery, flatware, gadgets, tools, knives, and brands like Cuisinart are featured.

Cooking.com
www.cooking.com

- Kitchen fixtures, large appliances, cutlery, cookbooks, and tools can be found at this site.

Crock-pot.com
www.crock-pot.com

- The Web site for Rival slow cookers, this site offers customer service, replacement parts, and recipes.

Kitchen.Manualsonline.com
http://kitchen.manualsonline.com

- Web site offers contact information for dozens of kitchen product manufacturers.

FIND INGREDIENTS

There are many resources for ingredients other than the grocery store

Catalogs and online resources

RESOURCE DIRECTORY

Amazon Grocery

www.agrocerydelivery.com/

- Amazon.com has a grocery delivery service. Offers general foods and hard-to-find items.

The Baker's Catalog

- From King Arthur Flour, this catalog offers cooking equipment and baking ingredients, including specialty flours and flavorings.

Peapod

www.peapod.com

- Online grocery store serving some areas of the United States.

Schwan's

www.schwans.com

- Home delivery service for groceries, serving parts of the United States.

Safeway.com

www.safeway.com

- Grocery chain offers delivery of food items, as well as recipes and tips for healthy living.

Farmers' markets

Farmers' Market Search
http://apps.ams.usda.gov/FarmersMarkets/
USDA site lets you search for a farmers' market by state, city, county, and zip code, as well as methods of payment.

Los Angeles Farmers' Markets
www.farmersmarketla.com
Los Angeles Farmers' Market Web site; the original farmers' market.

National Directory of Farmer's Markets
http://farmersmarket.com/
Site has index of U.S. farmers' markets listed by state.

METRIC CONVERSION TABLES
Approximate U.S. Metric Equivalents

Liquid Ingredients

U.S. MEASURES	METRIC	U.S. MEASURES	METRIC
1/4 TSP.	1.23 ML	2 TBSP.	29.57 ML
1/2 TSP.	2.36 ML	3 TBSP.	44.36 ML
3/4 TSP.	3.70 ML	1/4 CUP	59.15 ML
1 TSP.	4.93 ML	1/2 CUP	118.30 ML
1 1/4 TSP.	6.16 ML	1 CUP	236.59 ML
1 1/2 TSP.	7.39 ML	2 CUPS OR 1 PT.	473.18 ML
1 3/4 TSP.	8.63 ML	3 CUPS	709.77 ML
2 TSP.	9.86 ML	4 CUPS OR 1 QT.	946.36 ML
1 TBSP.	14.79 ML	4 QTS. OR 1 GAL.	3.79 L

Dry Ingredients

U.S. MEASURES	METRIC	U.S. MEASURES		METRIC
1/16 OZ.	2 (1.8) G	2 4/5 OZ.		80 G
1/8 OZ.	3 1/2 (3.5) G	3 OZ.		85 (84.9) G
1/4 OZ.	7 (7.1) G	3 1/2 OZ.		100 G
1/2 OZ.	15 (14.2) G	4 OZ.		115 (113.2) G
3/4 OZ.	21 (21.3) G	4 1/2 OZ.		125 G
7/8 OZ.	25 G	5 1/4 OZ.		150 G
1 OZ.	30 (28.3) G	8 7/8 OZ.		250 G
1 3/4 OZ.	50 G	16 OZ.	1 LB.	454 G
2 OZ.	60 (56.6) G	17 3/5 OZ.	1 LIVRE	500 G

HOTLINES & MANUFACTURERS

Find help with cooking problems and equipment manufacturers

Hotlines

Butterball Turkey Holiday Line
800-323-4848

- Hotline available year-round; answers questions about turkey cooking and preparation.

Empire Kosher Poultry Hotline
800-367-4734

- Year-round hotline answers questions about poultry.

Perdue
800-473-7383

- Year-round hotline helps with cooking questions, especially poultry products.

Reynolds Turkey Tips
800-745-4000

- Year-round hotline answers consumer questions about turkey preparation; free recipes.

USDA Meat and Poultry Hotline
800-535-4555

- Year-round line offers information about food safety, answers consumer questions about meat preparation.

Manufacturers of Equipment

All-Clad
www.all-clad.com/

- Company makes well-built equipment, especially pots and pans.

Cuisinart
www.cuisinart.com

- Company can completely outfit your kitchen, from ranges to stockpots.

GE Appliances
www.geappliances.com

- Outfit your entire kitchen with GE appliances. Online service and customer support.

Kitchenaid
www.kitchenaid.com/home.jsp

- Lots of high quality appliances offered, from refrigerators and stoves to slow cookers.

Rival
www.rivalproducts.com

- Manufacturer of the original Crock-Pot, with product information, recipes, and an online store.

237

GLOSSARY
Learn the language first

Adobo: A sauce made of garlic, vinegar, spices, and soy sauce used to season dishes.

Al dente: Italian phrase meaning "to the tooth" describes doneness of pasta.

Beat: To manipulate food with a spoon, mixer, or whisk to combine.

Bread: To coat chicken with crumbs or crushed crackers before baking or frying.

Brine: A mixture of salt, sugar, and water used to season chicken and turkey before cooking.

Broth: Liquid extracted from meats and vegetables, used as the basis for most soups.

Browning: Cooking step that caramelizes food and adds color and flavor before cooking.

Coat: To cover food in another ingredient, as to coat chicken breasts with breadcrumbs.

Chill: To refrigerate a food or place it in an ice-water bath to rapidly cool it.

Chop: To cut food into small pieces, using a chef's knife or a food processor.

Chowder: A soup thick with vegetables and meats, usually seafood, thickened with cream and cheese.

Cornish Hen: A very young chicken, sold whole. Usually stuffed and roasted.

Cutlet: A thin cut of chicken or turkey, either pounded thin or cut very thin to cook quickly.

Deglaze: To add a liquid to a pan used to sauté meats; this removes drippings and brown bits to create a sauce.

Dice: To cut food into small, even portions, usually about $\frac{1}{4}$ inch square.

Drippings: Brown bits made of meat, skin, and fat left in the pan after chicken is browned.

Flake: To break into small pieces; canned meats are usually flaked.

Fricassee: A dish made by stewing meats, especially chicken or turkey, with vegetables.

Gazpacho: A cold soup, usually made of tomatoes, that is pureed without cooking.

Grate: To use a grater or microplane to remove small pieces or shreds of skin or food.

Grill: To cook over coals or charcoal, or over high heat.

Marinate: To allow meats or vegetables to stand in a mixture of an acid and oil, to add flavor and tenderize.

Melt: To turn a solid into a liquid by the addition of heat.

Niçoise: Word means "as prepared in Nice," a town in France. Usually made with olives, tomatoes, and bell peppers.

Panfry: To cook quickly in a shallow pan, in a small amount of fat over relatively high heat.

Poultry: A broad category of birds kept for their eggs and meat, including chicken, turkey, Cornish hens, geese, and ducks.

Shred: To use a grater, mandoline, or food processor to create small strips of food.

Simmer: A state of liquid cooking, in which the liquid is just below a boil.

Slow cooker: An appliance that cooks food by surrounding it with low, steady heat.

Soup: A mixture of solids and liquids, served hot or cold, as a main dish or part of a multi-course meal.

Spatchcocked: A technique that removes the backbone and flattens chicken so it is easily grilled.

Toss: To combine food using two spoons or a spoon and a fork until mixed.

Whisk: Both a tool, which is made of loops of steel, and a method, which combines food until smooth.

INDEX

INDEX